GARDENING
WEEK BY WEEK

GARDENING
WEEK BY WEEK

DAVID SQUIRE

CHANCELLOR
PRESS

Photographic acknowledgments

All photographs reproduced in this book were supplied by
the author, except the following:

Frontispiece: Coloured paving slabs create added interest
in the garden throughout the year and dur-
ing the summer they harmonize with garden
plants (Harry Smith Horticultural Photographs, Essex).

Front cover: Spring flowering gardens create welcome
colour after a dreary and bare winter. Bulbs
and blossom trees are a perfect combination
(Harry Smith Horticultural Photographs,
Essex).

Back cover: Top left: Three kinds of cloche; top right:
Arranging rows of onions for careful ripening; bottom left: Raking dead grasses from
the lawn; bottom right: Edwards plums.

The author would like to thank the director of the Royal
Horticultural Society's Garden at Wisley, Surrey, for allow-
ing many of the photographs in this book to be taken and
also the many friends who made their gardens available for
photography.

This edition published in Great Britain 1993
by Chancellor Press
an imprint of Reed Consumer Books Limited
Michelin House, 81 Fulham Road, London SW3 6RB
and Auckland, Melbourne, Singapore and Toronto

Copyright © 1986 Reed International Books Limited
ISBN 1 851 52280 8

A CIP catalogue record for this book is available
at the British Library

Produced by Mandarin Offset
Printed in China

CONTENTS

Introduction 6
January 8
February 18
March 28
April 46
May 64
June 82
July 100
August 118
September 136
October 154
November 164
December 174
Glossary 184
Index 187

Above: Delphinium *'Thunderstorm' creates a dominant burst of colour during June and July and is useful for early summer colour in a mixed or herbaceous border.*

INTRODUCTION

Gardening is a year-through pursuit and a continuing and captivating hobby for millions of people. During spring and summer the weather and light encourage regular daily visits to the garden, perhaps to inspect and admire a choice plant that has just come into flower. During winter, however, gardening for many people is only possible at weekends. But whatever the size of your garden there is nearly always something to be done, even if it is just to remove dead leaves from around choice alpine plants during winter. And even the smallest of patio or courtyard gardens benefit from the regular removal of dead flowers from window-boxes and hanging-baskets during summer.

Gardens are also places in which to relax in seclusion and privacy. They are oases of peace and tranquillity where you can enjoy outside living and the beauty of your garden.

Increasingly, garden space is having to compete with encroachment from the house. Lean-to conservatories that conveniently bridge the gap between house and garden, patios and terraces with tables, chairs and sun-loungers, parasols and barbeque equipment all demand space.

For many people the whole nature of gardening has changed over the last decade or so. Jobs that were once physically demanding are now much easier with the wide range of powered garden tools now available. Demands on personal leisure time have increased and many gardeners are looking for convenience gardening where colour is quickly produced to last over a long period. Garden centres and nurseries selling plants in pots, ready for planting out, have both inspired and continued this change. They have also widened the whole spectrum of gardening for many people, offering garden furniture, tools and equipment. But there are still many gardeners who are dedicated to their gardens, reacting to seasonal changes and taking pleasure from the many and varied jobs in a garden.

This highly illustrated week-by-week guide to jobs in the garden has been planned to answer many of the questions put by gardeners each year. It may be about the how-and-when to aerate a lawn, how to prune roses, or when and how to sow runner beans? Or it might be when to sow seeds in a flower border, or even what shrub, climber or tree is in flower during a particular month? All these questions are answered here.

Right: The Californian Poppy, Eschscholzia californica, *is a hardy annual for sowing where it is to flower. The saucer-shaped flowers appear from June to October.*

This book is divided into the twelve months, with separate week-by-week sections in each. Within each of these sections suggestions for work that particular week are detailed, divided into work relevant to *Lawns, Flowers, Vegetables, Fruit* and *Greenhouses*. In addition, there are details of shrubs, trees and climbers in flower during the month, grouped according to their flower colour – *yellow and orange, white and cream, red and pink,* and *blue and mauve* and printed on an appropriately tinted background. *Bulbs, rock plants* and *border brighteners* in flower during the month are given in at-a-glance lists at the edges of the pages. In addition, each month there are lists of *biennials, perennials* and *annuals* that can be raised by seeds, together with the vital how and where information necessary for successful germination.

All this information is grouped under work for a particular week or plants in flower during the relevant month. However, Indian summers, rain-soaked summers and blizzards that last from Christmas through to early spring are all familiar to the gardener and to predict precisely when certain jobs should be done is like selecting the Derby winner on five consecutive years. However, it is possible to be about right for one particular area, three or four times out of five. There is, therefore, some variation within one area, but there is an even greater variation in the flowering times of plants in the south and in the north. For instance, in the Scilly Isles daffodils will flower during March and be nearly over by April, in the south they will be in full flower in April, but in the Midlands may still be in bud. There are a few areas in the north that are blessed with higher than average temperatures, where the west coast is washed by the Gulf Stream. Generally it is the north-east that suffers most from low temperatures and damaging cold winds. There great skill is needed in the choice of wind-tolerant plants.

Within this book all heights and spreads given for plants are those attainable after planting in good soil and ideal conditions after twenty or so years. In good conditions these may be exceeded, whereas in exposed and cold areas perhaps only half to three-quarters of these heights and spreads will be achieved. The heights and spreads given for climbers will also be affected by the structure supporting them, and if more space is available sideways then invariably that is the direction they will take.

From this it will be seen that gardening is the most perverse, inconstant, fascinating and demanding of all hobbies. And as it involves living plants it has an involvement not matched by any other hobby.

Above: The bright deep yellow heads of Achillea filipendula *'Coronation Gold' brighten borders from June to August. The flat heads are borne on plants 90 cm (3 ft) high.*

◇ JANUARY ◇

This is the season when there are fewest plants in flower in the garden, but those that do bring colour and brightness are particularly cherished. Few eyes would not give the *Hamamelis mollis* (Chinese witch hazel) with its rich golden-yellow spider-like flowers on bare branches a second glance, or the heavily spiced spider-like pale yellow and dark red centred flowers of *Hamamelis vernalis* (ozark witch hazel) or spicy scented *Chimonanthus praecox* 'Grandiflorus' (winter sweet).

Yellow is the dominant colour of winter and spring and many gardens have a *Jasminum nudiflorum* (winter jasmine) leaning against a north-facing wall where it creates colour from late autumn to early spring. It is not a climber, but a leaner, and so needs support to keep it in place. Its preference for a north-facing wall is because the flowers, if covered by frost, can thaw slightly before direct sun reaches them.

Helleborus niger (Christmas rose) with evergreen, leathery and deeply lobed leaves seldom bears flowers at Christmas: its everyday name refers to Old Christmas Day, 6 January. Its beautiful nearly 5 cm (2 in) wide saucer-shaped flowers are especially attractive behind a low and mound-forming clump of the pink-flowered *Erica herbacea* 'Springwood Pink'. White forms such as *E. herbacea* 'Springwood White' can also be used to create variation on the theme.

Few groups of flowering shrubs bring such reliable winter colour as the viburnums: the well-known *Viburnum × bodnantense* with highly fragrant rose-tinted white flowers on bare stems, the pink-tinged white-flowered *V. fragrans* and, perhaps the most widely grown, *V. tinus* (laurustinus). From early winter to early summer it is totally reliable with 5–10 cm (2–4 in) wide heads of white pink-budded flowers. The best form is 'Eve Price' with pink flowers.

Its evergreen bushiness makes it a superb screen, as well as a harmonizing partner for other viburnums and early-flowering rhododendrons.

Coloured barks can create striking areas of interest in perhaps an otherwise seasonally bare garden. *Acer griseum* (paperbark maple) is one of the best known and most widely grown coloured bark trees, with beautiful orange-brown bark that peels to reveal shades of cinnamon. It is exceptionally attractive when covered with snow. *Arbutus × andrachnoides*, with the influence of the Killarney strawberry tree in its blood, is also known as *A. × hybrida* and reveals cinnamon-red branches. The bark of the *A. unedo* (Killarney strawberry tree) is deep brown and shredding, and that of the ordinary strawberry tree is cinnamon-brown. The silver barks of birches are especially attractive when the branches are free of leaves. *Betula papyrifera* (paper birch or canoe birch) displays gleaming white bark that peels on old trees, and *B. utilis* (Himalayan birch) has creamy-white bark peeling in papery flakes. One of the most striking types, however, is the snakebarks, so called because of their striped barks. *Acer pensylvanicum* has bark with white and jade-green stripes, *A. capillipes* green bark striped white and *A. davidii* grey bark striped white.

Attractive plants during January need not depend solely on colour, but also on shape and interesting outlines. *Salix matsudana* 'Tortuosa', a form of the Pekin willow, creates a curious outline with twisted and contorted branches and twigs that are especially attractive against a bright blue winter sky. January need not be a dull month: there is a wealth of plants that can create colour, and the coloured-barked and interestingly branched types are not vulnerable to exceptionally cold weather.

Yellow-leaved conifers create an eye-catching display throughout the year, and especially during winter when in a snow-covered setting. Here, Chamaecyparis lawsoniana *'Winston Churchill' (left) and* Chamaecyparis lawsoniana *'President Roosevelt' (right) form an attractive focal point at the end of a lawn.*

JANUARY

**BULBS IN FLOWER
THIS MONTH**

◇

Cyclamen coum
Galanthus nivalis
(common snowdrop)

◇

FLOWERS

♦ Brush any snow from shrubs and trees gently before it freezes to prevent branches bending and breaking.
♦ Use your heel to firm back into the soil any shrubs and trees planted during the previous autumn which have been lifted by frost.

FRUIT

♦ Inspect fruits in store and remove any that are diseased and decaying. If left amid good fruits they soon cause all of them to rot. Check that the storage area is vermin-proof.
♦ Spray all fruit trees and bushes with tar-oil winter wash to kill overwintering eggs of insect pests. Thoroughly soak the tree or bush.

VEGETABLES

♦ Harvest the young shoots that have developed on chicory roots.
♦ Lift trench celery.
♦ Cover seakale crowns with inverted, large pots. Cover drainage holes with straw to exclude all light.

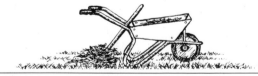

LAWNS

♦ Motor mowers not yet sent for servicing and repair should be seen to now. Hand-pushed-types also need checking, for wear and misalignment of the blades.
♦ Now is the time to clean, sharpen and oil all lawn equipment. If left their cutting edges become covered with rust that soon damages the metal and prevents them performing well in the garden during the following summer. If they are stored in a damp shed, place them in a plastic bag.

Right top: Variegated hollies are further enhanced when covered with snow or when seen against a ground-covering of snow.

GREENHOUSES

♦ Sow seeds, as recommended for this month. Ventilate the greenhouse carefully, avoiding draughts on the plants.

♦ Watering plants needs care during winter. Do not give them too much, which they will not be able to absorb when not growing quickly. Surplus water causes the compost to deteriorate to a soggy, airless mess that will not support plants either physically or nutritionally. Each year many plants are killed through being given too much water.

♦ Bulbs given as Christmas presents need to be checked to ensure the compost is not dry. If it is, stand the pot in a bowl of water until the moisture percolates to the surface. Then remove and allow excess water to drain away.

FLOWERS TO SOW THIS MONTH

BIENNIAL
LATHYRUS ODORATUS (sweet pea)
Sow 12 mm ($\frac{1}{2}$ in) deep in 15–20°C/60–68°F.

PERENNIALS
ALTHAEA ROSEA; now *Alcea rosea* (hollyhock)
Sow 6 mm ($\frac{1}{4}$ in) deep in 10–15°C/50–60°F.

ANEMONE CORONARIA (poppy anemone)
Sow 3 mm ($\frac{1}{8}$ in) deep in 10–15°C/50–60°F.

ANTIRRHINUM MAJUS (snapdragon): usually grown as half-hardy annual
Sow 3 mm ($\frac{1}{8}$ in) deep in 15–20°C/60–68°F.

AQUILEGIA VULGARIS (granny's bonnet)
Sow 3 mm ($\frac{1}{8}$ in) deep in 10–15°C/50–60°F.

ASCLEPIAS CURASSAVICA (milkweed/bloodflower)
Sow 6 mm ($\frac{1}{4}$ in) deep in 20–25°C/68–78°F.

CALCEOLARIA INTEGRIFOLIA; syn. *C. rugosa:* grown as half-hardy annual
Sow thinly and shallowly in 15–20°C/60–68°F.

CANNA (Indian shot)
Sow 12 mm ($\frac{1}{2}$ in) deep in 20–25°C/68–78°F.

CHRYSANTHEMUM PTARMICAEFLORUM (silver lace)
Sow 6 mm ($\frac{1}{4}$ in) deep in 15–20°C/60–68°F.

DIANTHUS CHINENSIS; syn. *D. sinensis* (Indian pink)
Sow (3 mm) ($\frac{1}{8}$ in) deep in 15–20°C/60–68°F.

LOBELIA ERINUS: grown as half-hardy annual
Sow thinly and shallowly in 15–20°C/60–68°F.

PETUNIA × HYBRIDA: grown as half-hardy annual
Sow thinly and shallowly in 15–20°C/60–68°F.

SALVIA PATENS: grown as half-hardy annual
Sow 6 mm ($\frac{1}{4}$ in) in 20–25°C/68–78°F.

SALVIA SPLENDENS: grown as half-hardy annual
Sow 6 mm ($\frac{1}{4}$ in) deep in 20–25°C/68–78°F.

VERBENA × HYBRIDA: grown as half-hardy annual
Sow 3 mm ($\frac{1}{8}$ in) deep in 15–20°C/60–68°F.

Left bottom: The large, silvery, plume-like heads of the Pampas Grass, Cortaderia selloana, assume further beauty when covered with snow and frost.

FLOWERS

♦ Keep paths free from snow, but after deep falls do not shovel it on top of small and delicate plants which are easily damaged.

♦ To free an area of ice on frozen ponds to relieve pressure on fish, place a kettle full of boiling water on the ice daily or float a tennis ball on the water before it freezes, clearing away the fresh ice each morning. Take care not to knock the ice, as this will kill the fish.

♦ Begin planning the flower garden. Do not wait until planting time arrives before planning the border.

FRUIT

♦ In good weather and if the soil is workable plant fruit trees and bushes.

♦ Dig the soil in preparation for strawberry planting. Mix in plenty of well-rotted manure or compost. Leave the surface with large lumps which frost will break down to a fine tilth.

VEGETABLES

♦ Sow early cauliflowers in gentle heat in a greenhouse to be ready for planting in March.

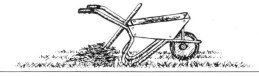

LAWNS

♦ Check all connections, plugs and sockets on electric grass cutters. Store all cables, plugs and sockets in a dry shed.

♦ Broken lawn edges not repaired in autumn can be patched if the lawn is dry. Cut out a rectangle encompassing the broken edge and reverse it so that the damaged part is in the lawn and the lawn edge is complete.

GREENHOUSES

♦ If your greenhouse is empty of plants during winter now is the time to clean it thoroughly. Wash and scrub all woodwork or metal parts, as well as the glass. Use a small plastic label to scrape dirt from between overlapping panes of glass. Clear away all debris from the soil and check that insects are not hiding under loose bricks.

♦ Remove flower heads as they fade. If left on the plants the rotting flowers encourage diseases to attack other flowers.

♦ Replace broken panes of glass if the greenhouse is empty.

♦ The ventilators frequently need repair during winter. If they are in need of drastic repair, remove them from the greenhouse and fix a piece of strong plastic over the vacant ventilator while it is being repaired. The hinges usually need some attention. Clean them and coat with oil so that they move freely.

IN FLOWER THIS MONTH

YELLOW AND ORANGE

SHRUBS

CHIMONANTHUS PRAECOX 'Grandiflorus' (winter sweet)
H: 2·4–3 m (8–10 ft) S: 2·4–3 m (8–10 ft)
Spicily scented deep yellow flowers with red centres. 'Luteus' has pure yellow flowers.

HAMAMELIS MOLLIS (Chinese witch hazel)
H: 1·8–2·4 m (6–8 ft) S: 1·8–2·4 m (6–8 ft)
Large deciduous, with rich golden-yellow spider-like and sweetly scented flowers clustered on bare stems. 'Pallida' has pale yellow flowers, and 'Brevipetala' has short, blunt-ended deep yellow petals.

HAMAMELIS VERNALIS (Ozark witch hazel)
H: 1·2–1·8 m (4–6 ft) S: 1·2–1·8 m (4–6 ft)
Deciduous with many small heavily scented spider-like pale yellow flowers with dark red centres.

MAHONIA BEALEI
H: 1·8–2·4 m (6–8 ft) S: 1·5–2·1 m (5–7 ft)
Leathery evergreen with lemon-yellow flowers in 10–15 cm (4–6 in) terminal clusters.

MAHONIA 'Charity'
H: 2·4–3 m (8–10 ft) S: 1·8–2·4 m (6–8 ft)
Spreading and ascending evergreen with fragrant deep yellow flowers in 23–30 cm (9–12 in) long poker-like arrangements.

MAHONIA LOMARIIFOLIA
H: 2·4–3 m (8–10 ft) S: 1·5–1·8 m (5–6 ft)
Evergreen with deep yellow 15–25 cm (6–10 in) erect spires of fragrant flowers.

Left: The spider-like rich golden-yellow flowers of the Chinese Witch Hazel, Hamamelis mollis, *are a treasure house of colour and scent.*

Right: Apples showing any sign of decay when being stored should be removed immediately. Fruits attacked by pests and diseases, as well as being roughly picked, soon develop rots when stored.

Below: The winter-flowering Erica herbacea 'Winter Beauty' (formerly 'King George') is a welcome sight now.

FLOWERS

♦ Protect *Helleborus niger*, the Christmas rose, with cloches from weather and birds.
♦ Watch out for slug damage during mild weather. Use slug-killing baits as soon as signs of attack are noticed.
♦ Prepare the ground for dahlias which will be planted out as soon as all risk of frost has passed. Some areas are not free from frost until late May or even the first week in June. Dig the soil thoroughly and add plenty of well-rotted manure or compost. Dahlias are gross-feeders and thrive on manure, which also helps retain moisture in the soil.

FRUIT

♦ Mulch gooseberry bushes with well-rotted manure or compost.
♦ Continue pruning established fruit trees, if not already completed. Burn all prunings.
♦ Inspect all apples and pears for canker. Cut out any infected tissue and paint the wound with a canker paint of bituminous wound paint.

VEGETABLES

♦ Harvest winter cabbages as they mature.

LAWNS

♦ When covered by snow the lawn edges are often inadvertently broken down so try to avoid treading on them.

Right: Dogwoods, Cornus alba, planted close to a garden pond, create coloured stems during winter, bringing invaluable colour during this dull season. The stems are also attractive when the pond is frozen.

GREENHOUSES

♦ Forced bulbs in bowls, such as daffodils and hyacinths, should be taken indoors when their growth is at the right stage.

♦ Greenhouse tomatoes can be sown in 16°C/61°F. Sow the seeds thinly in loam-based compost, water and cover with a piece of glass. After germination remove the glass and place the seedlings in a light part of the greenhouse. If left in a dull corner the seedlings become drawn up and leggy and will never become strong and healthy plants.

♦ Paraffin greenhouse heaters need checking before being used. Ensure that they are not leaking oil and that the wick is not burned out. It is better to replace it now than later.

IN FLOWER THIS MONTH

RED AND PINK

SHRUBS

ERICA × DARLEYENSIS 'Arthur Johnson'
H: 45–60 cm (18–24 in) S: 75–90 cm (2 ft 6 in–3 ft)
Spreading evergreen with magenta flowers in long sprays.

ERICA × DARLEYENSIS 'Jack H. Brummage'
H: 45–60 cm (18–24 in) S: 75–90 cm (2 ft 6 in–3 ft)
Evergreen yellow foliage that becomes gold then tinged red in winter. Deep pink flowers.

ERICA HERBACEA 'Adrienne Duncan'
H: 15–30 cm (6–12 in) S: 38–60 cm (15–24 in)
Evergreen dark bronze foliage with carmine red flowers.

ERICA HERBACEA 'Foxhollow'
H: 15–30 cm (6–12 in) S: 38–60 cm (15–24 in)
Evergreen yellow foliage, tinged red in winter, and pale pink flowers.

ERICA HERBACEA 'Myretoun Ruby'
H: 15–30 cm (6–12 in) S: 38–60 cm (15–24 in)
Evergreen dark foliage and deep rose-pink flowers.

ERICA HERBACEA 'Praecox Rubra'
H: 15–30 cm (6–12 in) S: 38–60 cm (15–24 in)
Evergreen foliage and deep rose-red flowers.

ERICA HERBACEA 'Ruby Glow'
H: 15–30 cm (6–12 in) S: 38–60 cm (15–24 in)
Evergreen bronze foliage and rich dark red flowers.

ERICA HERBACEA 'Springwood Pink'
H: 15–30 cm (6–12 in) S: 38–60 cm (15–24 in)
Evergreen with clear rose-pink flowers.

ERICA HERBACEA 'Vivellii'
H: 15–30 cm (6–12 in) S: 38–60 cm (15–24 in)
Evergreen bronze-red foliage in winter, and deep red flowers.

ERICA HERBACEA 'Winter Beauty', formerly 'King George'
H: 15–30 cm (6–12 in) S: 38–60 cm (15–24 in)
Evergreen with rose-pink flowers.

FLOWERS

♦ Order all seeds now in plenty of time for sowing.

♦ Examine all dahlias being stored as tubers and remove any that are showing signs of decay.

♦ Major structural changes are best carried out during the dormant season. Deciduous trees and shrubs can be moved while dormant. Wait until early spring to move evergreens, or even late autumn when the soil is warm.

♦ Prune and train ornamental vines on walls and pergolas.

FRUIT

♦ If not completed spray all fruit trees and bushes with tar-oil winter wash. Do not use on strawberry plants.

♦ Check all stakes and ties on fruit trees, replacing them as necessary. Ensure that the ties are not constricting the growth of trunks.

VEGETABLES

♦ Harvest leeks, trimming off roots and excessive leaves.

♦ Lift trench celery.

LAWNS

♦ In exceptionally mild areas the lawn may be producing top-growth. If the lawn is dry cut it with the cutters set high. Early cuts on wet lawns are best done with a hover-type mower as this does not cause skidding and destruction of the surface. If the lawn is extremely wet or covered with snow the best policy is to keep off it, as it can soon be seriously damaged.

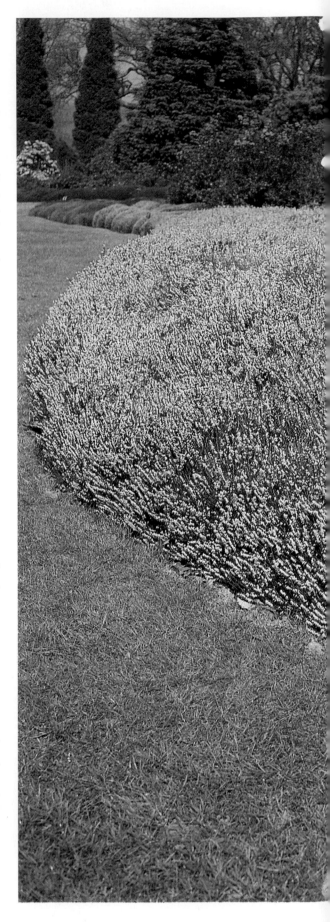

GREENHOUSES

♦ Bulbs that have been forced and produced plenty of growth may require unobtrusive staking. Use split canes and green twine.

♦ Prepare for boxing up chrysanthemum stools that are to be induced to produce cuttings. Clean all boxes and make sure there is a supply of clean compost.

♦ Sow cyclamen seeds for flowering during next winter. A temperature of 13–16°C/55–61°F is needed for rapid germination.

♦ Remove dead flowers from azaleas as soon as they fade. If left they will cause other blooms to decay. This also applies to other flowering plants for the home or greenhouse.

IN FLOWER THIS MONTH

CREAM AND WHITE

SHRUBS

CHIMONANTHUS PRAECOX; syn. *C. fragrans* (winter sweet)
H: 2·4–3 m (8–10 ft) S: 2·4–3 m (8–10 ft)
Spicily scented pale yellow flowers with purple centres.

ERICA × DARLEYENSIS 'Silver Bells'
H: 45–60 cm (18–24 in) S: 75–90 cm (30–36 in)
Spreading, ground-cover evergreen with white terminal flowers.

ERICA HERBACEA; formerly *E. carnea* 'Springwood White'
H: 15–30 cm (6–12 in) S: 38–60 cm (15–24 in)
Evergreen ground-cover plant.

ERICA LUSITANICA; syn. *E. codonodes*
H: 1·8–3 m (6–10 ft) S: 75–90 cm (30–36 in)
Evergreen with fragrant pink-budded white flowers amid apple-green leaves.

ERICA MEDITERRANEA 'W. T. Rackliff'; formerly *E. erigena* or *E. hibernica*
H: 75–90 cm (2 ft 6 in–3 ft) S: 90 cm–1·2 m (3–4 ft)
Dense evergreen with creamy-white bell-shaped flowers.

VIBURNUM × BODNANTENSE
H: 2·7–3·5 m (9–12 ft) S: 2·4–3 m (8–10 ft)
Deciduous with fragrant rose-tinted white flowers. 'Deben' has white flowers, pink in bud, and richly scented.

VIBURNUM FARRERI; syn. *V. fragrans*
H: 2·7–3·5 m (9–12 ft) S: 2·4–3 m (8–10 ft)
Deciduous with richly scented pink-tinged white flowers.

VIBURNUM TINUS (Laurustinus)
H: 2·1–3 m (7–10 ft) S: 1·8–2·1 m (6–7 ft)
Evergreen with pink-budded white flowers in flat heads.

Left: The winter-flowering **Erica herbacea** *'Springwood White' creates a dense ground-covering of white flowers.*

◇ F E B R U A R Y ◇

Bulbs burst upon the garden scene this month, perhaps heralding better weather to come. About now the well-known *Galanthus nivalis* (common snowdrop) raises its green-marked nodding white heads. Snowdrops are often confused with *Leucojum* (snowflakes). Snowdrops display three short inner petals and three long outer ones, whereas snowflakes have petals all the same size.

Eranthis hyemalis (winter aconite) foliage resembles that of aconites, and few bulbs are as appealing as these flowers peeping through a light fall of snow. *Cyclamen coum* continues to flower and is especially useful for dull areas under trees, and even on steep banks that are so often in need of a dash of winter colour. *Crocus biflorus* (Scotch crocus) flowers this month with purple-flushed white blooms. Other bulbs to look for are listed within this chapter.

A striking European native shrub in flower now is *Cornus mas* (cornelian cherry). It is bushy and twiggy with small fluffy clusters of golden-yellow flowers on naked branches from now to spring. At one time its exceedingly tough wood was used in central Europe for forks and ladder-spokes. Its common name derives from the red, pulpy, semi-translucent olive-sized fruits that in colour resemble a cornelian, which is a reddish form of chalcedony, a type of quartz used in jewellery.

Widely seen and admired is *Daphne mezereum* (mezereon) with dense clusters of purplish-red flowers. The stems are leafless at this time of year and the scented flowers can be easily seen. It looks superb grown with the bulbous *Iris reticulata* which displays 6·5–7·5 cm (2½–3 in) wide deep bluish-purple flowers blotched orange.

Later in the month in many areas the widely grown *Forsythia* × *intermedia* makes a spectacular show. The clouds of yellow flowers are a late winter joy in many gardens, and the plants easily grown. Perhaps it is for this reason that this reliable shrub does not always receive the praise it so richly deserves. Several forms are in flower now, including 'Lynwood' with rich yellow flowers, and bright yellow 'Spectabilis'. For extra large flowers try *Forsythia* 'Beatrix Farrand' with 4 cm (1½ in) wide rich yellow bells.

Herds of daffodils are good companions for forsythia and together they bring an impact of colour seldom achieved at any other time of year. Don't be mean when planting the daffodil bulbs, as just a few daffodil flowers looks worse than none at all. For exceptionally large gardens plant forsythias under *Acer saccharinum* (silver maple), with an underplanting of *Anemone blanda* (blue winter windflower or Grecian windflower).

In the rock garden many saxifragas are now producing colour and combine well with small bulbs such as *Crocus biflorus* (Scotch crocus).

Rhododendrons will now be creating colour and several look even better grouped with other plants that either harmonize or contrast with them. *Rhododendron* 'Christmas Cheer' with its compact and dense habit and pink-budded flowers that fade to white is an admirable companion for *Jasminum nudiflorum* (winter-flowering jasmine). Or position *Rhododendron* 'Tessa', with loose heads of purplish-pink flowers with crimson spots, in front of the winter-flowering jasmine and with an underplanting of *Narcissus bulbocodium* (hoop petticoat daffodil). This small and dainty miniature daffodil can also be set amid low winter-flowering heathers. The same can be done with *Narcissus cyclamineus*, a dainty bulb with a small trumpet and petals folded backwards.

Gardens need not be bare during this month, especially with the wealth of shrubs and bulbous plants that are so easily grown. Once planted these are the types of garden brighteners that create interest and colour from year to year without a great deal of seasonal attention. They are certainly value-for-money plants and candidates for all gardens.

Crocus naturalize around birches, creating a handsome late winter display. The sun, still low in the sky, highlights the silver bark as well as the bulbs. Take care that the newly-emerging bulbs are not trodden upon.

FLOWERS

♦ Fill gaps in wallflower beds with any spare plants which were heeled-in at the side of the bed, or any that were used to fill in gaps in shrub borders. Also, refirm those lifted by frost.

♦ Prune *Buddleia davidii*, butterfly bush, in the south. In very cold areas wait for a further few weeks before doing this as new shoots induced by the pruning may be damaged by frost.

♦ Prune dogwoods to encourage attractive stems with rich colours during autumn and winter.

FRUIT

♦ Established pear trees planted the previous year can be pruned now.

♦ Pear trees planted and treated as maidens the previous year will still not have developed a fruiting framework. Shorten the leader shoots to leave 20 cm (8 in) of new growth. And cut back lateral shoots to leave 15 cm (6 in) of new growth.

♦ Fruit trees growing in grassed orchards can be fed with a fertilizer high in nitrogen.

VEGETABLES

♦ Prepare the vegetable plot for the coming season. If not already completed dig it thoroughly, leaving the surface in relatively large pieces.

LAWNS

♦ Where stepping stones in the lawn have settled and created puddles, lift them and put sharp sand underneath. Use a straight-edged board to check that the stones are level with the surrounding lawn and will not catch on the mower blades.

FLOWERS TO SOW THIS MONTH

ANNUALS

AGERATUM HOUSTONIANUM
Sow 3 mm ($\frac{1}{8}$ in) deep in 10–15°C/50–60°F.

ALYSSUM MARITIMUM; now *Lobularia maritima*
Sow 6 mm ($\frac{1}{4}$ in) deep in 10–15°C/50–60°F.

ARCTOTIS × HYBRIDA (African daisy)
Sow 6 mm ($\frac{1}{4}$ in) deep in 10–15°C/50–60°F.

BEGONIA SEMPERFLORENS
Sow thinly and shallowly in 16°C/61°F.

CELOSIA ARGENTEA PLUMOSA (Prince of Wales' feather)
Sow 3 mm ($\frac{1}{8}$ in) deep in 20–25°C/68–78°F.

CLEOME SPINOSA; syn. *C. pungens* (spider flower)
Sow 3 mm ($\frac{1}{8}$ in) deep in 15–20°C/60–68°F.

DIDISCUS CAERULEUS; now *Trachymene caeruleus* (Queen Anne's lace/blue lace flower)
Sow 3 mm ($\frac{1}{8}$ in) deep in 15–20°C/60–68°F.

EMILIA FLAMMEA (tassel flower)
Sow 3 mm ($\frac{1}{8}$ in) deep in 15–20°C/60–68°F.

FELICIA BERGERIANA (kingfisher daisy)
Sow 3 mm ($\frac{1}{8}$ in) deep in 10–15°C/50–60°F.

GAILLARDIA PULCHELLA
Sow 6 mm ($\frac{1}{4}$ in) deep in 10–15°C/50–60°F.

GERBERA JAMESONII (Barberton daisy/Transvaal daisy)
Sow thinly and shallowly in 10–15°C/50–60°F.

IMPATIENS BALSAMINA (balsam/touch-me-not)
Sow 6 mm ($\frac{1}{4}$ in) deep in 15–20°C/60–68°F.

LATHYRUS ODORATUS (sweet pea)
Sow 12 mm ($\frac{1}{2}$ in) deep in 15–20°C/60–68°F.

MATTHIOLA INCANA (East Lothian stocks)
Sow 6 mm ($\frac{1}{4}$ in) deep in 15–20°C/60–68°F.

MOLUCELLA LAEVIS (Bells of Ireland/shell flower)
Sow 6 mm ($\frac{1}{4}$ in) deep in 15–20°C/60–68°F.

NEMESIA STRUMOSA
Sow 3 mm ($\frac{1}{8}$ in) deep in 15–20°C/60–68°F.

NICOTIANA ALATA: syn. *N. affinis* (tobacco plant)
Sow 3 mm ($\frac{1}{8}$ in) deep in 15–20°C/60–68°F.

PHLOX DRUMMONDII
Sow 6 mm ($\frac{1}{4}$ in) deep in 10–15°C/50–60°F.

TAGETES ERECTA (African marigold)
Sow 6 mm ($\frac{1}{4}$ in) deep in 15–20°C/60–68°F.

TAGETES PATULA (French marigold)
Sow 6 mm ($\frac{1}{4}$ in) deep in 15–20°C/60–68°F.

TAGETES TENUIFOLIA; syn. *T. signata* (marigold)
Sow 6 mm ($\frac{1}{4}$ in) deep in 15–20°C/60–68°F.

GREENHOUSES

♦ Sow seeds as recommended for this month. Also, sow sinningia (gloxinias), *Solanum capsicastrum* (winter cherry), tuberous begonias and primulas for greenhouse and indoor decoration.

♦ Place chrysanthemum stools into clean compost in boxes and place in a greenhouse. Water the compost and then give them a little heat and plenty of light.

♦ Box up dahlia tubers and treat them as for chrysanthemum stools.

♦ Water and ventilate the greenhouse, taking care to avoid draughts and excessive watering of plants. Remember to open the ventilators on the opposite side of the greenhouse from the prevailing wind.

Left: Few annuals have such attractive and delicate flowers as Didiscus caerulea, *the Queen Anne's Lace or Blue Lace Flower. Botanically, it is now called* Trachymene caerula, *although mostly it is known by its earlier name.*

Right: Marigolds are among the most popular and widely grown half-hardy bedding plants. Here, Tagetes patula *'Glowing Embers', a French Marigold, forms a neat edging to a border.*

BULBS IN FLOWER THIS MONTH

◇

Anemone blanda
(blue winter windflower/
Grecian windflower)

Chionodoxa gigantea;
syn. *C. grandiflora*

Chionodoxa luciliae
(glory of the snow)

Crocus biflorus
(Scotch crocus)

Crocus chrysanthus

Crocus susianus;
syn. *C. angustifolius*

Crocus tomasinianus

Cyclamen coum

Eranthis hyemalis
(winter aconite)

Eranthis × tubergenii

Galanthus nivalis
(common snowdrop)

Iris danfordiae

Iris reticulata

Narcissus bulbocodium
(hoop petticoat narcissus)

Narcissus cyclamineus
(cyclamen-flowered
narcissus)

◇

ROCK PLANTS IN FLOWER THIS MONTH

◇

Saxifraga burserana

Saxifraga × kewensis

◇

FLOWERS

◆ Rock gardens can be created now in a sunny position, not under trees where leaves and shade can be cast on it. If you do not have a suitable site, a well-drained mound can be formed. Position rocks so that they assume the lines of a natural strata: a random arrangement will create an eyesore and be a continuing disappointment.
◆ Feed established herbaceous borders. Spread well-rotted compost or manure between the cut-down plants. If the plants have not yet been tidied-up and cut down, do so before feeding them.
◆ Plant lily bulbs such as *Lilium regale*, the tiger lily (*Lilium tigrinum*), and *Lilium speciosum*.

FRUIT

◆ Cut down raspberry canes planted since the previous winter to 30 cm (1 ft) above the soil.
◆ Spray peaches against peach leaf-curl disease.
◆ Cover some strawberry plants with cloches to produce early crops.
◆ Apply a general-purpose fertilizer around fruit bushes and trees. Lightly hoe it in and mulch with well-rotted manure or compost.

VEGETABLES

◆ Plant shallots 15 cm (6 in) apart in rows 20–23 cm (8–9 in) apart.
◆ Sow salad onions 12 mm (½ in) deep in drills 13–15 cm (5–6 in) apart.

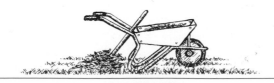

LAWNS

◆ Where bulbs were naturalized in the lawn cordon off the area to protect the emerging shoots from being trodden on.

FLOWERS TO SOW THIS MONTH

PERENNIAL
ALONSOA WARSCEWICZII (mask flower): grown as half-hardy annual
Sow 3 mm (⅛ in) deep in 10–15°C/50–60°F.

ALTHAEA ROSEA; now *Alcea rosea* (hollyhock)
Sow 6 mm (¼ in) deep in 10–15°C/50–60°F.

ANEMONE CORONARIA (poppy anemone)
Sow 3 mm (⅛ in) deep in 10–15°C/50–60°F.

ANTHEMIS NOBILIS (common chamomile)
Sow 3 mm (⅛ in) deep in 10–15°C/50–60°F.

ANTIRRHINUM MAJUS (snapdragon): grown as half-hardy or hardy annual
Sow 3 mm (⅛ in) deep in 15–20°C/60–68°F.

AQUILEGIA VULGARIS (granny's bonnet)
Sow 3 mm (⅛ in) deep in 10–15°C/50–60°F.

ASCLEPIAS CURASSAVICA (milkweed/blood flower)
Sow 6 mm (¼ in) deep in 20–25°C/68–78°F.

CALCEOLARIA INTEGRIFOLIA; syn. *C. rugosa*: grown as half-hardy annual
Sow thinly and shallowly in 15–20°C/60–68°F.

CANNA (Indian shot)
Sow 12 mm (½ in) deep in 20–25°C/68–78°F.

CATANANCHE CAERULEA (Cupid's dart)
Sow 3 mm (⅛ in) deep in 13°C/55°F.

CHRYSANTHEMUM PARTHENIUM: grown as annual
Sow 3 mm (⅛ in) deep in 15–20°C/60–68°F.

CHRYSANTHEMUM PTARMICAEFLORUM (silver lace)
Sow 6 mm (¼ in) deep in 15–20°C/60–68°F.

DIANTHUS CHINENSIS; syn. *D. sinensis* (Indian pink)
Sow 3 mm (⅛ in) deep in 15–20°C/60–68°F.

HELIOTROPIUM × HYBRIDUM (heliotrope/cherry pie): grown as half-hardy annual
Sow 6 mm (¼ in) deep in 15–20°C/60–68°F.

LOBELIA ERINUS: grown as half-hardy annual
Sow thinly and shallowly in 15–20°C/60–68°F.

MESEMBRYANTHEMUM CRINIFLORUM (Livingstone daisy): grown as half-hardy annual
Sow 3 mm (⅛ in) deep in 15–20°C/60–68°F.

PETUNIA × HYBRIDA: grown as half-hardy annual
Sow thinly and shallowly in 15–20°C/60–68°F.

SALVIA PATENS: grown as half-hardy annual
Sow 6 mm (¼ in) deep in 20–25°C/68–78°F.

SALVIA SPLENDENS: grown as half-hardy annual
Sow 6 mm (¼ in) deep in 20–25°C/68–78°F.

TROPAEOLUM PEREGRINUM (canary creeper): grown as half-hardy annual
Sow 12 mm (½ in) deep in 15–20°C/60–68°F.

VERBENA × HYBRIDA: grown as half-hardy annual
Sow 3 mm (⅛ in) deep in 15–20°C/60–68°F.

Right: Perpetual-flowering carnation cuttings can be taken from December to February. Detach sideshoots 10–13 cm (4–5 in) long from healthy plants and insert them in sharp sand. Place them in 16°C/61°F. When rooted, reduce the temperature to 10°C/50°F and pot up individually into small pots.

Right top: Verbena × hybrida 'Sparkle Hybrids' can be sown now to create a rich array of colourful flowers.

Right bottom; Lobelia erinus 'White Gem' is a beautiful half-hardy perennial grown as a half-hardy annual.

GREENHOUSES

♦ Syringe greenhouse grapevines with clean water to encourage the development of new growth.

♦ Check for signs of pests and diseases, spraying the plants as necessary.

♦ Forced bulbs can still be brought into the greenhouse or indoors.

♦ Bulbs that were forced into flower indoors during winter can be given less water and placed under greenhouse staging so that the foliage can die down naturally. Do not cut off the leaves.

♦ Fuchsia and pelargonium cuttings can be taken now, inserting them in well-drained rooting compost.

IN FLOWER THIS MONTH

YELLOW AND ORANGE

SHRUBS

CHIMONANTHUS PRAECOX 'Grandiflorus': see January

CORNUS MAS (cornelian cherry)
H: 2·4–3·5 m (8–12 ft) S: 1·8–3 m (6–10 ft)
Bushy, twiggy, deciduous shrub with clusters of small golden-yellow flowers on naked branches.

HAMAMELIS MOLLIS, H. VERNALIS, MAHONIA BEALEI, M. 'Charity', *M. LOMARIIFOLIA:* see January

MAHONIA PINNATA
H: 2·4–3 m (8–10 ft) S; 1·8–2·4 m (6–8 ft)
Prickly sea-green evergreen with slightly fragrant rich yellow flowers in 5–10 cm (2–4 in) wide clusters.

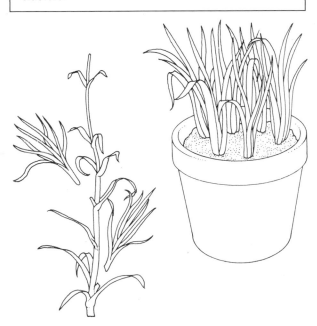

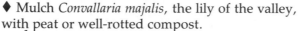

FLOWERS

FRUIT

Below: Cornus mas, *the Cornelian Cherry, is a large shrub or small tree with small yellow flowers on bare stems from February to April. It gains its common name from the bright red cherry-like fruits that follow the flowers. These resemble a cornelian, a reddish variety of chalcedony used in jewellery.*

♦ Mulch *Convallaria majalis,* the lily of the valley, with peat or well-rotted compost.

♦ Prune winter-flowering jasmine, *Jasminum nudiflorum,* as soon as the flowers have faded. In some areas it will continue flowering until early April.

♦ Trim winter-flowering heathers as soon as the flowers fade. Use sharp hedging shears to clip them.

♦ Examine dahlia tubers that are being stored for signs of decay.

♦ Roses affected by black spot last year should be tidied up by removing all leaves still on the soil's surface. Burn them rather than adding them to a compost heap.

♦ Cut off the tips from raspberry canes that grew the previous year and will bear fruit during the coming season. Prune off the top few inches of growth above the top supporting wire to concentrate their growth into buds that will bear fruit.

♦ Continue to inspect all fruits in store, removing those showing signs of decay.

♦ Control weeds among fruit trees and bushes with simazine.

♦ Apply fertilizers containing potash to apples, pears and plums.

♦ Cover strawberry plants to obtain an early crop of strawberries.

♦ Spray peach trees and nectarines against peach leaf curl.

VEGETABLES

♦ Sow parsnips 12 mm (½ in) deep in drills 30 cm (1 ft) apart.
♦ Thin lettuces sown the previous August for cutting in spring. Leave the seedlings 20–25 cm (8–10 in) apart.
♦ Sow onions in drills 12 mm (½ in) deep and 23–30 cm (9–12 in) apart.
♦ Harvest the young shoots that have developed on chicory roots.

LAWNS

♦ In mild areas the lawn will continue to develop top-growth. When the weather is suitable lightly cut the grass. If the mower shows any signs of skidding, stop immediately.

GREENHOUSES

♦ Pollinate peaches, almonds, nectarines and apricots growing in a greenhouse.
♦ Take cuttings of heliotrope, 7·5–10 cm (3–4 in) long, and insert them in a propagation frame at 16°C/61°F.
♦ Continue to sow tomato seeds to raise for planting in a greenhouse.
♦ Ventilate the greenhouse on warm days but take care not to create draughts.
♦ Re-pot ferns such as pteris and maidenhair fern and place them in a warm position.
♦ Freesias that have finished flowering can have their pots placed on their sides under the greenhouse bench to assist them to dry off. Position them away from water dripping from other plants.

Below: Winters can be brightened and given further interest by the cup-shaped flowers that are borne in pendulous tassel-like arrangements by Stachyrus chinensis, *a large deciduous shrub from China.*

IN FLOWER THIS MONTH

RED AND PINK

SHRUBS

CAMELLIA JAPONICA (common camellia)
H: 1·8–3·5 m (6–12 ft) S: 1·8–3 m (6–10 ft)
Evergreen, originally with red flowers 6·5–9 cm (2½–3½ in) wide, but now also available in white, and wide range of pinks and reds to purple and flower sizes up to 13 cm (5 in) wide. Single, semi-double, double, anemone and paeony forms are available.

DAPHNE MEZEREUM (mezereon)
H: 90 cm–1·5 m (3–5 ft) S: 60 cm–1·2 m (2–4 ft)
Deciduous with dense clusters of scented purplish-red flowers on leafless stems. A white form is also available.

DAPHNE ODORA
H: 1·5–1·8 m (5–6 ft) S: 1·2–1·5 m (4–5 ft)
Bushy evergreen with highly fragrant purple-pink flowers. 'Aureomarginata' displays leaves with creamy-white edges.

ERICA × DARLEYENSIS 'Arthur Johnson', *E. × D.* 'Jack H. Brummage', *E. HERBACEA* 'Adrienne Duncan', *E.H.* 'Foxhollow', *E. H.* 'Myretoun Ruby', *E.H.* 'Praecox Rubra', *E. H.* 'Ruby Glow', *E. H.* 'Springwood Pink', *E. H.* 'Vivellii': see January

WALL SHRUBS AND CLIMBERS

ABELIOPHYLLUM DISTICHUM
H: 90 cm–1·5 m (3–5 ft) S: 90 cm–1·5 m (3–5 ft)
Slow-growing deciduous wall shrub with star-shaped blush-pink flowers on bare stems.

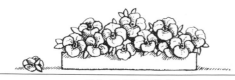

FLOWERS

♦ Cut down herbaceous plants not trimmed back in the autumn. In exceptionally cold areas leave this job for a further few weeks. Leaving the foliage on the plants helps to protect tender plants from frost damage in cold areas.

♦ Gladioli and anemone corms can be planted in mild areas. Ranunculus tubers can also be planted.

♦ Prepare the ground for further herbaceous and annual borders. Dig the soil thoroughly and remove all perennial weeds. Do not add such weeds to the compost heap; burn them instead.

♦ Prune *Hydrangea paniculata* and *H. arborescens* in mild areas.

FRUIT

♦ Autumn-fruiting raspberries will need pruning now. Cut out at ground level the canes that bore fruits during the previous autumn.

♦ Feed fruit trees growing in cultivated soil with a fertilizer high in nitrogen.

IN FLOWER THIS MONTH

WHITE AND CREAM

SHRUBS

CHIMONANTHUS PRAECOX, ERICA × DARLEYENSIS 'Silver Bells', *E. HERBACEA* 'Springwood White', *E. LUSITANICA, E. MEDITERRANEA* 'W. T. Rackliff: see January

LONICERA FRAGRANTISSIMA
H: 1·5–1·8 m (5–6 ft) S: 1·5–1·8 m (5–6 ft)
Partial evergreen with highly fragrant creamy-white flowers.

PACHYSANDRA TERMINALIS
H: 23–30 cm (9–12 in) S: 38–45 cm (15–18 in)
Sub-shrubby evergreen with 2·5–5 cm (1–2 in) long spikes of white flowers. 'Variegata' has white-edged leaves.

SARCOCOCCA HUMILIS
H: 45 cm (18 in)) S: 75–90 cm (30–36 in)
Thicket-forming and ground-covering evergreen with scented white flowers displaying pink anthers.

VIBURNUM × BODNANTENSE, V. FARRERI, V. TINUS: see January

VEGETABLES

♦ Harvest leeks, trimming off roots and excessive leaves.
♦ Feed asparagus beds with a general fertilizer.
♦ Thin lettuces sown under cloches the previous October to 15–23 cm (6–9 in) apart, depending on the vigour of the variety.

LAWNS

♦ Keep off the lawn if the surface is wet or frosted. When the surface is soft and wet it is easy to consolidate parts of the lawn, creating indentations and destroying the effect of any aeration treatment during the previous autumn or early winter.

GREENHOUSES

♦ Pot up achimines 2·5 cm (1 in) deep, six to a 13 cm (5 in) pot. Water them lightly and place in 16°C/61°F. Increase the amount of water given to them as they develop shoots.
♦ Pot up perpetual-flowering carnations and place in a light and cool position.
♦ Continue to sow seeds, as recommended for this month.
♦ Box up a few tubers of sinningia (gloxinia) and begonias. Set them in boxes of peat, 2·5–5 cm (1–2 in) apart, water and place in 18°C/64°F. When the shoots are developing strongly pot them up singly with loam-based compost.

Left: Hydrangea arborescens 'Grandiflora' *develops large heads of white flowers from July to September. It is a hardy deciduous shrub that can be pruned now. Cut back by half all the shoots that produced flowers during the previous year.*

◇ MARCH ◇

Whether this month is called late winter or early spring, the weather is often still very gloomy. It is therefore useful to have a dominant burst of colour in the garden, perhaps with the white-flowered *Magnolia stellata* (star magnolia) contrasting with deep sky-blue *Muscari botryoides* beneath it. *Muscari armeniacum* (grape hyacinth) flowers a little later, during April and May. *Magnolia denudata* can also be used, and like the star magnolia its size is suited to a small garden. It bears white, chalice-shaped fragrant flowers from now until May.

A beautiful deciduous tree often planted in streets is *Prunus cerasifera* 'Pissardii' (cherry plum), mainly grown for its beautiful dark red young leaves, although it also bears pink-budded white flowers. 'Pissardii' is in honour of Mr. Pissard, gardener to the Shah of Persia towards the latter part of the 1800s. In 1880 he sent a specimen to France and it soon became popular and widely grown. For pink flowers try *Prunus cerasifera* 'Nigra'. Both these trees, with distinctive dark foliage, make ideal backcloths for *Mahonia aquifolium* (Oregon grape). This is a suckering, hardy, evergreen shrub with dark green leathery leaves and fragrant, rich yellow flowers.

Another prunus tree flowering now is *Prunus sargentii*, with clear pink blossom and leaves that are orange and crimson during autumn. It it one of the earliest trees to assume colourful leaves in autumn.

For a scented March garden there are many candidates, including *Viburnum* 'Anne Russell' with clusters of pink-budded white flowers. *Viburnum × bodnantense* continues flowering this month, as does *Viburnum farreri* with its richly scented pink-tinged white flowers, *Chimonanthus praecox* (winter sweet), *Lonicera fragrantissima* and *Sarcococcoa humilis*, a ground-hugging evergreen with white flowers. All of these are worthy of consideration in a scented garden.

With the onset of early spring there is a greater range of colours in the garden. There are a multitude of shades of scarlet, yellow and orange among tulipa species. *Tulipa kaufmanniana* (water-lily tulip) displays star-like 10 cm (4 in) wide white flowers flushed yellow and red during March and April. Muscari and chionodoxas are bright blue, *Pulsatilla vulgaris* (pasque flower) violet or mauve, *Primula rosea* rose-pink, and the early daffodils yellow.

The Kaufmanniana tulips are splendid when planted with forsythia, or in a bed under the star magnolia.

The range of heathers in flower now is impressive, with colours to suit most tastes. *Erica × darleyensis*, a hybrid between *E. herbacea* and *E. mediterranea*, grows well in limy soil with terminal flowers in pink, purple and white. *E. herbacea*, previously known as *E. carnea*, is the best known and most widely grown heather. As well as producing flowers in shades of white or pink, many varieties have coloured foliage, such as 'Aurea' with golden-yellow leaves. *E. mediterranea* grows much higher, with flowers usually in shades of purple-pink. *E. lusitanica* is a similar height, with pink flowers.

Ribes sanguineum (flowering currant) does not come into flower until late this month, and blooms mainly in April, but *R. laurifolium* often flowers as early as February and then into March. The greenish-yellow flowers are in nodding 4–6·5 cm (1½–2½ in) long clusters. Flowers of one sex appear on one plant. The oval fruits are reddish at first and then purple, but occur only when male and female plants are grown together.

As soon as this month comes to an end we can look forward to a rush of spring flowers. Easter, with its herds of golden daffodils, is always a turning point in the gardener's calendar.

Herds of golden daffodils naturalize in grass and around shrubs and trees, bringing sparkle and further interest to a garden. Plant the bulbs in large and dominant clumps, rather than wide apart and sparse.

MARCH

BULBS IN FLOWER THIS MONTH

◇

Anemone blanda
(blue winter windflower/
Grecian windflower)

Anemone coronaria
(poppy anemone)

Chionodoxa gigantea;
syn. *C. grandiflora*

Chionodoxa luciliae
(glory of the snow)

Chionodoxa sardensis
(glory of the snow)

Crocus biflorus
(Scotch crocus)

Crocus tomasinianus

Crocus vernus;
syn. *C. neapolitanus*

Cyclamen coum

Eranthis hyemalis
(winter aconite)

Iris danfordiae

Iris reticulata

Muscari botryoides

Narcissus
(daffodil)

Narcissus bulbocodium
(hoop petticoat narcissus)

Narcissus cyclamineus
(cyclamen-flowered
narcissus)

Narcissus triandrus albus
(angel's tears)

Puschkinia scilloides
(striped squill)

Scilla bifolia
(two-leaf squill)

Scilla sibirica
(Siberian squill)

Tulipa fosteriana

Tulipa kaufmanniana

◇

FLOWERS

♦ Prepare the soil for sowing annuals. Fork the soil, removing all weeds and adding a general-purpose fertilizer after the surface has been raked level.

♦ Prune *Caryopteris* × *clandonensis*. Use secateurs to cut back the previous year's shoots to strong buds.

♦ Lift and divide snowdrop bulbs as soon as the flowers fade. Bulbs that become congested may eventually fail to flower.

FRUIT

♦ Winter-prune gooseberries. Cut back the shoots on two-year-old and newly planted plants by half.

♦ Prune maiden pear trees as soon as they start to grow in spring. Shorten the main shoot to 50 cm (20 in) high and prune back sideshoots to five buds.

VEGETABLES

♦ Sow onions in drills 12 mm (½ in) deep and 23–30 cm (9–12 in) apart.

♦ Top-dress lettuces that have been sown for cutting in spring. Use a balanced fertilizer at 70 grams a square metre (2 oz a square yard).

♦ Remove straw covering globe artichokes and top-dress with a general fertilizer.

♦ Sow cauliflowers in a seedbed for planting out in June.

♦ Sow summer spinach 12 mm (½ in) deep in drills 30 cm (1 ft) apart.

♦ Sow radishes thinly in drills 12 mm (½ in) deep between now and early September.

♦ Sow parsnips 12 mm (½ in) deep in drills 30 cm (1 ft) apart.

Right: Cleome spinosa, *the Spider Flower from the West Indies, can be sown now to produce large spider-like heads of flowers from June to the frosts of autumn.*

FLOWERS TO SOW THIS MONTH

ANNUALS

ADONIS AESTIVALIS (pheasant's eye)
Sow 6 mm (¼ in) deep *in situ*.

AGERATUM HOUSTONIANUM
Sow 3 mm (⅛ in) deep in 10–15°C/50–60°F.

ALYSSUM MARITIMUM; now *Lobularia maritima*
Sow 6 mm (¼ in) deep in 10–15°C/50–60°F.

AMARANTHUS CAUDATUS (love-lies-bleeding)
Sow 3 mm (⅛ in) deep *in situ*.

AMARANTHUS HYPOCHONDRIACUS (prince's feather/pygmy torch)
Sow 3 mm (⅛ in) deep in 15°C/60°F.

ARCTOTIS × HYBRIDA (African daisy)
Sow 6 mm (¼ in) deep in 10–15°C/50–60°F.

ASPERULA ORIENTALIS; syn. *A. azurea/A. setosa* (annual woodruff)
Sow 6 mm (¼ in) deep *in situ*.

BEGONIA SEMPERFLORENS
Sow thinly and shallowly in 16°C/61°F.

BRACHYCOME IBERIDIFOLIA (Swan River daisy)
Sow 6 mm (¼ in) deep *in situ*.

CALENDULA OFFICINALIS (pot marigold/English marigold)
Sow 12 mm (½ in) deep *in situ*.

CALLISTEPHUS CHINENSIS (China aster)
Sow 6 mm (¼ in) deep in 16°C/61°F.

CELOSIA ARGENTEA PLUMOSA (Prince of Wales' feather)
Sow 3 mm (⅛ in) deep in 20–25°C/68–78°F.

CENTAUREA CYANUS (Cornflower)
Sow 12 mm (½ in) deep *in situ*.

CHRYSANTHEMUM CARINATUM; syn. *C. tricolor*
Sow 6 mm (¼ in) deep *in situ*.

CLARKIA ELEGANS
Sow 6 mm (¼ in) deep *in situ*.

CLARKIA PULCHELLA
Sow 6 mm (¼ in) deep *in situ*.

CLEOME SPINOSA; syn. *C. pungens* (spider flower)
Sow 3 mm (⅛ in) deep in 15–20°C/60–68°F.

CONSOLIDA AJACIS (larkspur)
Sow 6 mm (¼ in) deep *in situ*.

CONVOLVULUS TRICOLOR; syn. *C. minor*
Sow 12 mm (½ in) deep *in situ*.

COREOPSIS TINCTORIA (tickseed)
Sow 6 mm (¼ in) deep *in situ*.

DIDISCUS CAERULEUS; now *Trachymene caeruleus* (Queen Anne's lace/blue lace flower)
Sow 3 mm (⅛ in) deep in 15–20°C/60–68°F.

DIMORPHOTHECA AURANTIACA (star of the veldt)
Sow 6 mm (¼ in) deep *in situ*.

ECHIUM LYCOPSIS; syn. *E. plantagineum* (viper's bugloss)
Sow 6 mm (¼ in) deep *in situ*.

EMILA FLAMMEA (tassel flower)
Sow 3 mm (⅛ in) deep in 15–20°C/60–68°F.

ESCHSCHOLZIA CALIFORNICA (Californian poppy)
Sow 6 mm (¼ in) deep *in situ*.

FELICIA BERGERIANA (kingfisher daisy)
Sow 3 mm (⅛ in) deep in 10–15°C/50–60°F.

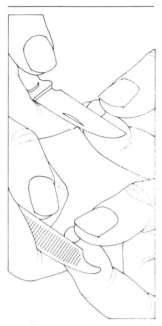

Above: Large seeds with hard coats can be encouraged to germinate more rapidly by either shallowly nicking the seed's coat with a penknife or using a nail-file to scrape away part of the covering.

MARCH

ROCK PLANTS IN FLOWER THIS MONTH

◇

Aubrieta deltoidea
Erinus alpinus
Saxifraga × apiculata
Saxifraga × borisii
Saxifraga burserana
Saxifraga 'Cranbourne'
Saxifraga × kewensis
Saxifraga 'Riverslea'
Saxifraga oppositifolia

◇

FLOWERS TO SOW THIS MONTH

ANNUALS

GAILLARDIA PULCHELLA
Sow 6 mm (¼ in) deep in 10–15°C/50–60°F.

GERBERA JAMESONII (Barberton daisy/Transvaal daisy)
Sow thinly and shallowly in 10–15°C/50–60°F.

GILIA LUTEA (stardust)
Sow 6 mm (¼ in) deep *in situ*.

GODETIA GRANDIFLORA
Sow 6 mm (¼ in) deep *in situ*.

GOMPHRENA GLOBOSA (bachelor's buttons)
Sow 6 mm (¼ in) deep in 20–25°C/68–78°F.

GYPSOPHILA ELEGANS
Sow 6 mm (¼ in) deep *in situ*.

HELIANTHUS ANNUUS (sunflower)
Sow 12 mm (½ in) deep *in situ*.

HIBISCUS TRIONUM (flower-of-an-hour)
Sow 6 mm (¼ in) deep *in situ*.

IBERIS UMBELLATA (candytuft)
Sow 6 mm (¼ in) deep *in situ*.

IMPATIENS BALSAMINA (balsam/touch-me-not)
Sow 6 mm (¼ in) deep in 15–20°C/60–68°F.

IPOMOEA PURPUREA; syn. *Convolvulus major*
Sow 12 mm (½ in) deep *in situ*.

IPOMOEA VIOLACEA; syn. *I. rubro-caerulea* (morning glory)
Sow 12 mm (½ in) deep in 15–20°C/60–68°F.

KOCHIA SCOPARIA 'Trichophylla' (summer cypress/ burning bush)
Sow 3 mm (⅛ in) deep in 15–20°C/60–68°F.

LATHYRUS ODORATUS (sweet pea)
Sow 12 mm (½ in) deep in 15–20°C/60–68°F.

LAVATERA TRIMESTRIS (mallow)
Sow 12 mm (½ in) deep *in situ*.

LIMNANTHES DOUGLASII (poached egg plant)
Sow 3 mm (⅛ in) deep *in situ*.

LINARIA MAROCCANA (Toadflax)
Sow 3 mm (⅛ in) deep *in situ*.

LYCHNIS VISCARIA
Sow 6 mm (¼ in) deep *in situ*.

MALCOLMIA MARITIMA (Virginian stock)
Sow 6 mm (¼ in) deep *in situ*.

MATTHIOLA BICORNIS (night-scented stock)
Sow 6 mm (¼ in) deep *in situ*.

MATTHIOLA INCANA (East Lothian stocks)
Sow 6 mm (¼ in) deep in 15–20°C/60–68°F.

MENTZELIA LINDLEYI
Sow 6 mm (¼ in) deep *in situ*.

MOLUCELLA LAEVIS (bells of Ireland/shell flower)
Sow 6 mm (¼ in) deep in 15–20°C/60–68°F.

NEMESIA STRUMOSA
Sow 3 mm (⅛ in) deep in 15–20°C/60–68°F.

NEMOPHILA MENZIESII (baby blue eyes)
Sow 6 mm (¼ in) deep *in situ*.

NICOTIANA ALATA; syn. *N. affinis* (tobacco plant)
Sow 3 mm (⅛ in) deep in 15–20°C/60–68°F.

NIGELLA DAMASCENA (love-in-a-mist)
Sow 6 mm (¼ in) deep *in situ*.

PAPAVER RHOEAS (field poppy/Shirley poppy)
Sow 6 mm (¼ in) deep *in situ*.

PHLOX DRUMMONDII
Sow 6 mm (¼ in) deep in 10–15°C/50–60°F.

RESEDA ODORATA (mignonette)
Sow 3 mm (⅛ in) deep *in situ*.

TAGETES ERECTA (African marigold)
Sow 6 mm (¼ in) deep in 15–20°C/60–68°F.

TAGETES PATULA (French marigold)
Sow 6 mm (¼ in) deep in 15–20°C/60–68°F.

TAGETES TENUIFOLIA; syn. *T. signata* (marigold)
Sow 6 mm (¼ in) deep in 15–20°C/60–68°F.

THUNBERGIA ALATA (black-eyed Susan)
Sow 6 mm (¼ in) deep in 20–25°C/68–78°F.

ZINNIA ELEGANS
Sow 6 mm (¼ in) deep in 15–20°C/60–68°F.

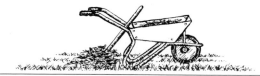

LAWNS

♦ Grass cutting will soon be necessary in all areas. Even if the grass is long, don't cut it closely. Mowing lawns too closely now may ruin it for the rest of the year. For the first cut set the blades of the mower high, gradually reducing the cutting height to 12–18 mm (½–¾ in) high.

♦ Lawn edges will need trimming with edging shears.

♦ When digging borders next to lawns always place a board along the edge to prevent it being damaged. Lawn edges that are wet are easily damaged and become an eye-sore.

GREENHOUSES

♦ Continue to sow seeds, as recommended for this month.

♦ Prick out seedlings into boxes or pots of compost as soon as they are large enough to handle.

♦ Stop schizanthus plants to encourage the formation of further sideshoots. Nip out the growing tips.

♦ Take cuttings of chrysanthemums, 7·5 cm (2½ in) long, and insert them in equal parts of peat and sharp sand. Place in a propagation frame with bottom heat, preferably about 15°C/59°F.

♦ Sow greenhouse-flowering plants for flowering later in the year and during winter.

FLOWERS TO SOW THIS MONTH

PERENNIALS

ALONSOA WARSCEWICZII (mask flower): grown as half-hardy annual
Sow 3 mm (⅛ in) deep in 10–15°C/50–60°F.

ALSTROEMERIA LIGTU (Peruvian lily)
Sow 18 mm (¾ in) deep in cool greenhouse.

ALYSSUM SAXATILE (gold dust)
Sow 6 mm (¼ in) deep in a cool greenhouse.

ANEMONE CORONARIA (poppy anemone)
Sow 3 mm (⅛ in) deep in 10–15°C/50–60°F.

ANTHEMIS NOBILIS (common chamomile)
Sow 3 mm (⅛ in) deep in 10–15°C/50–60°F.

ANTIRRHINUM MAJUS (snapdragon): usually grown as half-hardy annual
Sow 3 mm (⅛ in) deep in 15–20°C/60–68°F.

AQUILEGIA VULGARIS (granny's bonnet)
Sow 3 mm (⅛ in) deep in 10–15°C/50–60°F.

ARABIS ALPINA (wall cress/rock cress)
Sow 3 mm (⅛ in) deep in a cool greenhouse.

ASCLEPIAS CURASSAVICA (milkweed/bloodflower)
Sow 6 mm (¼ in) deep in 20–25°C/68–78°F.

ASTER NOVI-BELGII (Michaelmas daisy)
Sow 6 mm (¼ in) deep in 15–20°C/60–68°F.

CALCEOLARIA INTEGRIFOLIA; syn. *C. rugosa:* grown as half-hardy annual
Sow thinly and shallowly in 15–20°C/60–68°F.

CANNA (Indian shot)
Sow 12 mm (½ in) deep in 20–25°C/68–78°F.

CATANANCHE CAERULEA (Cupid's dart)
Sow 3 mm (⅛ in) deep in 13°C/55°F.

CERASTIUM TOMENTOSUM (snow-in-summer)
Sow 6 mm (¼ in) deep in a seed bed.

CHRYSANTHEMUM PARTHENIUM: grown as annual
Sow 3 mm (⅛ in) deep in 15–20°C/60–68°F.

DIANTHUS CHINENSIS (Indian pink)
Sow 3 mm (⅛ in) deep in 15–20°C/60–68°F.

HELIOTROPIUM × HYBRIDUM (heliotrope/cherry pie): grown as half-hardy annual
Sow 6 mm (¼ in) deep in 15–20°C/60–68°F.

LOBELIA ERINUS: grown as half-hardy annual
Sow thinly and shallowly in 15–20°C/60–68°F.

LYCHNIS CHALCEDONICA (Jerusalem cross)
Sow 6 mm (¼ in) deep *in situ.*

MESEMBRYANTHEMUM CRINIFLORUM (Livingstone daisy): grown as half-hardy annual
Sow 3 mm (⅛ in) deep in 15–20°C/60–68°F.

PETUNIA × HYBRIDA: grown as half-hardy annual
Sow thinly and shallowly in 15–20°C/60–68°F.

SALVIA PATENS: grown as half-hardy annual
Sow 6 mm (¼ in) deep in 20–25°C/68–78°F.

SALVIA SPLENDENS: grown as half-hardy annual
Sow 6 mm (¼ in) deep in 20–25°C/68–78°F.

TROPAEOLUM PEREGRINUM (canary creeper): grown as half-hardy annual
Sow 12 mm (½ in) deep in 15–20°C/60–68°F.

VERBENA × HYBRIDA: grown as half-hardy annual
Sow 3 mm (⅛ in) deep in 15–20°C/60–68°F.

Shrubs sold in containers can be planted at any time when the soil is not frozen or too wet. First, thoroughly water the compost while the plant is still in the container (top picture). Dig a hole large enough to accommodate the roots and fork over the soil in the base. At the same time add a sprinkling of bonemeal. When planting a shrub or tree in a lawn, place the soil on a large piece of sacking to prevent the grass being spoiled. Form a mound of soil at the base of the hole, so that when the plant is placed on top the soil-ball is slightly lower than the surrounding soil. Remove the container from the soil-ball (centre picture). Return the soil to the hole and firm it around the roots. Use the heel of your shoe to firm the soil (bottom picture). Afterwards, water the soil to enable the soil particles to settle closely around the roots.

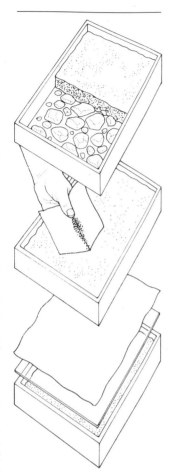

Above: When sowing seeds in boxes or pots ensure that the container is well drained and that moisture-retentive yet well-drained compost is used. Seeds are often sprinkled on to the compost directly from a packet. But a better method is to put some seed into a V-shaped piece of white paper and to tap the side with a pencil so that seed sowing is more controlled.
Water the compost by standing the container in a bowl of water until moisture rises to the surface. Watering the surface directly scatters the seeds and washes them into a heap at one side of the box. Cover the seeds with a pane of glass and a sheet of paper until germination has taken place. The newspaper keeps the seeds in the dark and the pane of glass increases the temperature slightly.

Right: Temporary shelving can be easily fixed up in a greenhouse by suspending pieces of wood from the glazing bars. However, ensure that water does not drip on to plants below.

FLOWERS

◆ Plant herbaceous plants now, as soon as the ground is ready. In cold areas wait for a further few weeks before doing this job. Carefully plan the border on paper before setting new plants in the ground.

◆ Plant gladioli corms, ranunculus tubers and lily bulbs.

◆ Lift and divide large clumps of herbaceous plants, replanting the young and healthy parts from around the outside.

IN FLOWER THIS MONTH

YELLOW AND ORANGE

SHRUBS

CHIMONANTHUS PRAECOX 'Grandiflorus': see January

CORNUS MAS: see February

CORYLOPSIS PAUCIFLORA
H: 1·5–1·8 m (5–6 ft) S: 1·5–2·4 m (5–8 ft)
Hardy deciduous, with drooping cowslip-scented pale yellow flowers.

FORSYTHIA 'Beatrix Farrand'
H: 1·8–2·4 m (6–8 ft) S: 1·8–2·4 m (6–8 ft)
Deciduous with 4 cm (1½ in) wide rich yellow flowers with orange throats.

FORSYTHIA × INTERMEDIA 'Lynwood'
H: 1·8–2·4 m (6–8 ft) S: 2·1–2·4 m (7–8 ft)
Deciduous with rich yellow flowers. Very floriferous. 'Spectabilis' bears bright yellow flowers.

HAMAMELIS MOLLIS: see January

MAHONIA AQUIFOLIUM
H: 90 cm–1·5 m (3–5 ft) S: 1·5–1·8 m (5–6 ft)
Evergreen with dark green spine-toothed leaflets and fragrant rich yellow flowers in clusters 7·5–13 cm (3–5 in) wide.

MAHONIA 'Charity', *M. LOMARIIFOLIA*: see January

MAHONIA PINNATA: see February

STACHYRUS PRAECOX
H: 2·4–3 m (8–10 ft) S: 2·4–3 m (8–10 ft)
Deciduous with pendulous pale yellow flowers on bare stems.

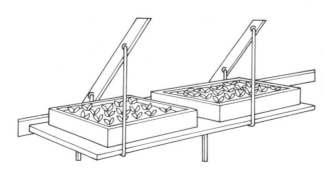

FRUIT

♦ New blackcurrant bushes can still be planted (*see* page 156). Re-firm those planted earlier which have been lifted and loosened by frost.
♦ Spray blackcurrants against gall mite, also known as big bud mite.
♦ Spray gooseberries against gooseberry mildew just before the flowers open, repeating a fortnight later.
♦ Spray cane fruits against cane spot and spur blight.

Left: Forsythia and daffodils form a harmonious combination for spring colour.

Below: Magnolia × loebneri 'Leonard Messel' is among the many glorious magnolias that grace gardens in spring.

VEGETABLES

LAWNS

Right: Pelargonium cuttings can be rooted now by taking them from over-wintered plants and inserting them in equal parts peat and sharp sand. Place on a greenhouse bench and cover with newspaper to help reduce the loss of moisture from the cuttings. Pot up the cuttings when rooted.

Below: Prunus sargentii, from Korea and Japan, produces clusters of clear pink flowers during late March and into early April.

♦ Sow salad onions 12 mm (½ in) deep in drills 13–15 cm (5–6 in) apart.

♦ Harvest lettuce sown under cloches the previous October.

♦ Top-dress and hoe in 70 grams a square metre (2 oz per square yard) of sulphate of ammonia.

♦ Sow broad beans 10 cm (4 in) apart in drills 75 mm (3 in) deep and 25 cm (10 in) apart.

♦ Prepare runner bean trenches, adding plenty of well-rotted manure or compost.

♦ Harvest winter cabbages as they mature.

♦ Sow celery seed in a heated greenhouse at 13°C/55°F.

♦ Plant seakale crowns 5 cm (2 in) deep and 38 cm (15 in) apart in rows 45 cm (18 in) apart.

♦ Where soil alongside lawns has fallen against the edges it should be removed. Use a spade to tidy up the edges which helps to improve drainage, as well as creating a neat appearance.

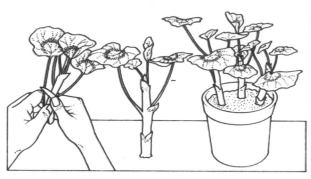

IN FLOWER THIS MONTH

RED AND PINK

TREES

PRUNUS × AMYGDALO-PERSICA 'Pollardii'
H: 6–7·5 m (20–25 ft) S: 6–7·5 m (20–25 ft)
Deciduous with rich pink almond-like flowers on bare branches.

PRUNUS DULCIS; syn. *P. amygdalus* (common almond)
H: 5·4–7·5 m (18–25 ft) S: 5·4–7·5 m (18–25 ft)
Deciduous with large clear pink flowers on naked branches.

PRUNUS CERASIFERA 'Nigra' (cherry plum)
H: 6–7·5 m (20–25 ft)) S: 5·4–6 m (18–20 ft)
Deciduous with blue-purple leaves and pink flowers.

PRUNUS 'Pandora'
H: 4·5–6 m (15–20 ft) S: 3–5·4 m (10–18 ft)
Deciduous hybrid with soft pink flowers.

PRUNUS SARGENTII
H: 7·5–9 m (25–30 ft) S: 5·4–7·5 m (18–25 ft)
Deciduous with young bronze-red leaves and clusters of clear pink flowers.

PRUNUS × YEDOENSIS (Yoshino cherry)
H: 6–7·5 m (20–25 ft) S: 7·5–9 m (25–30 ft)
Deciduous with pale pink buds opening to white flowers.

SHRUBS

CAMELLIA JAPONICA: see February

CHAENOMELES JAPONICA (Maule's quince)
H: 90 cm (3 ft) S: 1·5–1·8 m (5–6 ft)
Deciduous with orange-red apple-blossom flowers.

CHAENOMELES SPECIOSA 'Cardinalis' (Japanese quince/japonica)
H: 1·5–1·8 m (5–6 ft) S: 1·2–1·5 m (4–5 ft)
Deciduous with crimson to dark red flowers. 'Crown of Gold' has rich crimson flowers and 'Fascination' orange-red flowers.

DAPHNE MEZEREUM, D. ODORA: see February

ERICA × DARLEYENSIS 'Arthur Johnson', *E. × D.* 'Jack H. Brummage', *E. HERBACEA* 'Adrienne Duncan', *E. H.* 'Foxhollow', *E. H.* 'Myretoun Ruby', *E. H.* 'Praecox Rubra', *E. H.* 'Ruby Glow', *E. H.* 'Springwood Pink', *E. H.* 'Vivellii': see January

ERICA MEDITERRANEA 'Brightness'
H: 90 cm (3 ft) S: 90 cm–1·2 m (3–4 ft)
Evergreen with bright rose-pink bells.

PRUNUS TRILOBA
H: 3–4·5 m (10–15 ft) S: 3–3·5 m (10–12 ft)
Small, twiggy, deciduous, with double 2·5 cm (1 in) wide clear pink flowers.

WALL SHRUB

ABELIA DISTICHUM: see February

Right: Few conifers are as eye-catching and distinctive as the dwarf and conical Picea glauca 'Albertina Conica'. It is ideal for a rock garden or in a bed of conifers and heathers.

GREENHOUSES

♦ Take cuttings of dahlias, fuchsias and pelargoniums, as well as perpetual-flowering carnations.
♦ Check all plants for pests and diseases, spraying and fumigating as necessary.
♦ As soon as forced bulbs finish flowering move them to a sheltered, cool position. Stop watering them so that they can dry off naturally.
♦ Spray vines with clean water.
♦ Remove dead flowers from all plants to encourage the development of further blooms and discourage diseases.
♦ Do not allow the soil around grapevines, peaches and almonds to become dry. A check in growth at this stage will diminish the crop.

Right: The Star Magnolia, **Magnolia stellata,** *is one of the best-known magnolias, with fragrant 7·5–10 cm (3– 4 in) wide flowers during March and April.*

FLOWERS

♦ Plant unsprouted dahlia tubers and cover them with peat or well-decomposed compost.
♦ Bulbs that have finished flowering indoors can be planted between shrubs.
♦ Prune bush and climbing roses.
♦ Remove cloches and panes of glass from choice alpines.

FRUIT

♦ Raspberry canes can still be planted. Immediately they are planted cut them down to 30 cm (1 in) above soil level. Canes produced during the coming season will not bear fruit until the following year.
♦ Pollinate apricot, peaches and nectarines.
♦ Place cloches over strawberries to encourage early fruits.
♦ Spray apple and pear trees to prevent scab disease attacking the fruits during the coming year.

VEGETABLES

♦ Sow Brussels sprouts in a seedbed.
♦ Plant cauliflowers sown under gentle heat in January. Plant 60 cm (2 ft) apart in rows 60 cm (2 ft) apart.
♦ Sow carrots thinly in drills 12 mm ($\frac{1}{2}$ in) deep and 20 cm (8 in) apart.
♦ Prepare trenches for celery, 30 cm (1 ft) deep and 38–45 cm (15–18 in) wide. Add manure to the bottom of the trench and return soil to within 10 cm (4 in) of soil-level.
♦ Thin summer spinach to 75 mm (3 in) apart, then later to 15 cm (6 in) apart, when they will develop into sturdy plants.
♦ Sow early garden peas 10 cm (4 in) apart in drills 5 cm (2 in) deep.
♦ Detach sucker-like growths from established globe artichokes and plant them 60 cm (2 ft) apart in rows 75–90 cm (2 ft 6 in–3 ft) apart.

IN FLOWER THIS MONTH

WHITE AND CREAM

SHRUBS

ARBUTUS ANDRACHNE (Grecian strawberry tree)
H: 3·5–4·5 cm (12–15 ft) S: 2·4–3 m (8–10 ft)
Evergreen, tender when young, with white flowers
in terminal clusters and cinnamon-red peeling
bark.

CHAENOMELES SPECIOSA 'Nivalis' (Japanese quince/
japonica)
H: 1·5–1·8 m (5–6 ft) S: 1·2–1·5 m (4–5 ft)
Deciduous with pure white bowl-shaped flowers
up to 5 cm (2 in) wide.

ERICA × DARLEYENSIS 'Silver Bells', *E. HERBACEA*
'Springwood White', *E. LUSITANICA, E.
MEDITERRANEA* 'W. T. Rackliff: see January

LONICERA FRAGRANTISSIMA: see February

MAGNOLIA STELLATA (star magnolia)
H: 2·4–3 m (8–10 ft) S: 2·4–3·5 m (8–12 ft)
Deciduous shrub, often a small tree, with 7·5–
10 cm (3–4 in) wide star-shaped fragrant white
flowers.

PACHYSANDRA TERMINALIS: see February

PIERIS FLORIBUNDA
H: 1·2–1·8 cm (4–6 ft) S: 1·2–1·8 m (4–6 ft)
Leathery evergreen with white, waxy, lily-of the-
valley-like flowers in 7·5–10 cm (3–4 in) wide
dropping clusters.

SPIRAEA THUNBERGII
H: 1·5–1·8 m (5–6 ft) S: 1·8–2·1 m (6–7 ft)
Deciduous, with white, star-like flowers in arching
sprays which appear before the leaves.

VIBURNUM 'Anne Russell'
H: 1·8–2·4 m (6–8 ft) S: 1·5–1·8 m (5–6 ft)
Evergreen with clusters of fragrant pink-budded
white flowers.

VIBURNUM × BODNANTENSE, V. TINUS: see January

*Below: Special propagation
frames with soil-warming
equipment are ideal for
raising plants. In addition,
small glass-covered frames
are useful as an intermediary
stage for plants between the
rooting frame and being
placed on the greenhouse
benching.*

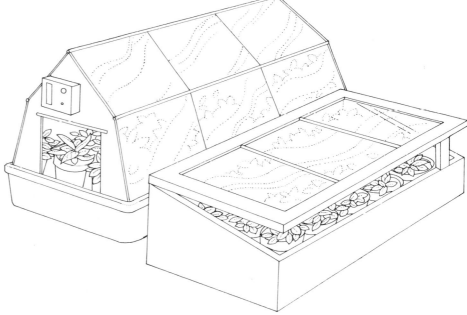

Above: From now and until late April or early May, hanging-baskets can be planted with half-hardy annuals so that the plants are well developed before the baskets are placed outside. Place the wire-framed basket in the top of a large pot and line the base with sphagnum moss or black or green plastic. If plastic is used it will, after the basket is planted, have to be pierced with holes to ensure good drainage. Place plants in the basket, with some pointing out of the sides so that they can trail. Water the basket and suspend it in a greenhouse until it can be placed outside.

L A W N S

◆ Remove leaves and any other rubbish that may have blown on the lawn during winter with a stiff brush, such as a besom, or a wire lawn rake.
◆ Brush and scatter worm casts. If left they may be stepped on and flattened, creating muddy patches and suffocating fine grasses.

G R E E N H O U S E S

◆ Pot up cyclamen seedlings into larger pots. The small corm should be set at soil-level: if left exposed it will become dry and hard, if too deep it will not be able to develop and expand properly.
◆ Harden off sweet peas sown earlier in a greenhouse.
◆ Pot on all plants that are filling their pots with roots.
◆ Continue to take cuttings of dahlias, as well as heliotrope, verbena and coleus. Insert them in sandy compost.
◆ Plant a few more sinningia (gloxinia) and begonia tubers, setting them 2·5 cm (1 in) apart in boxes of peat. As soon as the shoots sprout pot them separately.

Above: Gloxinia and tuberous-rooted begonias can be planted in boxes of peat. As soon as shoots develop on them, plant up separately into pots.

Right: This widely-grown, slow-growing and compact rhododendron, 'Blue Diamond', produces rich lavender-blue flowers during late March and April.

MARCH

FLOWERS

♦ Remove dead flower heads from bulbs that have finished flowering to conserve the strength of the bulbs.

FRUIT

♦ Check gooseberry, red currants and white currants for low-growing or damaged shoots, which should be cut out. These fruit bushes, unlike blackcurrants, need to be grown on a short stem, often known as a 'leg'.
♦ Protect blossom on wall-trained trees when frost is forecast.

IN FLOWER THIS MONTH

BLUE AND MAUVE

SHRUBS
VINCA MINOR (lesser periwinkle)
H: 5–10 cm (2–4 in) S: 90 cm–1 m (3 ft–3 ft 6 in)
Spreading sub-shrub with 18–25 cm ($\frac{3}{4}$–1 in) wide blue flowers. 'Atropurpurea' has deep purple flowers, 'Azurea Flore-pleno' blue, and 'Bowles Variety' azure-blue.

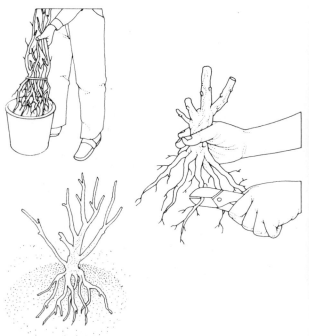

Far left: **Chamaecyparis obtusa** *'Nana Aurea' is an ideal dwarf golden conifer for a rock garden.*

Centre: Roses can be planted now. First, thoroughly moisten the roots by dipping them in a bucket of water. Then, trim off long or damaged roots. Position the plants in the soil so that the old soil mark seen on the stem is an inch or so below the surface of the soil. This allows for natural settlement of the soil around the plant.

Left: **Picea abies** *'Inverta' creates an interesting feature in a large rock garden.*

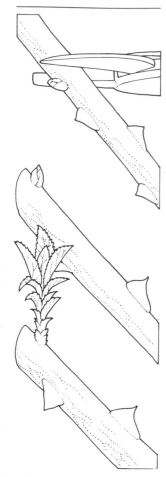

Above: When pruning roses take care to make all cuts just above a bud. If the cut is too far above the bud the end will rot and encourage diseases to enter. If the cut is too close to the bud it will be damaged.

VEGETABLES

♦ Plant early potatoes 15 cm (6 in) deep and 30 cm (1 ft) apart in rows 60 cm (2 ft) apart.

♦ Thin parsnips to 15 cm (6 in) apart.

♦ Summer lettuce can be sown from now until late July or early August.

♦ Plant onion sets 10 cm (4 in) apart in rows 25–30 cm (10–12 in) apart.

♦ Sow endive from now until late July, 12 mm ($\frac{1}{2}$ in) deep in rows 25–30 cm (10–12 in) apart.

♦ Prick out celery seedlings into boxes and harden off in a frame.

♦ Remove pots from over seakale and cut the shoots when 15 cm (6 in) long.

♦ Sow summer spinach 12 mm ($\frac{1}{2}$ in) deep in drills 30 cm (1 ft) apart.

LAWNS

♦ Lawn rollers can be used to settle lightly turf lifted by winter frost, often necessary if the turf was newly laid during the previous autumn. Other than for this job the roller is best not used on lawns.

GREENHOUSES

♦ Support young growths on schizanthus plants unobtrusively.

♦ Continue to sow seeds, as recommended for this month.

♦ Prick out congested seedlings. Hold them gently by their leaves, taking care not to squeeze the stems.

♦ Ventilate the greenhouse whenever necessary, avoiding draughts. Open the ventilators on the lee side.

♦ Increase the frequency of watering, without saturating the compost continually. It is better to water a plant thoroughly and then to allow the compost to become moderately dry than to keep it continually wet.

Right: Amelanchier lamarkii, the North American Snowy Mespilus or June Berry, displays masses of white, starry flowers in spring. It is a deciduous small tree, and bears the flowers before the leaves are fully developed.

◇ **APRIL** ◇

Flowering trees are the essence of spring to many gardeners, and few trees bring more pleasure than *Prunus subhirtella*, the spring cherry, with small, pale pink flowers during March and April. There are many forms, including *P. s.* 'Pendula' with a slender weeping habit and small blush-pink flowers in March and April, but not dominant. *P. s.* 'Pendula Plena Rosea' (weeping spring cherry) is also weeping, with semi-double rose-pink flowers during March and into April. If your garden is small and narrow try *Prunus* 'Amanogawa' (Lombardy poplar cherry). It rises to 6–7·5 m (20–25 ft) after 20 or so years and with a spread of only 1·2–1·8 m (4–6 ft) there are few gardens that cannot accommodate it. Its clusters of slightly fragrant soft pink flowers are splendid. Several other flowering cherry trees in flower now are recommended in the following pages.

Magnolia × soulangiana with its chalice-shaped white flowers stained rose-purple can be fitted into many gardens. Several forms are available, including 'Lennei' with large goblet-shaped rose-purple flowers, white within. Slightly smaller is *M. liliiflora* with 7·5–10 cm (3–4 in) wide chalice-shaped reddish-purple flowers. It looks magnificent when in a lawn, where it acts as a spring focal point.

Rhododendrons are now filling many gardens with colour, but if your garden is limy or you live in a cold, northerly area try the ornamental crabs. They are hardy, deciduous, floriferous and very reliable for a spring burst of colour. The broad-headed *Malus × eleyi* creates a picture of deep wine-red single flowers, 2·5 cm (1 in) wide, while *M. × purpurea* is upright with single purple flowers towards the end of this month. An underplanting of wallflowers creates an even more impressive scene. For double flowers plant the American hybrids such as 'American Beauty' with red flowers and bronze leaves, 'Pink Perfection' with clear pink flowers, or the beautifully small-garden sized 'Snowcloud' with pure white flowers. Even after 20 or so years it reaches only 4·5 m (15 ft) high and 3–3·5 m (10–12 ft) wide. If, however, you have plenty of space try a combination of the wide-spreading *Malus baccata mandshurica*, with fragrant white flowers, and a ground carpeting of polyanthus. This combination is best seen from a distance.

Polyanthus can also be used in combination with daffodils. Set the daffodils about 30 cm (1 ft) apart in a bed of pink or red polyanthus or densely plant a circular bed with polyanthus and circle it with *Arabis caucasica* 'Flore Plena' with double white flower clusters.

One of the earliest flowering herbaceous plants is *Doronicum plantangineum* with its bright green heart-shaped leaves and golden-yellow flowers. Several fine forms are available, including 'Miss Mason' with 6·5 cm (2½ in) wide bright yellow flowers, and 'Harpur Crew' with 7·5 cm (3 in) wide golden-yellow flowers. Both combine well in a medley mixture with tulips and forget-me-nots.

Daffodils, with their great versatility happily blend with the silver-grey foliage of *Lavandula spica* (Old English lavender). The best form to use is *Lavandula spica* 'Hidcote' (also sold as *L. nana atropurpurea*) which rises to only 45–60 cm (1½–2 ft) and displays purple-blue flowers from July to September. The daffodils give extra colour to the lavender's foliage. A hedge of lavender with daffodils set along in it on the sunny side is a spring joy. Use a deep yellow large-faced variety.

As April draws to an end a wealth of tulips will burst into flower to combine with other plants in spring-bedding schemes before in their turn yielding to the yearly massed colour of summer-bedding schemes.

Spring-flowering cherry trees create a dominant array of blossom. Here, the weeping Prunus subhirtella *'Pendula' with an underplanting of daffodils creates an attractive display against a clear blue sky.*

FLOWERS

♦ Continue to remove the faded flower heads from bulbs.

♦ Bulbs flowered indoors can be planted in bare areas between deciduous trees and shrubs. This will help to create colour around trees and shrubs that do not create a dominant display until mid or late summer.

♦ Continue to plant lily bulbs and gladioli corms.

♦ Delphiniums, herbaceous phlox and lupins can be increased from root cuttings.

FRUIT

♦ Apply sulphate of potash to the soil around gooseberry bushes, at 25 grams a square metre (¾ oz a square yard).

♦ Prune plums and gages as soon as the sap starts rising. If pruned in winter there is a risk of silver leaf disease infecting the trees.

♦ Spray all fruit trees and bushes with pesticides and insecticides before bud-burst or after petal fall.

♦ Avoid using these sprays when pollinating insects are active.

Below: Lavatera trimestris *'Silver Oak' is a spectacular and delicately-coloured hardy annual for sowing now and flowering from July to September.*

FLOWERS TO SOW THIS MONTH

ANNUALS AND BIENNIALS

ADONIS AESTIVALIS (pheasant's eye)
Sow 6 mm (¼ in) deep *in situ*.

ALYSSUM MARITIMUM; now *Lobularia maritima*
Sow 6 mm (¼ in) deep *in situ*.

AMARANTHUS CAUDATUS (love-lies-bleeding)
Sow 3 mm (⅛ in) deep *in situ*.

AMARANTHUS TRICOLOR (Joseph's coat)
Sow 3 mm (⅛ in) deep in 15–20°C/60–68°F.

ANCHUSA CAPENSIS
Sow 12 mm (½ in) deep *in situ*.

ASPERULA ORIENTALIS; syn. *A. azurea/A. setosa* (annual woodruff)
Sow 6 mm (¼ in) deep *in situ*.

BRACHYCOME IBERIDIFOLIA (Swan River daisy)
Sow 6 mm (¼ in) deep *in situ*.

CALENDULA OFFICINALIS (pot marigold/English marigold)
Sow 12 mm (½ in) deep *in situ*.

CAMPANULA MEDIUM (Canterbury bell)
Sow 6 mm (¼ in) deep in a seed bed.

CELOSIA ARGENTEA PLUMOSA (Prince of Wales' feather)
Sow 3 mm (⅛ in) deep in 20–25°C/68–78°F.

CENTAUREA CYANUS (Cornflower)
Sow 12 mm (½ in) deep *in situ*.

CENTAUREA MOSCHATA (sweet sultan)
Sow 6 mm (¼ in) deep *in situ*.

CHRYSANTHEMUM CARINATUM; syn. *C. tricolor*
Sow 6 mm (¼ in) deep *in situ*.

CLARKIA ELEGANS
Sow 6 mm (¼ in) deep *in situ*.

CLARKIA PULCHELLA
Sow 6 mm (¼ in) deep *in situ*.

CONSOLIDA AJACIS (larkspur)
Sow 6 mm (¼ in) deep *in situ*.

CONVOLVULUS TRICOLOR; syn. *C. minor*
Sow 12 mm (½ in) deep *in situ*.

COREOPSIS TINCTORIA (tickseed)
Sow 6 mm (¼ in) deep *in situ*.

VEGETABLES

♦ Sow kohlrabi thinly in drills 12 mm (½ in) deep and 38 cm (15 in) apart.
♦ Sow leeks in a seedbed, 12 mm (½ in) deep.
♦ Thin onion seedlings 50–75 mm (2–3 in) apart.
♦ Sow leaf lettuce such as 'Salad Bowl' 12 mm (½ in) deep in rows 25–30 cm (10–12 in) apart.
♦ Plant seakale crowns 5 cm (2 in) deep, 38 cm (15 in) apart in rows 45 cm (18 in) apart.
♦ Sow cauliflowers for planting out in June.
♦ Sow Brussels sprouts in a seedbed.

Above: Seedlings, as well as pots or boxes of seeds that have not yet germinated, are best watered by standing the containers in a bowl of water until moisture rises to the surface.

FLOWERS TO SOW THIS MONTH

COSMOS BIPINNATUS (cosmea)
Sow 6 mm (¼ in) deep *in situ*.

COTULA BARBATA (pincushion plant)
Sow 6 mm (¼ in) deep *in situ*.

DIMORPHOTHECA AURANTIACA (star of the veldt)
Sow 6 mm (¼ in) deep *in situ*.

ECHIUM LYCOPSIS; syn. *E. platagineum* (viper's bugloss)
Sow 6 mm (¼ in) deep *in situ*.

EMILIA FLAMMEA (tassel flower)
Sow 6 mm (¼ in) deep *in situ*.

ESCHSCHOLZIA CALIFORNICA (Californian poppy)
Sow 6 mm (¼ in) deep *in situ*.

FELICIA BERGERIANA (kingfisher daisy)
Sow 3 mm (⅛ in) deep in 10–15°C/50–60°F.

GILIA LUTEA (stardust)
Sow 6 mm (¼ in) deep *in situ*.

GODETIA GRANDIFLORA
Sow 6 mm (¼ in) deep *in situ*.

GOMPHRENA GLOBOSA (bachelor's buttons)
Sow 6 mm (¼ in) deep in 20–25°C/68–78°F.

GYPSOPHILA ELEGANS
Sow 6 mm (¼ in) deep *in situ*.

HELIANTHUS ANNUUS (sunflower)
Sow 12 mm (½ in) deep *in situ*.

HIBISCUS TRIONUM (flower-of-an-hour)
Sow 6 mm (¼ in) deep *in situ*.

IBERIS UMBELLATA (candytuft)
Sow 6 mm (¼ in) deep *in situ*.

IMPATIENS BALSAMINA (balsam/touch-me-not)
Sow 6 mm (¼ in) deep in 15–20°C/60–68°F.

IPOMOEA PURPUREA; syn. *Convolvulus major*
Sow 12 mm (½ in) deep *in situ*.

IPOMOEA VIOLACEA; syn. *I. rubro-caerulea* (morning glory)
Sow 12 mm (½ in) deep in 15–20°C/60–68°F.

LATHYRUS ODORATUS (sweet pea)
Sow 12 mm (½ in) deep *in situ*.

LAVATERA TRIMESTRIS (mallow)
Sow 12 mm (½ in) deep *in situ*.

LIMNANTHES DOUGLASII (poached egg plant)
Sow 3 mm (⅛ in) deep *in situ*.

LINARIA MAROCCANA (toadflax)
Sow 3 mm (⅛ in) deep *in situ*.

LYCHNIS VISCARIA
Sow 6 mm (¼ in) deep *in situ*.

MALCOLMIA MARITIMA (Virginian stock)
Sow 6 mm (¼ in) deep *in situ*.

MATTHIOLA BICORNIS (night-scented stock)
Sow 6 mm (¼ in) deep *in situ*.

MATTHIOLA INCANA (ten-week stocks/perpetual-flowering stocks/trysomic stocks)
Sow 6 mm (¼ in) deep *in situ*.

NEMESIA STRUMOSA
Sow 3 mm (⅛ in) deep in 15–20°C/60–68°F.

NEMOPHILA MENZIESII (baby blue eyes)
Sow 6 mm (¼ in) deep *in situ*.

NICANDRA PHYSALOIDES (apple of Peru/shoo fly plant)
Sow 6 mm (¼ in) deep *in situ*.

NICOTIANA ALATA; syn. *N. affinis* (tobacco plant)
Sow 3 mm (⅛ in) deep in 15–20°C/60–68°F.

NIGELLA DAMASCENA (love-in-a-mist)
Sow 6 mm (¼ in) deep *in situ*.

PAPAVER RHOEAS (field poppy/Shirley poppy)
Sow 6 mm (¼ in) deep *in situ*.

PAPAVER SOMNIFERUM (opium poppy)
Sow 6 mm (¼ in) deep *in situ*.

PHLOX DRUMMONDII
Sow 6 mm (¼ in) deep in 10–15°C/50–60°F.

RESEDA ODORATA (mignonette)
Sow 3 mm (⅛ in) deep *in situ*.

SCABIOSA ATROPURPUREA (sweet scabious)
Sow 12 mm (½ in) deep *in situ*.

THUNBERGIA ALATA (black-eyed Susan)
Sow 6 mm (¼ in) deep in 20–25°C/68–78°F.

TROPAEOLUM MAJUS (nasturtium)
Sow 12 mm (½ in) deep *in situ*.

ZINNIA ELEGANS
Sow 6 mm (¼ in) deep in 15–20°C/60–68°F.

APRIL

ROCK PLANTS IN FLOWER THIS MONTH

◇

Aethionema 'Warley Rose'

Alyssum saxatile 'Flore-pleno'
(gold dust)

Aubrieta deltoidea

Draba aizoides

Draba bryoides;
syn. *D. rigida bryoides*

Draba rigida

Erinus alpinus

Saxifraga × apiculata

Saxifraga × borisii

Saxifraga burserana

Saxifraga 'Cranbourne'

Saxifraga oppositifolia

◇

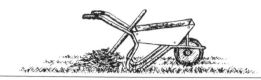

LAWNS

◆ Prepare sites in readiness for sowing grass seed. If the site is still wet and sticky this job is best left for a further few weeks. Dig the site – if not prepared during early winter – and break up the surface soil. Rake level, removing all stones over 5 cm (2 in) in diameter. Leave smaller ones as they assist drainage. Ensure all perennial weeds have been removed.

GREENHOUSES

◆ If the greenhouse is becoming congested with boxes of seedlings, additional shelves can be often temporarily fitted by suspending them from wires attached to the roofing bars. But take care as they may easily be tipped over. Also, drips of water from them will splash over lower plants.

◆ Pot on plants such as tuberous begonias, gloxinias, chrysanthemums and cyclamen.

◆ Plant greenhouse tomato plants into pots or growing-bags.

◆ Sow tomatoes for planting outside later in the year.

◆ Spray or fumigate plants as soon as pests and diseases are seen, following the maker's instructions.

Below: When repotting spiky cacti the plant can be held in a narrow strip of soft cardboard or rolled paper.

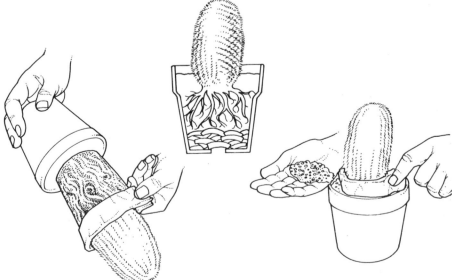

FLOWERS TO SOW THIS MONTH

PERENNIALS

ACHILLEA FILIPENDULA
Sow 6 mm (¼ in) deep in a seed bed.

ACHILLEA MILLEFOLIUM
Sow 6 mm (¼ in) deep in a seed bed.

ACHILLEA PTARMICA
Sow 6 mm (¼ in) deep in a seed bed.

AGRIMONY EUPATORIA (agrimony/cocklebur)
Sow 6 mm (¼ in) deep in a seed bed.

ANCHUSA AZUREA; syn. *A. italica*
Sow 12 mm (½ in) deep in a seed bed.

ANEMONE CORONARIA (poppy anemone)
Sow 3 mm (⅛ in) deep in 10–15°C/50–60°F.

AQUILEGIA VULGARIS (granny's bonnet)
Sow 6 mm (¼ in) deep in a seed bed.

AQUILEGIA ALPINA
Sow 6 mm (¼ in) deep in a seed bed.

ARABIS ALPINA (wall cress/rock cress)
Sow 3 mm (⅛ in) deep in a cool greenhouse.

ASTER NOVI-BELGII (Michaelmas daisy)
Sow 6 mm (¼ in) deep in 15–20°C/60–68°F or 12 mm (½ in) deep *in situ.*

AUBRIETA DELTOIDEA
Sow 6 mm (¼ in) deep in a seed bed.

CATANANCHE CAERULEA (Cupid's dart)
Sow 6 mm (¼ in) deep in a cold frame.

CENTRANTHUS RUBER; syn. *Kentranthus ruber* (valerian)
Sow 6 mm (¼ in) deep in a seed bed.

CERASTIUM TOMENTOSUM (snow-in-summer)
Sow 6 mm (¼ in) deep in a seed bed.

CHRYSANTHEMUM MAXIMUM (shasta daisy)
Sow 6 mm (¼ in) deep *in situ.*

ECHINOPS RITRO (globe thistle)
Sow 12 mm (½ in) deep in a seed bed.

ERIGERON SPECIOSUS (midsummer daisy)
Sow 6 mm (¼ in) deep in a seed bed.

GEUM CHILOENSE
Sow 6 mm (¼ in) deep in a cold frame.

HESPERIS MATRONALIS (sweet rocket)
Sow 6 mm (¼ in) deep in a seed bed.

LYCHNIS CHALCEDONICA (Jerusalem cross)
Sow 6 mm (¼ in) deep *in situ.*

MESEMBRYANTHEMUM CRINIFLORUM (Livingstone daisy): grown as half-hardy annual
Sow 3 mm (⅛ in) deep in 15–20°C/60–68°F.

BORDER BRIGHTENERS IN FLOWER THIS MONTH

Anemone coronaria
(poppy anemone)

Bellis perennis
(daisy)

Cheiranthus cheiri

Left: Calendula officinalis, *the Pot Marigold, is superb for both the garden and in pots in a greenhouse. It flowers from May to the frosts of autumn.*

Right: Pyrus salicifolia 'Pendula', a form of the Willow-leaved Pear, is a graceful deciduous small tree with silvery willow-like leaves.

IN FLOWER THIS MONTH

YELLOW AND ORANGE

SHRUBS

BERBERIS DARWINII (Darwin's berberis)
H: 1·8–3 m (6–10 ft) S: 1·8–3 m (6–10 ft)
Evergreen with small holly-like leaves and crimson-tinted yellow flowers, followed by blue berries.

BERBERIS LINEARIFOLIA
H: 2·4–3 m (8–10 ft) S: 90 cm–1·2 m (3–4 ft)
Slow-growing deep glossy evergreen with rich orange flowers. 'Orange King' with orange and apricot flowers is the best form.

CYTISUS PURGANS
H: 90 cm–1·2 m (3–4 ft) S: 90 cm–1·2 m (3–4 ft)
Deciduous with pea-shaped rich golden-yellow fragrant flowers.

FORSYTHIA 'Beatrix Farrand', *F.* × *INTERMEDIA* 'Lynwood': see March

KERRIA JAPONICA
H: 1·2–1·8 m (4–6 ft) S: 1·2–1·5 m (4–5 ft)
Deciduous with yellow-orange flowers 4 cm (1½ in) wide. 'Pleniflora' has double orange-yellow flowers.

MAHONIA AQUIFOLIUM: see March

MAHONIA PINNATA: see February

RIBES ALPINUM
H: 90 cm–1·5 m (3–5 ft) S: 90 cm–1·2 m (3–4 ft)
Deciduous with greenish-yellow flowers in 4 cm (1½ in) long clusters.

RIBES AUREUM (golden currant/buffalo currant)
H: 1·8–2·4 m (6–8 ft) S: 1·2–1·5 m (4–5 ft)
Deciduous with tubular bright yellow clove-scented flowers.

ULEX EUROPAEUS (gorse/furze/whin)
H: 1·5–2·1 m (5–7 ft) S: 1·5–2·4 m (5–8 ft)
Hardy, spiny evergreen with pea-shaped golden-yellow flowers. 'Plenus' has double yellow flowers, and is smaller.

FLOWERS

♦ Sow seeds, as recommended.
♦ Prune forsythia as it finishes flowering.

FRUIT

♦ Apply sulphate of ammonia at 70 grams a square metre (2 oz a square yard) around blackberry and hybrid berry plants.
♦ Thin the fruits of nectarines and peaches when the size of marbles to enable the remaining fruits to develop fully.

BULBS IN FLOWER
THIS MONTH
◇

Anemone blanda
(blue winter windflower/
Grecian windflower)

Anemone coronaria
(poppy anemone)

Chionodoxa gigantea;
syn. *C. grandiflora*
(glory of the snow)

Chionodoxa sardensis
(glory of the snow)

Cyclamen repandum

Fritillaria imperialis
(crown imperial)

Fritillaria meleagris
(snake's head fritillary)

Hyacinthus orientalis
(common hyacinth)

Muscari armeniacum
(grape hyacinth)

Muscari botryoides

Narcissus
(daffodil)

Narcissus jonquilla
(wild jonquil)

Narcissus × odorus
(campernelle jonquil)

Narcissus poeticus
(poet's narcissus)

Narcissus pseudonarcissus
(wild daffodil/Lent lily)

Narcissus triandrus albus
(angel's tears)

Ornithogalum nutans

Ornithogalum umbellatum
(star of Bethlehem)

Puschkinia scilloides
(striped squill)

Tulipa – early double, early
single, triumph and Darwin
hybrids

Tulipa fosteriana

Tulipa greigii
◇

VEGETABLES

◆ Thin summer lettuce to 23–30 cm (9–12 in) apart.

◆ Remove pots from over seakale and cut the shoots when 15 cm (6 in) long.

◆ Sow carrots thinly in drills 12 mm ($\frac{1}{2}$ in) deep and 20 cm (8 in) apart.

◆ Harvest spring cabbage, cutting them off at soil-level.

◆ Sow winter cabbage for harvesting from early November to spring. Sow seeds 18 mm ($\frac{3}{4}$ in) deep in drills 15 cm (6 in) apart in a seedbed.

◆ Prepare new asparagus beds. Dig trenches 38 cm (15 in) wide and 25–30 cm (10–12 in) wide. Leave a ridge of friable soil along the base of the trench.

LAWNS

◆ Final soil preparation for seed sowing can be completed. To consolidate the soil evenly systematically tread it, shuffling sideways across the plot, consolidating a strip about 30 cm (1 ft) wide at each crossing. A garden roller is not advisable as unless it is kept moving at a slow and steady pace it consolidates some areas more than others. Rake the surface level and then rake a well-balanced lawn fertilizer into the top 25 mm (1 in) of soil. The same soil preparation is needed for either the sowing of seed or when laying turf.

GREENHOUSES

◆ Feed greenhouse plants that are in their final pots. They will also need frequent watering at this stage when they have plentiful leaves.

◆ Cyclamen plants that have finished flowering will need drying. Place the pots on their sides under the greenhouse staging in a dry place.

◆ Harden off bedding plants sown under glass and previously pricked off into boxes. Place them in a cold frame to protect them from frost.

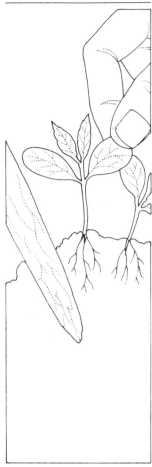

Above: Young seedlings need careful treatment when being pricked off into boxes or pots. Water the compost a few hours before doing this job, and gently lever up just a few seedlings at a time. If too many are disturbed their roots will dry out before they are pricked off. Hold each seedling by its first leaf and form a hole in the compost with a pencil or small dibber. Then, gently lever soil against the roots.

Left: Euphorbia wulfenii, *also known as* Euphorbia veneta, *is a bushy evergreen shrub with terminal heads of bright yellowish-green flower bracts in late spring and early summer. Here, positioned at the top of a flight of steps, it creates a dominant display.*

Right: Ipheion uniflorum, *the Spring Star Flower from South America, creates a mass of star-shaped and scented white to violet-blue flowers during April and May. It is ideal for the edges of borders or paths, or for planting in a rock garden.*

FLOWERS

♦ Plant out hardened off chrysanthemum plants into well-prepared soil.

♦ Continue to remove dead flower heads from bulbs, which tidies them up and produces stronger bulbs.

♦ Harden off bedding plants sown under glass earlier in the year.

♦ Lift and divide hardy chrysanthemums over-wintered outdoors. Re-pot the healthy parts from around the outside of the clump.

♦ Continue to plant out bulbs flowered indoors among deciduous trees and shrubs.

♦ Continue to sow seeds, as recommended for this month. This will ensure that the garden is burgeoned with colour in summer.

FRUIT

♦ Lightly hoe around established raspberry canes to remove weeds. Do not hoe deeply or the roots will be damaged. At the same time feed the plants with 25 grams a square metre ($\frac{3}{4}$ oz per square yard) of sulphate of potash.

VEGETABLES

♦ Thin carrots to 5 cm (2 in) apart.

♦ Thin endive to 23–30 cm (9–12 in) apart.

♦ Sow summer spinach 12 mm ($\frac{1}{2}$ in) deep in drills 30 cm (1 ft) apart.

♦ Plant asparagus crowns 38–45 cm (15–18 in) apart along the ridge in the asparagus trench prepared during the previous week. Cover the crowns with 5 cm (2 in) of soil.

♦ Harvest asparagus spears from established beds when 15 cm (6 in) high.

♦ Sow salad onions 12 mm ($\frac{1}{2}$ in) deep in drills 13–15 cm (5–6 in) apart.

♦ Sow garden peas 10 cm (4 in) apart in drills 5 cm (2 in) deep.

♦ Support garden peas with pea-sticks or wire-netting secured at either end of the row.

When sowing seeds in seed boxes, place coarse drainage material in the base, then a layer of peat. Top up with seed compost and strike level with a straight-edged piece of wood (top picture). Use a flat-surfaced square or oblong piece of wood to firm the surface level (centre picture). Fine seeds can be scattered thinly on the surface, while large seeds are best spaced apart (bottom picture). Fine soil can then be sieved over the surface.

IN FLOWER THIS MONTH

RED AND PINK

TREES

MALUS × ELEYI
H: 6–7·5 m (20–25 ft) S: 4·5–6 m (15–20 ft)
Round-headed deciduous, with single 2·5 cm (1 in)
wide deep wine-red flowers.

PRUNUS 'Accolade'
H: 6–9 m (20–30 ft) S: 4·5–6 m (15–20 ft)
Deciduous with semi-double rich pink flowers.

PRUNUS 'Asano'
H: 6–9 m (20–30 ft) S: 4·5–7·5 m (15–25 ft)
Upright deciduous, with double deep pink flowers.

PRUNUS 'Amanogawa'
H: 6–7·5 m (20–25 ft) S: 1·8–2·4 m (6–8 ft)
Narrow, upright deciduous, with dense clusters of
fragrant soft pink flowers.

PRUNUS PERSICA 'Prince Charming' (common
peach)
H: 4.5–6 m (15–20 ft) S: 4.5–6 m (15–20 ft)
Deciduous with double rose-red flowers.

PRUNUS SUBHIRTELLA 'Pendula Plena Rosea'
H: 3–4·5 m (10–15 ft) S: 3–6 m (10–20 ft)
Deciduous with drooping branches bearing semi-
double rose-pink flowers.

SHRUBS

CAMELLIA JAPONICA: see February

CHAENOMELES JAPONICA, C. SPECIOSA 'Cardinalis':
see March

ERICA × DARLEYENSIS 'Arthur Johnson', *E. × D.* 'Jack
H. Brummage', *E. HERBACEA* 'Adrienne Duncan', *E.
H.* 'Foxhollow', *E. H.* 'Myretoun Ruby', *E. H.*
'Praecox Rubra', *E. H.* 'Springwood Pink', *E. H.*
'Vivellii': see January

ERICA MEDITERRANEA 'Brightness': see March

MAGNOLIA × SOULANGIANA 'Lennei'
H: 3–4·5 m (10–15 ft) S: 3–5·4 m (10–18 ft)
Deciduous with 13–15 cm (5–6 in) wide rose-purple
flowers on bare branches.

PRUNUS TENELLA 'Fire Hill'
H: 60 cm–1·2 m (2–4 ft) S: 90 cm–1·5 m (3–5 ft)
Deciduous with rose-crimson flowers on stiff stems.

PRUNUS GLANDULOSA 'Sinensis'
H: 1·2–1·5 m (4–5 ft) S: 1·2–1·5 m (4–5 ft)
Deciduous with bright pink double flowers.

PRUNUS TRILOBA: see March

RIBES SANGUINEUM 'Pulborough Scarlet'
H: 1·8–2·4 m (6–8 ft) S: 1·5–2·1 m (5–7 ft)
Deciduous with rich red flowers.

RIBES SPECIOSUM
H: 1·8–2·4 m (6–8 ft) S: 1·2–1·5 m (4–5 ft)
Deciduous with bright red fuchsia-like flowers in
pendent clusters.

*Right: The distinctive 7.5–10 cm (3–4 in) wide dark
reddish-purple and chalice-shaped flowers of* Magnolia
liliiflora *'Nigra' are stunningly attractive from April to
July. It forms a deciduous shrub 1·8–2·4 cm (6–8 ft) high
and is ideal for a small garden. In some catalogues it is
listed as* Magnolia × soulangiana *'Nigra'.*

LAWNS

♦ Sow lawn seed about a week after adding the fertilizer (*see* previous week). Select a seed mixture suitable for the site's shadiness and likely wear and tear. Mixtures with fine-bladed grasses should be reserved for ornamental areas where wear is restricted.

♦ Sow seed evenly at 35–70 grams a square metre (1–2 oz a square yard). For accurate distribution mark yard-square areas with string. Alternatively, halve the seed mixture and broadcast half in one direction and the rest in the other. Rake the seed lightly into the surface. If the soil is dry use a very light roller or the roller on a lawn mower to firm the seeds into the surface.

GREENHOUSES

♦ Sow melons and cucumbers for growing in a greenhouse. Sow two seeds in each pot, thinning them to the strongest seedling later. They need a temperature of 18°C/64°F for rapid germination.

♦ Pot on chrysanthemums rooted earlier in the year.

♦ Early tomatoes sown earlier in the year and planted in a greenhouse will now be producing sideshoots. Remove these by bending and snapping them sideways.

♦ Hanging-baskets can be planted up now in readiness for placing outside as soon as all risk of frost has passed. Line baskets with grey or black polythene or sphagnum moss and fill with such plants as trailing geraniums, lobelia, verbena, pendulous fuchsias, packing compost around them. If the basket is lined with polythene pierce it to allow excess water to escape. While the plants are becoming established and before it can safely be placed outside hang up the basket or place it on top of a very large pot. Keep the compost well watered.

♦ Continue to sow seeds, as recommended for this month.

♦ As the greenhouse becomes packed with plants, some can be put into a garden frame to harden off. However, on cold nights the frames may require a covering of sacking.

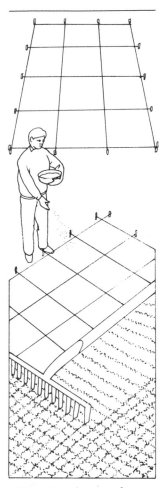

Above: Sow lawn seed now (see Lawns, above).

FLOWERS

♦ Plant water-lilies and other water plants. Select the vigour of water-lilies to suit the size of the pond. Over-vigorous plants in small areas will create too much foliage and eventually kill other plants.

FRUIT

♦ Prune peaches and nectarines as soon as the buds start to develop.

Below: Prunus 'Ukon' is a Japanese Cherry with a spreading nature displaying semi-double white flowers tinged green during April. It is deciduous, with leaves that turn rusty-red or purplish-brown in autumn.

VEGETABLES

♦ Sow maincrop potatoes 15 cm (6 in) deep and 38 cm (15 in) apart in rows 75 cm (30 in) apart to ensure that they have plenty of room for the tubers to develop fully later in the year.
♦ Sow radishes 12 mm ($\frac{1}{2}$ in) deep.
♦ Lettuces for cutting in spring must be watered during dry periods.
♦ Summer lettuce can be sown now, and until early August.
♦ Thin kohlrabi to 15 cm (6 in) apart.
♦ Sow cardoons, 45 cm (18 in) apart in rows 75 cm (30 in) apart.
♦ Thin summer spinach to 75 mm (3 in) apart, then later to 15 cm (6 in) apart.

IN FLOWER THIS MONTH

WHITE AND CREAM

TREES

AMELANCHIER LAMARCKII (snowy mespilus/June berry)
H: 4·5–7·5 m (15–25 ft) S: 4·5–6 m (15–20 ft)
Deciduous with abundant clusters of starry white flowers. Leaves colour well in autumn.

PRUNUS AVIUM (gean/wild cherry)
H: 9–12 m (30–40 ft) S: 6–9 m (20–30 ft)
Pyramidal deciduous, with cup-shaped single white flowers. 'Plena' bears double white flowers.

PRUNUS 'Shirotae'; syn. *P.* 'Kojima' (Japanese cherry)
H: 5·4–7·5 m (18–25 ft) S: 9–10·5 m (30–35 ft)
Wide-spreading deciduous, with single or semi-double snow-white flowers.

PRUNUS 'Ukon'
H: 4·5–6 m (15–20 ft) S: 5·4–7·5 m (18–25 ft)
Spreading deciduous, with semi-double white flowers tinged green.

PRUNUS 'Umeniko'
H: 4·5–6 m (15–20 ft) S: 1·5–1·8 m (5–6 ft)
Narrow upright deciduous, with pure white 2·5 cm (1 in) wide flowers.

PYRUS NIVALIS
H: 4·5–7·5 m (15–25 ft) S: 4·5–7·5 m (15–25 ft)
Deciduous with white and woolly young leaves and pure white flowers.

PYRUS SALICIFOLIA 'Pendula' (willow-leaved pear)
H: 4·5–6 m (15–20 ft) S: 4·5–5·4 m (15–18 ft)
Deciduous with silvery foliage and creamy-white flowers.

SHRUBS

ARBUTUS ANDRACHNE: see March

ARCTOSTAPHYLOS UVA-URSI (red bearberry)
H: 10–15 cm (4–6 in) S: 75 cm–1 m (2 ft 6 in–3 ft 6 in)
Ground-hugging evergreen with pendulous urn-shaped pink-flushed white flowers followed by glossy red berries.

CHANOMELES SPECOSA 'Nivalis': see March

ERICA ARBOREA ALPINA
H: 1·8–3 m (6–10 ft) S: 1·8–4 m (6–8 ft)
Evergreen tree heath with fresh green leaves and slightly scented white flowers.

ERICA × DARLEYENSIS 'Silver Bells', *E. HERBACEA* 'Springwood White', *E. LUSITANICA:* see January

MAGNOLIA × SOULANGIANA
H: 3–4·5 m (10–15 ft) S: 3–5·4 m (10–18 ft)
Deciduous, often tree-like with 13–15 cm (5–6 in) wide chalice-shaped white flowers appearing before the leaves. 'Alba Superba' has scented white flowers.

MAGNOLIA STELLATA: see March

× OSMAREA BURKWOODII
H: 1·8–3 m (6–10 ft) S: 1·8–2·4 m (6–8 ft)
Hardy evergreen with fragrant tubular white flowers.

PIERIS FLORIBUNDA: see March

PRUNUS × CISTENA (purple-leaf sand cherry)
H: 90 cm–1·5 m (3–5 ft) S: 1·2–1·5 m (4–5 ft)
Deciduous rich red leaves and white flowers.

SKIMMIA JAPONICA 'Fragrans'
H: 90 cm 1·5 m (3–5 ft) S: 1·5–1·8 m (5–6 ft)
Slow-growing evergreen with strongly scented white flowers.

SPIRAEA × ARGUTA (foam of May/bridal wreath)
H: 1·8–2·4 m (6–8 ft) S: 1·5–2·1 m (5–7 ft)
Deciduous with white flowers on arching stems.

SPIRAEA THUNBERGII, VIBURNUM 'Anne Russell': see March

VIBURNUM × BODNANTENSE: see January

VIBURNUM CARLESII
H: 1·2–1·5 m (4–5 ft) S: 1·2–1·5 m (4–5 ft)
Rounded deciduous, with heavily scented pink-budded white flowers.

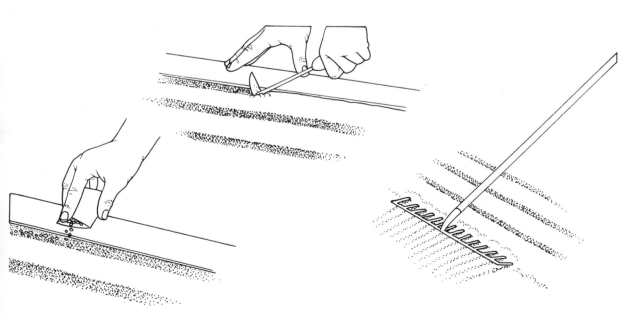

Left: When sowing hardy annuals in the garden, always prepare the soil to a fine tilth. Use a straight-edged board or a garden line, together with an onion hoe or small draw hoe. Sow the seeds thinly and then rake soil over them. Take care not to rake deeply and so disturb the seeds.

Right: Flowering crab trees create their best display during late April and May. When used in a front garden do not plant them too close to the boundary, as the branches may eventually spread over the pavement. Also, in autumn the fruits may fall on the path and make it slippery. White picket fencing blends well with this magnificent flowering tree.

LAWNS

♦ Stretch black cotton thread over the site between sticks pushed in at the side to thwart birds attracted by newly sown lawn seed.

♦ Lawn seed germinates within seven to 10 days from being sown. If the weather is hot and dry during this period thoroughly, but lightly, water the soil so that the top few inches are moist. Just dampening the surface soil will do more harm than good. Alternatively, if the site is small, a sheet of clear polythene can be stretched over it until germination has occurred.

♦ Feed established lawns with a quick-acting lawn fertilizer at 70 grams a square metre (2 oz a square yard). Use a fertilizer mixture with about equal parts of nitrogen, phosphate and potash.

GREENHOUSES

♦ Continue to remove sideshoots from tomato plants. As soon as the first fruits are formed apply a liquid fertilizer.

♦ Pot up chrysanthemums.

♦ Young growths on grapevines should be nipped back to two leaves beyond the fruit truss.

♦ Check for pests and diseases that often start to build up at this time of year. Use a fungicide or pesticide as soon as they are seen.

♦ Continue to prick out congested seedlings into boxes or pots.

♦ Harden off bedding plants that are well established in their boxes. Place them in a cold frame. If you do not have a cold frame, place the boxes in the shelter of a south or west-facing wall and cover the plants with sacking draped over a framework when frosts are forecast.

IN FLOWER THIS MONTH

BLUE AND MAUVE

SHRUBS
VINCA MAJOR (greater periwinkle)
H: 15–30 cm (6–12 in) S: 90 cm–1·2 m (3–4 ft)
Wide spreading sub-shrub with 25–30 mm (1–1¼ in) wide bright blue flowers. 'Elegantissima'/ 'Variegata' has variegated foliage and pale purple-blue flowers.
VINCA MINOR: see March

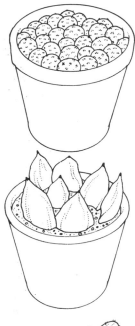

Above: Cacti can be increased in several ways; by removing and rooting offsets; taking leaf cuttings; or by removing stems that can be rooted.

◇ **MAY** ◇

Tulips now abound in gardens, occasionally on their own but often with other spring-flowering plants. The combinations in which they can be used are nearly endless and much depends on the ingenuity of the gardener. Forget-me-nots, wallflowers, violas and daisies are the more common companions for tulips, and a few to consider are a yellow viola planted with the scarlet and gold 'Keizerskroon', a carpet of a pale blue forget-me-not and a planting of the scarlet and gold single early tulip 'Keizerskroon', and a triple combination of a deep blue forget-me-not, the yellow 'Mrs. John T. Scheepers' and the orange-red 'President Hoover'. If your eye fancies a salmon, yellow and orange-red mixture try a carpet of the salmon *Cheiranthus cheiri* 'Easter Queen' and a mixture of the orange-red 'President Hoover' and the yellow 'Mrs. John T. Scheepers'. For a blue and red spring-bedding mixture try blue *Aubrieta deltoidea* and 'Red Emperor'.

Tulips also blend well with *Bellis perennis* (daisies). Blue parrot types make an eye-catching picture with the daisies, and for a slightly rarer taste light blue forget-me-nots and blue parrot tulips can be combined. There are colour combinations and plants for all tastes, and it is well worth a visit to public gardens at this time of year to make notes about arrangements you like.

Rock gardens are a special delight when plants can be used in eye-catching combinations. The 5–10 cm (2–4 in) high *Phlox subulata* (alpine moss pink) in a pink form such as 'Alexander's Surprise', the sub-shrubby *Lithodora diffusa* 'Heavenly Blue' at 10 cm (4 in) high and the 45 cm (1½ ft) high yellow-flowered *Genista pilosa* form a superb trio of plants and colour. *Lithodora diffusa*, by the way, is often better known by its earlier name *Lithospermum diffusum*.

Besides the genista, many other members of the broom family flower during early summer. *Genista januensis* (Genoa broom) is a rare shrub, but a common broom is *Ulex europaeus* (gorse), a spiny, tangled shrub with honeyed-fragrance and pea-like golden-yellow flowers. The best form is *U. e.* 'Plenus', a double-flowered and compact type. Beware of too large patches of it as it can dominate all other colours nearby.

Cytisus scoparius (common broom) with its many forms makes a stunning impact. One of the brightest is 'Golden Sunlight' with rich yellow flowers. But if your liking is for a member of the broom family against a wall you will not be disappointed with *Cytisus battandieri*. It creates pineapple-scented golden-yellow flowers in 10 cm (4 in) long heads. It can be grown as a free-standing shrub in a border, but it is often better against a south-facing wall. Other broom members in flower include *Cytisus × praecox* (Warminster broom), *Cytisus × beanii* which is ideal for rock gardens, and *Cytisus albus* (white broom).

May is also the month for *Syringa vulgaris* (common lilac) which provides a wealth of flowers, usually highly scented, from white through to deep purple. 'Blue Hyacinth' displays mauve-budded lavender-blue flowers, 'Congo' rich pink heads, 'Massena' deep purple, 'Maud Notcutt' white, 'Vestale' pure white, and 'Souvenir de Alice Harding' double and alabaster-white. A beautiful combination is the richly yellow laburnum and a dark blue lilac. Alternatively, the laburnum looks good when cascading over red, pink, apricot or orange azaleas. But do not try this combination unless the soil is slightly acid.

May – early summer – is a wonderful month for flowers. There is a sense of newness and brightness about all the flowers, unlike the dying months of autumn and early winter.

Yellow-flowered plants are most welcome in spring, and especially those that are able to brighten the moist surrounds of a stream or garden pond. Lysichiton americanus, the Skunk Cabbage from Canada and North America, reveals golden-yellow arum-like flowers that brighten the often dark surface of water.

FLOWERS

♦ Remove spring-bedding plants as they fade. Discard such plants as forget-me-nots and wall-flowers, but lift and heel-in all bulbs on a spare piece of ground to die down naturally.

♦ Thin annuals sown *in situ*.

♦ Hoe shallowly to remove all weeds.

♦ Do not be tempted to plant out bedding plants too early. In the south-west it is likely that the risk of frost has passed, but in many other areas there is a risk of frost up to the first week in June.

♦ Remove sideshoots from exhibition sweet peas.

♦ Plant outdoor-flowering chrysanthemums.

♦ Thin out excessive shoots on delphiniums.

♦ Stake and support herbaceous plants as they develop. Put twiggy sticks in early so that the young shoots grow up and through them, eventually hiding the supports. Delphiniums require stronger supports such as bamboo canes.

VEGETABLES

♦ Sow asparagus peas 10 cm (4 in) apart in drills 25 mm (1 in) deep and 30–38 cm (12–15 in) apart.

♦ Sow kohlrabi thinly in drills 12 mm (½ in) deep and 38 cm (15 in) apart.

♦ Sow leaf lettuces such as 'Salad Bowl' 12 mm (½ in) deep in rows 25–30 cm (10–12 in) apart.

♦ Sow endive 12 mm (½ in) deep in rows 25–30 cm (10–12 in) apart.

♦ Sow runner beans 15 cm (6 in) apart and 5 cm (2 in) deep in rows 60 cm (2 ft) apart. When supporting them with poles it is usually easier to put the supports in first.

♦ Harvest early sowings of summer spinach.

♦ Sow haricot beans 5 cm (2 in) deep, 10 cm (4 in) apart in rows 38–45 cm (15–18 in) apart.

♦ Sow French beans 75 mm (3 in) apart and 5 cm (2 in) deep in drills 38–45 cm (15–18 in) apart, so that they will develop properly.

Far left: Garden cloches are invaluable for raising early crops of vegetables. Many forms of cloche are available, three can be seen here. The centre type is covering a crop of broadbeans.

Left below: A slope is not essential for the making of a rock garden. If you want a rock garden but have only a flat site, select a well-drained position away from trees, place clean brick rubble at the base and use well-drained and weed-free loam to build up the mound. Large rocks can be used to produce a natural outcrop of rocks.

Below: Birds can be a problem in a greenhouse in spring and summer. Their entry can be prevented by fixing wire-netting over the ventilators.

FRUIT

♦ Mulch established raspberry canes with well-rotted manure or compost to keep the soil moist, prevent weeds germinating and to feed the plants.

♦ Spray all fruits against pests and diseases before the flowers are fully open, or when they are over.

♦ Remove runners from strawberry plants to direct all their energy into the production of fruits.

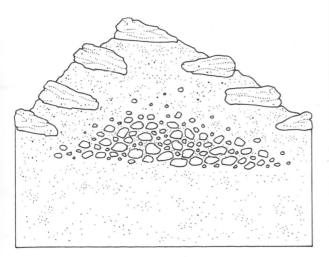

BORDER BRIGHTENERS IN FLOWER THIS MONTH

◇

Anemone coronaria
(poppy anemone)

Bellis perennis
(daisy)

Calendula officinalis
(pot marigold/English marigold)

Cheiranthus × allionii
(Siberian wallflower)

Cheiranthus cheiri

Lobelia erinus

Lychnis viscaria

Viola × wittrockiana
(pansy)

◇

Right: Few eyes are not captivated by Limnanthus douglasii, *the Poached Egg Plant. It is an annual that can be sown where it is to flower.*

FLOWERS TO SOW THIS MONTH

ANNUALS AND BIENNIALS

ADONIS AESTIVALIS (pheasant's eye)
Sow 6 mm (¼ in) deep *in situ*.

ALYSSUM MARITIMUM; now *Lobularia maritima*
Sow 6 mm (¼ in) deep *in situ*.

AMARANTHUS CAUDATUS (love-lies-bleeding)
Sow 3 mm (⅛ in) deep *in situ*.

ANCHUSA CAPENSIS
Sow 12 mm (½ in) deep *in situ*.

ASPERULA ORIENTALIS; syn. *A. azurea/A. setosa* (annual woodruff)
Sow 6 mm (¼ in) deep *in situ*.

BRACHYCOME IBERIDIFOLIA (Swan River daisy)
Sow 6 mm (¼ in) deep *in situ*.

CALENDULA OFFICINALIS (pot marigold/English marigold)
Sow 12 mm (½ in) deep *in situ*.

CAMPANULA MEDIUM (Canterbury bell)
Sow 6 mm (¼ in) deep in a seed bed.

CENTAUREA CYANUS (cornflower)
Sow 12 mm (½ in) deep *in situ*.

CENTAUREA MOSCHATA (sweet sultan)
Sow 6 mm (¼ in) deep *in situ*.

CHRYSANTHEMUM CARINATUM; syn. *C. tricolor*
Sow 6 mm (¼ in) deep *in situ*.

CLARKIA ELEGANS
Sow 6 mm (¼ in) deep *in situ*.

CLARKIA PULCHELLA
Sow 6 mm (¼ in) deep *in situ*.

CONSOLIDA AJACIS (larkspur)
Sow 6 mm (¼ in) deep *in situ*.

CONVOLVULUS TRICOLOR; syn. *C. minor*
Sow 12 mm (½ in) deep *in situ*.

COREOPSIS TINCTORIA (tickseed)
Sow 6 mm (¼ in) deep *in situ*.

COSMOS BIPINNATUS (cosmea)
Sow 6 mm (¼ in) deep *in situ*.

COTULA BARBATA (pincushion plant)
Sow 6 mm (¼ in) deep *in situ*.

DIMORPHOTHECA AURANTIACA (star of the veldt)
Sow 6 mm (¼ in) deep *in situ*.

ECHIUM LYCOPSIS; syn. *E. plantagineum* (viper's bugloss)
Sow 6 mm (¼ in) deep *in situ*.

EMILIA FLAMMEA (tassel flower)
Sow 6 mm (¼ in) deep *in situ*.

ERYSIMUM ALPINUM (alpine wallflower/fairy wallflower)
Sow 6 mm (¼ in) deep in a seed bed.

ESCHSCHOLZIA CALIFORNICA (Californian poppy)
Sow 6 mm (¼ in) deep *in situ*.

GILIA LUTEA (stardust)
Sow 6 mm (¼ in) deep *in situ*.

GYPSOPHILA ELEGANS
Sow 6 mm (¼ in) deep *in situ*.

HELIANTHUS ANNUUS (sunflower)
Sow 12 mm (½ in) deep *in situ*.

HIBISCUS TRIONUM (flower-of-an-hour)
Sow 6 mm (¼ in) deep *in situ*.

LAWNS

♦ Water newly sown lawns if the weather is dry. Established lawns will need cutting with the blades set 12–18 mm (½–¾ in) high.

♦ Newly sown grass soon reaches 75 mm (3 in) high when it should be cut. Use a sharp-bladed mower that will cut the grass at 5 cm (2 in) high without tearing out grass seedlings from the soil. During its first year do not cut the grass lower than 5 cm (2 in) high.

GREENHOUSES

♦ Continue to harden off bedding plants, placing them in a cold frame.

♦ Sow primulas, calceolarias and cinerarias to produce plants for greenhouse and indoor decoration.

♦ Water all plants regularly and ventilate the greenhouse as necessary.

♦ Plant cucumbers and melons in their growing positions in a greenhouse.

FLOWERS TO SOW THIS MONTH

IBERIS UMBELLATA (candytuft)
Sow 6 mm (¼ in) deep *in situ*.

IPOMOEA PURPUREA; syn. *Convolvulus major*
Sow 12 mm (½ in) deep *in situ*.

LATHYRUS ODORATUS (sweet pea)
Sow 12 mm (½ in) deep *in situ*.

LAVATERA TRIMESTRIS (mallow)
Sow 12 mm (½ in) deep *in situ*.

LIMNANTHES DOUGLASII (poached egg plant)
Sow 3 mm (⅛ in) deep *in situ*.

LINARIA MAROCCANA (toadflax)
Sow 3 mm (⅛ in) deep *in situ*.

LUNARIA ANNUA (honesty)
Sow 12 mm (½ in) deep in a seed bed.

LYCHNIS VISCARIA
Sow 6 mm (¼ in) deep *in situ*.

MALCOLMIA MARITIMA (Virginian stock)
Sow 6 mm (¼ in) deep *in situ*.

MATTHIOLA BICORNIS (night-scented stock)
Sow 6 mm (¼ in) deep *in situ*.

MENTZELIA LINDLEYI
Sow 6 mm (¼ in) deep *in situ*.

MYOSOTIS SYLVATICA (forget-me-not)
Sow 6 mm (¼ in) deep in a seed bed.

NEMOPHYLLA MENZIESII (baby blue eyes)
Sow 6 mm (¼ in) deep *in situ*.

NICANDRA PHYSALOIDES (apple of Peru/shoo fly plant)
Sow 6 mm (¼ in) deep *in situ*.

NIGELLA DAMASCENA (love-in-a-mist)
Sow 6 mm (¼ in) deep *in situ*.

PAPAVER RHOEAS (field poppy/Shirley poppy)
Sow 6 mm (¼ in) deep *in situ*.

PAPAVER SOMNIFERUM (opium poppy)
Sow 6 mm (¼ in) deep *in situ*.

RESEDA ODORATA (mignonette)
Sow 3 mm (⅛ in) deep *in situ*.

SCABIOSA ATROPURPUREA (sweet scabious)
Sow 12 mm (½ in) deep *in situ*.

TROPAEOLUM MAJUS (nasturtium)
Sow 12 mm (½ in) deep *in situ*.

Above: Spring is the time to encourage young children to take an interest in the garden. Sowing a packet of hardy seeds and looking after the plants during the rest of the year will capture Michael's interest for many months.

Left: When filling ponds with water through a hose-pipe tie a piece of cloth over the end to minimize the force of the water.

FLOWERS

♦ Prune *Prunus triloba* and *P. glandulosa* as soon as they have finished flowering. Cut back flowered shoots to two or three buds of their bases.

♦ Stop outdoor-flowering chrysanthemums by nipping out the terminal buds and a piece of the stem, encouraging the plant to develop side-shoots.

♦ Rambler roses will be making strong growths from their bases which should be tied up to supports.

♦ Divide violets.

♦ Support gladioli in exposed areas.

FRUIT

♦ Hoe between strawberry plants and place a layer of straw between them to prevent the developing fruits resting on the soil and becoming dirty.

♦ Tie raspberry canes to the wires as they develop.

VEGETABLES

♦ Harvest lettuce sown the previous August.

♦ Thin summer lettuce to 23–30 cm (9–12 in) apart.

♦ Sow beetroot in small groups 13 cm (5 in) apart in drills 5 cm (2 in) deep and 30 cm (1 ft) apart.

♦ Sow radishes 12 mm ($\frac{1}{2}$ in) deep.

♦ Sow ridge cucumbers on well-prepared mounds.

♦ Sow chicory 12 mm ($\frac{1}{2}$ in) deep in drills 25–30 cm (10–12 in) apart.

♦ Plant celery in a trench, in two rows 23 cm (9 in) apart, with 20–25 cm (8–10 in) between the plants.

♦ Transplant Brussels sprouts to their growing positions, 75–90 cm (2 ft 6 in–3 ft) apart in rows 90 cm (3 ft) apart. Firm the soil thoroughly.

♦ Sow winter cabbage for harvesting from early November to spring. Sow seeds 18 mm ($\frac{3}{4}$ in) deep in drills 15 cm (6 in) apart in a seedbed.

FLOWERS TO SOW THIS MONTH

PERENNIALS

ACHILLEA FILIPENDULA
Sow 6 mm ($\frac{1}{4}$ in) deep in a seed bed.

ACHILLEA MILLEFOLIUM
Sow 6 mm ($\frac{1}{4}$ in) deep in a seed bed.

ACHILLEA PTARMICA
Sow 6 mm ($\frac{1}{4}$ in) deep in a seed bed.

ALTHAEA ROSEA; now *Alcea rosea* (hollyhock)
Sow 12 mm ($\frac{1}{2}$ in) deep *in situ.*

ANCHUSA AZUREA; syn. *A. italica*
Sow 12 mm ($\frac{1}{2}$ in) deep in a seed bed.

ANEMONE CORONARIA (poppy anemone)
Sow 3 mm ($\frac{1}{8}$ in) deep in 10–15°C/50–60°F.

AQUILEGIA VULGARIS (granny's bonnet)
Sow 6 mm ($\frac{1}{4}$ in) deep in a seed bed.

AQUILEGIA ALPINA
Sow 6 mm ($\frac{1}{4}$ in) deep in a seed bed.

ARENARIA MONTANA (sandwort)
Sow 6 mm ($\frac{1}{4}$ in) deep in a cold frame.

ASTER NOVI-BELGII
Sow 12 mm ($\frac{1}{2}$ in) deep *in situ.*

AUBRIETA DELTOIDEA
Sow 6 mm ($\frac{1}{4}$ in) deep in a seed bed.

BELLIS PERENNIS (daisy): grown as biennial
Sow 6 mm ($\frac{1}{4}$ in) deep in a seed bed.

CATANANCHE CAERULEA (Cupid's dart)
Sow 6 mm ($\frac{1}{4}$ in) deep in a cold frame.

CENTRANTHUS RUBER; syn. *Kentranthus ruber*
(valerian)
Sow 6 mm ($\frac{1}{4}$ in) deep in a seed bed.

CHEIRANTHUS × ALLIONII (Siberian wallflower):
grown as hardy biennial
Sow 6 mm ($\frac{1}{4}$ in) deep in a seed bed.

CHEIRANTHUS CHEIRI: grown as hardy biennial
Sow 6 mm ($\frac{1}{4}$ in) deep in a seed bed.

CHRYSANTHEMUM MAXIMUM (shasta daisy)
Sow 6 mm ($\frac{1}{4}$ in) deep *in situ.*

DELPHINIUM ELATUM
Sow 6 mm ($\frac{1}{4}$ in) deep in a seed bed.

DIANTHUS BARBATUS (sweet William): grown as
hardy biennial
Sow 6 mm ($\frac{1}{4}$ in) deep in a seed bed.

DIGITALIS PURPUREA (foxglove)
Sow thinly and shallowly in a cold frame.

ECHINOPS RITRO (globe thistle)
Sow 12 mm ($\frac{1}{2}$ in) deep in a seed bed.

ERIGERON SPECIOSUS (midsummer daisy)
Sow 6 mm ($\frac{1}{4}$ in) deep in a seed bed.

GEUM CHILOENSE
Sow 6 mm ($\frac{1}{4}$ in) deep in a cold frame.

HESPERIS MATRONALIS (sweet rocket)
Sow 6 mm ($\frac{1}{4}$ in) deep in a seed bed.

LYCHNIS CHALCEDONICA (Jerusalem cross)
Sow 6 mm ($\frac{1}{4}$ in) deep *in situ.*

Left: Chrysanthemum maximum, *the well-known Shasta Daisy from the Pyrenees, creates a massed display of single white flowers with golden centres from June to August. It is a hardy perennial that can be raised from seed sown now.*

BULBS IN FLOWER THIS MONTH

◇

Allium aflatunensis

Cyclamen repandum

Fritillaria meleagris
(snake's head frittilary)

Hyacinthus orientalis
(common hyacinth)

Muscari armeniacum
(grape hyacinth)

Muscari botryoides

Ornithogalum nutans

Ornithogalum umbellatum
(star of Bethlehem)

Puschkinia scilloides
(striped squill)

Scilla peruviana
(Cuban lily)

Tulipa – triumph, lily-flowered, cottage, Darwin, and parrot types

◇

Below: Berberis darwinii 'Prostrata' is a beautiful shrub with golden-yellow flowers during April and May.

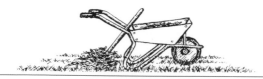

LAWNS

♦ New lawns can be created by laying turves. These lawns can be used within several months from being formed. Thorough preparation of the soil is essential, in the same manner as when creating a lawn from seed (*see* page 59). Lay the turves in rows with the joints staggered. Brush clean sifted soil – about 1·1 kg per square metre (2 lb a square yard) – into the joints. If the surface is dry use a light roller to firm the turves into position.

♦ Selective lawn weedkillers can be used when established lawns are growing strongly. If a fertilizer treatment was given a few weeks ago now is the right time to apply weedkillers. Don't use weedkillers if the soil is too dry or wet, or on windy days and follow the maker's instructions. Do not cut the grass for at least three days afterwards and do not put the mowings on the compost heap.

IN FLOWER THIS MONTH

YELLOW AND ORANGE

TREES

CARAGANA ARBORESCENS (pea tree)
H: 4·5–7·5 m (15–25 ft) S: 4·5–5·4 m (15–18 ft)
Shrubby deciduous with yellow pea-like flowers.

LABURNUM × WATEREI
H: 3–5·4 m (10–18 ft) S: 3·5–4·5 m (12–15 ft)
Deciduous hybrid, with 25–30 cm (10–12 in) long pendulous clusters of pea-shaped yellow flowers. 'Vossii' has larger clusters of flowers.

SHRUBS

BERBERIS CANDIDULA
H: 60 cm (2 ft) S: 60 cm (2 ft)
Small, dome-shaped evergreen with yellow flowers followed by blue-black berries.

BERBERIS DARWINII: see April

BERBERIS × RUBROSTILLA
H: 1·2–1·5 m (4–5 ft) S: 1·5–2·1 m (5–7 ft)
Compact deciduous with yellow flowers followed by coral-red berries.

BERBERIS × STENOPHYLLA
H: 2·4–3 m (8–10 ft) S: 3–3·5 m (10–12 ft)
Vigorous evergreen with golden-yellow flowers.

COROKIA COTONEASTER (wire-netting bush)
H: 90 cm–1·2 m (3–4 ft) S: 90 cm–1·5 m (3–5 ft)
Evergreen with stiff, intertwined branchlets and small star-like yellow flowers.

CORONILLA GLAUCA
H: 90 cm–1·2 m (3–4 ft) S: 1·2–1·5 m (4–5 ft)
Evergreen with clusters of pea-shaped bright yellow flowers.

GREENHOUSES

♦ At this time of year the greenhouse and cold frames are packed with plants. If more plants are ready to be hardened off space can be made by placing boxes of plants already in the cold frame into the shelter of a south- or west-facing wall.

♦ Many plants will need shading from strong sunlight, either by painting white shading material on the outside of the glass or with blinds inside. Blinds are preferable as they can be rolled down according to the weather.

♦ Continue to remove sideshoots from tomato plants: if left, they create a tangled mass of growth and deprive the fruits of food.

♦ Maintain vigilance for the presence of pests and diseases. These can soon build up into epidemic proportions if left unattended. Pests and diseases spread especially rapidly when the greenhouse is packed with just one type of plant, such as tomatoes and cucumbers.

IN FLOWER THIS MONTH

YELLOW AND ORANGE

CYTISUS SCOPARIUS 'Golden Sunlight' (common broom)
H: 1·8–2·4 m (6–8 ft) S: 1·8–2·4 m (6–8 ft)
Deciduous with evergreen appearance and rich yellow pea-shaped flowers.

CYTISUS × BEANII
H: 45–60 cm (18–24 in) S: 75–90 cm (24–36 in)
Deciduous with golden-yellow pea-shaped flowers.

CYTISUS PURGANS: see April

GENISTA HISPANICA (Spanish gorse)
H: 75 cm–1·2 m (2 ft 6 in–4 ft) S: 1·5–2·4 m (5–8 ft)
Deciduous with spiny stems and golden-yellow pea-shaped flowers.

GENISTA LYDIA
H: 60–90 cm (2–3 ft) S: 1·2–1·8 m (4–6 ft)
Low-growing deciduous with bright yellow pea-shaped flowers.

GENISTA PILOSA
H: 30–45 cm (12–18 in) S: 60–90 cm (2–3 ft)
Low-growing, often prostrate, deciduous, with small pea-shaped yellow flowers.

KERRIA JAPONICA: see April

PIPTANTHUS LABURNIFOLIUS
H: 2·4–3·5 m (8–12 ft) S: 2·4–3 m (8–10 ft)
Slightly tender deciduous, with erect 5–7·5 cm (2–3 in) clusters of bright yellow sweat-pea-like flowers.

POTENTILLA FRUTICOSA 'Farreri'
H: 1·2–1·5 m (4–5 ft) S: 1·2–1·5 m (4–5 ft)
Deciduous with small butter-yellow flowers. 'Katherine Dykes' has primrose-yellow flowers.

ULEX EUROPAEUS: see April

Above: Cuttings of early-flowering greenhouse chrysanthemums can be taken now, with late-flowering ones rooted in June. Take cuttings 5–6·5 cm (2–2½ in) long and remove the lower leaves. Trim the stems just below a leaf-joint and insert them in pots of equal parts peat and sharp sand. Place them in a plastic bag, sealed with an elastic band.

Left: Sorbus aria 'Lutescens', a form of the Common Whitebeam, has creamy-white young leaves. It creates an attractive spring focal point in a garden.

IN FLOWER THIS MONTH

RED AND PINK

TREES

AESCULUS × CARNEA 'Briottii' (Red horse chestnut)
H: 4·5–6 m (15–20 ft) S: 2·4–3·5 m (8–12 ft)
Deciduous with mid-green palm-shaped leaves and deep pink 15–20 cm (6–8 in) high candles of flowers.

CRATAEGUS LAEVIGATA 'Coccinea Plena' (Paul's double scarlet thorn)
H: 4·5–6 m (15–20 ft) S: 4·5–5·4 m (15–18 ft)
Deciduous with double scarlet flowers. 'Rosea Pleno-flore' has double pink flowers.

MALUS CORONARIA 'Charlottae'
H: 4·5–5·4 m (15–18 ft) S: 3·5–6 m (12–20 ft)
Broad-headed and deciduous, with scented, large, semi-double shell-pink flowers.

MALUS 'Pink Perfection'
H: 5·4–6 m (18–20 ft) S: 3·5–5·4 m (12–18 ft)
Deciduous American hybrid with scented clear pink double flowers.

MALUS 'Royalty'
H: 4·5–6 m (15–20 ft) S: 3–4·5 m (10–15 ft)
Rich purple deciduous foliage, pink flowers and bright reddish-purple fruits.

MALUS 'Van Eseltine'
H: 4·5–6 m (15–20 ft) S: 3–3·5 m (10–12 ft)
Stiffly-erect deciduous with scarlet-budded semi-double pink flowers.

PRUNUS PADUS 'Purple Queen'
H: 6–7·5 m (20–25 ft) S: 4·5–5·4 m (15–18 ft)
Deciduous with pale pink flowers in slender tassels 7·5–10 cm (3–4 in) long.

PRUNUS 'Kanzan'
H: 7·5–9 m (25–30 ft) S: 5·4–7·5 m (18–25 ft)
Deciduous with double purple-pink flowers.

PRUNUS 'Pink Perfection'
H: 6–7·5 m (20–25 ft) S: 5·4–6 m (18–20 ft)
Upright deciduous hybrid cherry with carmine-budded double rosy-pink flowers.

PRUNUS 'Shirofugen'
H: 6–7·5 m (20–25 ft) S: 5·4–9 m (18–30 ft)
Spreading, strong-growing deciduous cherry with pink-budded flowers that open to white and then change to purple-pink.

SHRUBS

CAMELLIA JAPONICA: see February

CERCIS SILIQUASTRUM (Judas tree)
H: 5·4–6 m (15–20 ft) S: 3–4·5 m (10–15 ft)
Wide-spreading deciduous with pea-shaped rose-purple flowers.

CISTUS × PURPUREUS
H: 1·2–1·5 m (4–5 ft) S: 1·2 m (4 ft)
Upright bushy deciduous with 5–7·5 cm (2–3 in) wide reddish-pink flowers.

CRINODENDRON HOOKERIANUM
H: 3–4·5 m (10–15 ft) S: 1·8–3 m (6–10 ft)
Upright dense evergreen with urn-shaped, waxy, rich crimson pendent flowers.

Right: Prunus padus, *the Bird Cherry, is distinctive with its slender 7.5–13 cm (3–5 in) long tassels of almond-scented white flower in May.*

Below: Yucca filamentosa
'Variegatum' is eye-catching
and remains attractive
throughout the year. Its
leaves are distinctively
striped with yellow
and green.

IN FLOWER THIS MONTH

RED AND PINK

CYTISUS SCOPARIUS 'Burkwoodii'
H: 1·8–2·1 m (6–7 ft) S: 1·8–2·1 m (6–7 ft)
Deciduous, but appears evergreen, with rich crimson-red pea-like flowers. 'Killiney Red' has bright red, 'Killiney Salmon' salmon-red and 'Windlesham Ruby' ruby-red flowers.

DAPHNE × BURKWOODII 'Somerset'
H: 90 cm–1·2 m (3–4 ft) S: 90 cm–1·2 m (3–4 ft)
Semi-evergreen with soft mauve-pink flowers.

EMBOTHRIUM LANCEOLATUM (Chilean fire bush)
H: 4·5–5·4 m (15–18 ft) S: 2·1–3 m (7–10 ft)
Suckering evergreen with bright orange-scarlet flowers.

ERICA MEDITERRANEA 'Brightness': see March

KOLKWITZIA AMABILIS 'Pink Cloud' (beauty bush)
H: 1·8–3 m (6–10 ft) S: 1·2–2·4 m (4–8 ft)
Upright deciduous, with clear pink flowers.

LEPTOSPERMUM SCOPARIUM 'Chapmanii' (manuka/tea tree)
H: 1·8–3 m (6–10 ft) S: 1·5–2·1 m (5–7 ft)
Slightly tender evergreen with bright rose-red flowers. 'Red Damask' has double and dark red and 'Roseum Multipetalum' double and rose-pink flowers.

MAGNOLIA × SOULANGIANA: see April

RIBES SANGUINEUM 'Pulborough Scarlet',
R. SPECIOSUM: see April

ROBINIA HISPIDA (rose acacia)
H: 1·8–3 m (6–10 ft) S: 1·8–2·4 m (6–8 ft)
Deciduous with large rose-pink pea-shaped flowers.

SYRINGA VULGARIS (common lilac)
H: 2·4–3·5 m (8–12 ft) S: 1·5–3 m (5–10 ft)
Deciduous, with many varieties such as 'Congo' (dark lilac-red), 'Charles Joly' (purplish-red), 'Sensation' (purplish-red), 'Souvenir de L'Spath' (wine red) and 'Elinor' (dark purplish-red buds opening to pale lilac).

SYRINGA MICROPHYLLA 'Superba'
H: 1·2–1·5 m (4–5 ft) S: 1·2–1·5 m (4–5 ft)
Deciduous with rose-pink fragrant flowers.

WEIGELA 'Abel Carriere'
H: 1·5–1·8 m (5–6 ft) S: 1·5–2·4 m (5–8 ft)
Spreading deciduous, with rosy-carmine flowers with yellow throats.

WEIGELA 'Bristol Ruby'
H: 1·5–1·8 m (5–6 ft) S: 1·5–2·4 m (5–8 ft)
Deciduous with bright ruby-red flowers.

WEIGELA 'Newport Red'
H: 1·5–1·8 m (5–6 ft) S: 1·5–2·4 m (5–8 ft)
Deciduous with dark red flowers.

CLIMBER

CLEMATIS MONTANA 'Rubens'
H: 3–7·5 m (10–25 ft) S: 3–6 m (10–20 ft)
Deciduous with slightly scented 5 cm (2 in) wide pale pink flowers.

FLOWERS

♦ Watch out for aphids on roses, and spray as necessary.
♦ Thin out hardy annuals already sown and producing a large number of congested seedlings.
♦ Continue to sow seeds, as indicated.

FRUIT

♦ If you have a fruit cage over your fruit trees and bushes open one side to let pollinating insects in.
♦ Bark-ring apple and pear trees if necessary.
♦ Remove blossom from both two- and three-year-old fruit trees.
♦ Control weeds in between soft fruits by hoeing or using herbicides.

VEGETABLES

♦ Water summer lettuce if the weather is dry.
♦ Harvest spring cabbage, cutting them off at soil-level.
♦ Earth-up potatoes as necessary.
♦ Sow carrots thinly in drills 12 mm ($\frac{1}{2}$ in) deep and 20 cm (8 in) apart. Also, thin carrots sown earlier in the year.
♦ Sow summer spinach 12 mm ($\frac{1}{2}$ in) deep in drills 30 cm (1 ft) apart.
♦ Sow sweet corn outdoors in blocks of plants rather than long, single rows.
♦ Thin cardoon seedlings to leave one seedling at each station.
♦ Support garden peas with sticks or wire-netting supported at either end of the row.

LAWNS

♦ Lawn edges slightly damaged during winter and early spring can be trimmed back with an edging-iron to form a larger flower border.
♦ Severely damaged edges will need to be repaired by cutting out and reversing the damaged part.

GREENHOUSES

♦ Feed tuberous-rooted begonias as soon as their roots fill the pots. They will probably need feeding every 10 days at this stage.
♦ Water hanging-baskets waiting to be placed outside when all risk of frost has passed. If they are suspended from the roof take care that drips of water do not fall on to plants beneath them and cause them to rot.
♦ Take cuttings of hydrangeas to produce strong plants for next year. When treated with a hormone rooting powder they produce roots very quickly.
♦ Inspect the plants regularly for attack from pests and diseases and spray immediately they are seen.

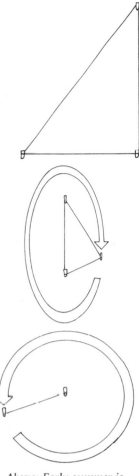

Above: Early summer is often the time for planning new flower borders and beds. Here are detailed ways to produce right-angles, ovals and circles.

Left: Philadelphus coronarius 'Aureus', *a form of the Mock Orange, displays bright golden-yellow foliage in spring that turns greenish-yellow in summer. It is a superb shrub for a garden, creating interest from spring to autumn, when the leaves fall.*

MAY

IN FLOWER THIS MONTH

WHITE AND CREAM

TREES

CRATAEGUS × LAVALLEI
H: 4·5–6 m (15–20 ft) S: 3–4·5 m (10–15 ft)
Almost thornless deciduous ornamental thorn with white flowers in 5–7·5 cm (2–3 in) wide clusters.

CRATAEGUS LAEVIGATA 'Alba Plena' (hawthorn/may)
H: 4·5–6 m (15–20 ft) S: 4·5–5·4 m (15–18 ft)
Deciduous with sweetly scented white flowers.

DAVIDIA INVOLUCRATA (handkerchief tree)
H: 5·4–7·5 m (18–25 ft) S: 3–5·4 m (10–18 ft)
Deciduous with large creamy-white bracts, often up to 18 cm (7 in) long.

MALUS 'Golden Hornet'
H: 4·5–5·4 m (15–18 ft) S: 3–4·5 m (10–15 ft)
Deciduous crab apple with single white flowers followed by bright yellow fruits.

MALUS 'John Downie'
H: 7·5–9 m (25–30 ft) S: 4·5–7·5 m (15–25 ft)
Erect deciduous crab apple with single white flowers and crimson-flushed yellow fruits.

MALUS 'Red Sentinel'
H: 3–4·5 m (10–15 ft) S: 2·4–3·5 m (8–12 ft)
Deciduous with single white flowers followed by bright scarlet glossy fruits.

MALUS 'Snowcloud'
H: 3·5–4·8 m (12–16 ft) S: 3–3·5 m (10–12 ft)
Free-flowering deciduous American crab apple with pure white double flowers.

MESPILUS GERMANICA (medlar)
H: 4·5–7·5 m (15–25 ft) S: 4·5–6 m (15–20 ft)
Spreading deciduous, with large white flowers and edible brown fruits.

PRUNUS PADUS 'Grandiflora' (bird cherry)
H: 6–9 m (20–30 ft) S: 4·5–6 m (15–20 ft)
Deciduous with 7·5–13 cm (3–5 in) long tassels of almond-scented white flowers.

PRUNUS SERRULA
H: 6–7·5 m (20–25 ft) S: 4·5–5·4 m (15–18 ft)
Deciduous with white flowers and peeling reddish-brown bark.

SORBUS ARIA (common whitebeam)
H: 4·5–6 m (15–20 ft) S: 3–4·5 m (10–15 ft)
Deciduous with silvery-white young leaves and creamy-white flowers.

SORBUS AUCUPARIA (rowan/mountain ash)
H: 4·5–7·5 m (15–25 ft) S: 2·4–3·5 m (8–12 ft)
Deciduous with white flowers in 10–15 cm (4–6 in) wide clusters.

SHRUBS

CHAENOMELES SPECIOSA 'Nivalis': see March

CHOISYA TERNATA (Mexican orange blossom)
H: 1·5–1·8 m (5–6 ft) S: 1·8–2·4 m (6–8 ft)
Evergreen with fragrant star-like flowers and aromatic foliage.

CISTUS × ANGUILARI
H: 1·2–1·5 m (4–5 ft) S: 1·2–1·5 m (4–5 ft)
Bushy evergreen with 7·5 cm (3 in) wide pure white flowers.

CISTUS × CYPRIUS
H: 1·8–2·4 m (6–8 ft) S: 1·8–2·7 m (6–9 ft)
Olive-green evergreen with 7·5 cm (3 in) wide crimson-blotched white flowers.

CYTISUS ALBUS (white Portugal broom)
H: 1·5–1·8 m (5–6 ft) S: 1·5–1·8 m (5–6 ft)
Bushy, deciduous, upright shrub with many small pea-shaped white flowers.

CYTISUS PRAECOX 'Albus'
H: 1·5–1·8 m (5–6 ft) S: 1·5–1·8 m (5–6 ft)
Deciduous with tumbling masses of white pea-like flowers.

HALESIA CAROLINA (snowdrop tree)
H: 4·5–6 m (15–20 ft) S: 6–7·5 m (20–25 ft)
Often tree-like deciduous, with silver-white bell-shaped flowers.

MAGNOLIA SIEBOLDII
H: 3–4·5 m (10–15 ft) S: 3–4·5 m (10–15 ft)
Deciduous with 7·5 cm (3 in) wide pendent bowl-shaped white flowers.

MAGNOLIA × SOULANGIANA, × OSMAREA BURKWOODII: see April

PIERIS FLORIBUNDA: see March

PONCIRUS TRIFOLIATA (Japanese bitter orange)
H: 1·5–2·1 m (5–7 ft) S: 1·8–2·1 m (6–7 ft)
Spiny deciduous, with sweetly scented large white flowers.

RUBUS × TRIDEL 'Benenden'
H: 1·8–2·4 m (6–8 ft) S: 2·4–3 m (8–10 ft)
Ornamental deciduous bramble with saucer-shaped bright white flowers up to 5 cm (2 in) wide and with masses of yellow stamens.

SKIMMIA JAPONICA, SPIRAEA × ARGUTA: see April

SYRINGA VULGARIS 'Maud Notcutt'
H: 2·4–3·5 m (8–12 ft) S: 1·5–3 m (5–10 ft)
Deciduous with single white flowers in large clusters. 'Vestale' is a scented white variety.

VIBURNUM × BURKWOODII
H: 1·8–2·4 m (6–8 ft) S: 2·4–3 m (8–10 ft)
Evergreen with pink-budded sweetly scented waxy flowers.

VIBURNUM CARLESII: see April

VIBURNUM PLICATUM
H: 2·4–3 m (8–10 ft) S: 3–4·5 m (10–15 ft)
Deciduous with horizontal branches bearing 5–7·5 cm (2–3 in) clusters of white flowers.

VIBURNUM RHYTIDOPHYLLUM
H: 3–4·5 m (10–15 ft) S: 3–4·5 m (10–15 ft)
Evergreen with 7·5–10 cm (3–4 in) wide flat heads of white flowers.

CLIMBERS

CLEMATIS MONTANA (mountain clematis)
H: 3–7·5 m (10–25 ft) S: 3–6 m (10–20 ft)
Sprawling deciduous, with slightly scented pure white flowers up to 5 cm (2 in) wide.

WISTERIA VENUSTA
H: 7·5–9 m (25–30 ft) S: 4·5–7·5 m (15–25 ft)
Deciduous with fragrant white flowers in 10–15 cm (4–6 in) long clusters. Also, *W. floribunda* 'Alba' and *W. sinensis* 'Alba'.

FLOWERS

♦ Plant summer bedding plants that have been thoroughly hardened off.

♦ Where naturalized bulbs are overcrowded, lift and replant them.

♦ Water and mulch gladioli and lilies.

FRUIT

♦ Keep the grass short in orchards.

♦ During dry weather water fruit bushes and trees, especially when growing as wall-trained specimens. Soil around walls is often much drier than ground in the open.

♦ Gooseberry fruits can be thinned if large dessert fruits are desired.

♦ Spray to control pests and diseases, following the manufacturer's instructions.

VEGETABLES

♦ Sow carrots thinly in drills 12 mm ($\frac{1}{2}$ in) deep and 20 cm (8 in) apart. Also, thin out carrots sown earlier.

♦ Summer lettuce can be sown from now until early August.

♦ Harvest leaf-type lettuces such as 'Salad Bowl'.

♦ Harvest asparagus spears when 15 cm (6 in) high.

♦ Plant leeks in holes 15 cm (6 in) deep and 20 cm (8 in) apart in rows 30–38 cm (12–15 in) apart. Just drop a plant in a hole made by a dibber and water it in. Do not pack the hole with soil.

♦ Sow salad onions 12 mm ($\frac{1}{2}$ in) deep in drills 13–15 cm (5–6 in) apart.

♦ Sow garden peas 10 cm (4 in) apart in drills 5 cm (2 in) deep.

♦ Harvest asparagus spears when 15 cm (6 in) high.

♦ During spring it is especially important to keep the plants free from weeds. Seedlings newly emerging are soon suffocated by weeds, and they also encourage the presence of pests.

By late May and early June the lawn will have received its initial summer onslaught of wear and tear from children and dogs. Holes created by vigorous play can be filled with friable soil and sown with seed, but this often results in the area being trodden upon and soil scattered over the rest of the lawn. However, a quick repair job can be carried out by placing a square piece of board over the hole and cutting around it with a spade or edging-iron. The square of turf can be lifted on a spade and the same wooden template used to cut a fresh piece of turf to fit the area. Fill up any cracks with friable soil.

IN FLOWER THIS MONTH

BLUE AND MAUVE

TREES

PAULOWNIA TOMENTOSA
H: 3·5–7·5 m (12–25 ft) S: 3–4·5 m (10–15 ft)
Hardy deciduous, with fragrant lavender-blue foxglove-like flowers, 4–5 cm (1½–2 in) long.

SHRUBS

CEANOTHUS 'Cascade'
H: 1·8–3 m (6–10 ft) S: 1·8–2·4 m (6–8 ft)
Hardy evergreen with 6·5 cm (2½ in) long clusters of small rich blue flowers.

CEANOTHUS 'Delight'
H: 1·8–3 m (6–10 ft) S: 1·8–2·4 m (6–8 ft)
Bushy erect evergreen with 5–7·5 cm (2–3 in) long clusters of bright blue flowers.

CEANOTHUS DENTATUS
H: 1·8–3 m (6–10 ft) S: 1·8–2·4 m (6–8 ft)
Evergreen with rounded clusters of small blue flowers.

CEANOTHUS THYRSIFLORUS
H: 1·8–3 m (6–10 ft) S: 1·8–2·4 m (6–8 ft)
Very hardy evergreen with light blue flowers in clusters up to 7·5 cm (3 in) long.

ROSMARINUS OFFICINALIS (rosemary)
H: 1·8–2·1 m (6–7 ft) S: 1·5–1·8 m (5–6 ft)
Erect evergreen with 18 mm (¾ in) long mauve flowers. 'Miss Jessop's Upright' has lighter mauve flowers on a vigorous, upright plant.

SYRINGA VULGARIS (lilac)
H: 2·4–3·5 m (8–12 ft) S: 1·5–3 m (5–10 ft)
Hardy deciduous with pyramidal flower clusters. 'Blue Hyacinth' has lavender-blue and fragrant, 'Firmament' light lavender-blue, 'Katherine Havemeyer' scented, double purple-lavender and 'Michael Buchner' scented, double lavender flowers.

VINCA MINOR: see March
VINCA MAJOR: see April

CLIMBERS

ABUTILON VITIFOLIUM
H: 2·4–4·5 m (8–15 ft) S: 1·8–3 m (6–10 ft)
Slightly tender deciduous with palm-shaped leaves and 5 cm (2 in) wide lavender or mauve flowers.

CLEMATIS 'Barbara Jackman'
H: 3·5–4·5 m (12–15 ft) S: 3–3·5 m (10–12 ft)
Deciduous with bluish-purple 13 cm (5 in) wide flowers bearing plum-coloured bars.

CLEMATIS 'Lasurstern'
H: 3·5–4·5 m (12–15 ft) S: 3–3·5 m (10–12 ft)
Deciduous with deep lavender-blue flowers.

CLEMATIS 'Mrs. Cholmondeley'
H: 3·5–4·5 m (12–15 ft) S: 3–3·5 m (10–12 ft)
Deciduous with lavender-blue petals tipped purple.

CLEMATIS MACROPETALA
H: 3–3·5 m (10–12 ft) S: 1·8–2·4 m (6–8 ft)
Deciduous with 5–7·5 cm (2–3 in) wide nodding bell-shaped light and dark blue flowers.

WISTERIA FLORIBUNDA (Japanese wisteria)
H: 7·5–9 m (25–30 ft) S: 3·5–4·5 m (12–15 ft)
Deciduous with fragrant 25–30 cm (10–12 in) long pendulous bunches of pea-shaped violet-blue flowers. 'Macrobotrys' has lilac-blue and purple flowers in pendulous clusters up to 90 cm (3 ft) long.

WISTERIA SINENSIS (Chinese wisteria)
H: 15–21·5 m (50–70 ft) S: 7·5–9 m (25–30 ft)
Deciduous with densely packed 20–30 cm (8–12 in) long clusters of fragrant mauve flowers.

ROCK PLANTS IN FLOWER THIS MONTH
◇

Aethionema grandiflorum
(Persian candytuft)

Aethionema 'Warley Rose'

Alyssum saxatile 'Flore-pleno'

Antennaria dioica

Aquilegia alpina
(alpine columbine)

Aquilegia flabellata 'Nana Alba'

Armeria maritima 'Alba'
(thrift)

Armeria maritima 'Vindictive'
(thrift)

Aubrieta deltoidea

Erinus alpinus

Gentiana verna
(spring gentian)

Geranium cinereum

Geranium farreri;
syn. *G. napuligerum*

Geranium subcaulescens

Helichrysum milfordiae;
syn. *H. marginatum*

Iberis sempervirens

Lewisia cotyledon

Sedum spathulifolium

Silene acaulis

Thymus nitidus

Veronica prostrata
◇

LAWNS

GREENHOUSES

♦ Hollows and bumps can be levelled by using an edging-iron or spade to cut back the turf and either adding or removing soil.
♦ New lawns can still be created by sowing seed or laying turves (*see* pages 59 and 72).

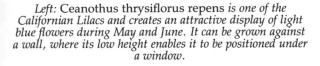

Left: Ceanothus thrysiflorus repens *is one of the Californian Lilacs and creates an attractive display of light blue flowers during May and June. It can be grown against a wall, where its low height enables it to be positioned under a window.*

♦ Pot up hydrangea cuttings as soon as they have developed roots. Set them individually into small pots, using loam-based compost.
♦ Pot on all plants that fill their pots: a congested mass of roots will stunt plants permanently.
♦ Chrysanthemums for flowering outdoors in pots can be moved to a firm-based, wind-sheltered and well-drained area outdoors. If the plants are placed on a soft base a heavy rain storm will cause the pots to move.
♦ If birds and cats are invading the greenhouse during the day when the door is open, make a wood-framed wire-mesh screen for the entrance. If birds are entering through ventilators, place mesh over them.

◇ JUNE ◇

Rose-growers will be overwhelmed with flowers this month. It is the time when there is a wealth of colour from roses of all types. It is difficult to find a garden without at least one rose bush. They look good on their own, of course, but when combined with other plants that either extend the colour scheme or bring contrast or harmony with the roses it is a further delight. For instance, the hybrid tea 'Ophelia' with a height of 75 cm (2½ ft) and with fragrant, small, silvery-pink flowers shading to yellow combines well with the light mauve *Viola* 'Maggie Mott'. Climbing roses are good companions for other climbers. The eye-catching May and June flowering *Rosa ecacae* 'Helen Knight' displays 5 cm (2 in) wide saucer-shaped clear yellow flowers amid fern-like leaves, and when grown with *Clematis montana* (mountain clematis) makes a beautiful picture against a sunny wall. The rambler 'Albertine' that rises to about 5·4 m (18 ft) with double copper-pink and richly scented flowers makes a good companion for *Lonicera periclymenum* 'Belgica' (early Dutch honeysuckle). It produces purple-red and yellow flowers during May and June. Alternatively, plant a clear pale blue delphinium in front of rose 'Albertine'. If pale sulphur-yellow flowers are more to your taste then use *Verbascum* 'Gainsborough' instead of the delphinium.

Another climbing pair is the superb *Rosa banksiae* 'Lutea', a form of the Banks's rose with double yellow flowers, with the pale blue flowers of a wisteria.

A tough and cold-resistant combination of plants is *Vitus vinifera* 'Purpurea' (Teinturier grape) with large, coarsely lobed leaves first claret-red and then rich purple in autumn, and the silver-leaved *Artemisia arborescens* at 1 m (3½ ft) high and with silver-white leaves. It has the bonus of small, round, yellow flowers during June and July. An alternative plant for the artemisia is the silver-grey-leaved *Senecio* 'Sun-shine', which also has daisy-like yellow flowers during midsummer.

Herbaceous borders are now starting to create large splashes of colour. One of the most dominant of all reds is *Lychnis chalcedonica* (scarlet lychnis) which rises to 75 cm (2½ ft) with bright scarlet flowers in dense flattened heads. It is often too dominant in colour to be set too close to other plants, but can be combined with red sweet-Williams. Set these in front of the scarlet lychnis, with at least twice as many sweet-William plants as the lychnis for the right balance.

The scarlet lychnis can also be planted in a shaded, moist, woodland or naturalized setting, as can *Meconopsis betonicifolia* (blue Himalayan poppy). Its sky-blue 6·5–7·5 cm (2½–3 in) wide delicate flowers are borne during June and July. When grown in a large drift with primulas such as the *Primula pulverulenta* 'Bartley Strain' with stems tiered with pink flowers and the *Primula helodoxa* with bright tiers of yellow flowers it is a stunning and most rewarding sight. But they do need shade and moist soil.

Many lilies are now in flower, including *Lilium candidum* (madonna lily) with trumpet-shaped white flowers heavily peppered with golden pollen, *Lilium hansonii* with pale orange-yellow flowers peppered with brown spots, *Lilium pyrenaicum* and *Lilium rubellum*.

By the end of this month bedding plants planted out into the garden during the first week of this month – after all risk of frost had passed – will be establishing themselves and preparing for a dominant show of colour during the rest of summer. Hardy annuals sown in the open soil will also be growing rapidly and covering the soil with shoots. The continuing cycle of fresh flowers bursting on the garden continues, as it should in a well-planned garden.

Spring bedding plants create borders with strong colour impact and can be planted to form attractive patterns that can be changed each year. Take care not to set the plants in the garden too early, as they may then be damaged by late frosts.

FLOWERS TO SOW THIS MONTH

ANNUALS AND BIENNIALS

CAMPANULA MEDIUM (Canterbury bell)
Sow 6 mm (¼ in) deep in a seed bed.

CLARKIA ELEGANS
Sow 6 mm (¼ in) deep *in situ*.

CLARKIA PULCHELLA
Sow 6 mm (¼ in) deep *in situ*.

ERYSIMUM ALPINUM (alpine wallflower/fairy wallflower)
Sow 6 mm (¼ in) deep in a seed bed.

LUNARIA ANNUA (honesty)
Sow 12 mm (½ in) deep in a seed bed.

MATTHIOLA INCANA (Brompton stock)
Sow 6 mm (¼ in) deep in a seed bed.

MYOSOTIS SYLVATICA (forget-me-not)
Sow 6 mm (¼ in) deep in a seed bed.

VIOLA × WITTROCKIANA (pansy)
Sow 6 mm (¼ in) deep in a seed bed.

Below: Roses burst upon gardens this month. The climbing rose 'Meg' flowers mainly during June and July, with single pink and apricot blooms. It is well suited to growing on a small wall, where it grows up to 3·5 m (12 ft) high.

FLOWERS

♦ Plant summer bedding plants in containers.
♦ Support herbaceous plants, using twiggy sticks or canes.
♦ Tie up the shoots on delphiniums to prevent damage by gusting winds.
♦ Ensure sweet peas do not become dry. Thoroughly water the plants and then mulch them.
♦ Spray regularly against pests and diseases, especially if greenflies are present.
♦ Sow seeds, as indicated.
♦ Lift and divide congested clumps of primulas that have flowered.

FRUIT

♦ Blackberries and hybrid berries will produce new canes throughout summer. Tie these into the supporting wires.

VEGETABLES

♦ Thin endive to 23–30 cm (9–12 in) apart.
♦ Harvest salad onions.
♦ Thin beetroot to one seedling every 13 cm (5 in).
♦ Thin ridge cucumbers to leave one seedling on each mound.
♦ Plant out cauliflowers sown in a seedbed in March or April.
♦ Harvest early sowings of summer spinach.
♦ Thin chicory seedlings to 20 cm (8 in) apart.
♦ Harvest spring cabbage, cutting them off at soil-level.
♦ Transplant Brussels sprout plants to their growing positions, 75–90 cm (2 ft 6 in–3 ft) apart in rows 90 cm (3 ft) apart. Firm the soil thoroughly.
♦ Keep the soil hoed between the crops, but take care not to sever any roots. Soil that is kept open and not with a crusty top will absorb rain quickly and not run off the top, washing away the soil. Also, the soil needs to have access to air if the many soil organisms are to function.

The versatile Aubrieta deltoidea *can be used in rock gardens as well as on walls, where it creates a beautiful array of purple to rose-lilac flowers during March and June.*

Hosta fortunei *'Albopicta', one of the variegated Plantain Lilies, creates colour over a long period in both large rock gardens and borders. The pale green leaves are variegated buff-yellow when young, becoming glaucous green by July.*

BORDER BRIGHTENERS IN FLOWER THIS MONTH

◇

Adonis aestivalis
(pheasant's eye)

Ageratum houstonianum

Alonsoa warscewiczii
(mask flower)

Alyssum maritimum;
now *Lobularia maritima*

Anchusa azurea;
syn. *A. italica*

Anemone coronaria
(poppy anemone)

Aquilegia vulgaris
(granny's bonnet)

Aquilegia alpina

Actotis × hybrida
(African daisy)

Begonia semperflorens

Bellis perennis
(daisy)

Brachycome iberidifolia
(Swan River daisy)

Calendula officinalis
(pot marigold/English
marigold)

Campanula medium
(Canterbury bell)

Centaurea cyanus
(cornflower)

Centaurea moschata
(sweet sultan)

Cheiranthus × allionii
(Siberian wallflower)

Cheiranthus cheiri

Chrysanthemum carinatum;
syn. *C. tricolor*

Cleome spinosa
(spider flower)

Consolida ajacis
(larkspur)

Dianthus barbatus
(sweet William)

LAWNS

♦ When using a lawn mower during summer remember to keep children and pets off the lawn. Also, wear a stout pair of shoes and keep your feet away from the blades. With electric-types ensure that the cable is not severed. Start cutting the grass at the lawn edge nearest the power supply, moving away from that point so that there is less chance of the cable being severed.

♦ Never adjust motor mowers with either the power cable or spark plug lead still connected.

GREENHOUSES

♦ Plant out all bedding plants as soon as possible. Most areas are now free from frost. Before planting them, thoroughly soak the compost with water. Plants that are dry at their roots do not transplant easily and take a long time to become established. Also water the flower bed they are to be planted in a day or so beforehand.

♦ Thin grape bunches by about a third.

♦ Re-pot cyclamen into their final pots, taking care not to bury the corms.

♦ Take cuttings of regal pelargoniums. They root readily in equal parts of peat and sharp sand.

♦ Move hanging-baskets outside into their flowering positions. Suspend them from a firm support where they can be watered easily.

♦ Azaleas, primulas, calceolarias and winter cherries can be placed in a cold frame as soon as the bedding plants are moved.

Below: Many vegetable seedlings will need thinning now, such as onions. Pull out the ones not required, taking care not to disturb those that are left.

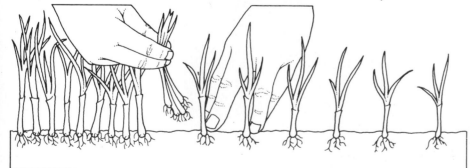

FLOWERS TO SOW THIS MONTH

PERENNIALS

ACHILLEA FILIPENDULA
Sow 6 mm (¼ in) deep in a seed bed.

ACHILLEA MILLEFOLIUM
Sow 6 mm (¼ in) deep in a seed bed.

ACHILLEA PTARMICA
Sow 6 mm (¼ in) deep in a seed bed.

ALTHAEA ROSEA; now *Alcea rosea* (hollyhock)
Sow 12 mm (½ in) deep *in situ.*

ANCHUSA AZUREA; syn. *A. italica*
Sow 12 mm (½ in) deep in a seed bed.

AQUILEGIA VULGARIS (granny's bonnet)
Sow 6 mm (¼ in) deep in a seed bed.

ARENARIA MONTANA (sandwort)
Sow 3 mm (⅛ in) deep in a cold frame.

AUBRIETA DELTOIDEA
Sow 6 mm (¼ in) deep in a seed bed.

BELLIS PERENNIS (daisy): grown as hardy biennial
Sow 6 mm (¼ in) deep in a seed bed.

CATANANCHE CAERULEA (Cupid's dart)
Sow 6 mm (¼ in) deep in a cold frame.

CENTRANTHUS RUBER; syn. *Kentranthus ruber*
(valerian)
Sow 6 mm (¼ in) deep in a seed bed.

CHEIRANTHUS × ALLIONII (Siberian wallflower):
grown as hardy biennial
Sow 6 mm (¼ in) deep in a seed bed.

CHEIRANTHUS CHEIRI: grown as hardy biennial
Sow 6 mm (¼ in) deep in a seed bed.

CHRYSANTHEMUM MAXIMUM (shasta daisy)
Sow 6 mm (¼ in) deep *in situ.*

DELPHINIUM ELATUM
Sow 6 mm (¼ in) deep in a seed bed.

DIANTHUS BARBATUS (sweet William): grown as
hardy biennial
Sow 6 mm (¼ in) deep in a seed bed.

DIGITALIS PURPUREA (foxglove)
Sow thinly and shallowly in a cold frame.

ECHINOPS RITRO (globe thistle)
Sow 12 mm (½ in) deep in a seed bed.

ERIGERON SPECIOSUS (midsummer daisy)
Sow 6 mm (¼ in) deep in a seed bed.

GEUM CHILOENSE
Sow 6 mm (¼ in) deep in a cold frame.

HESPERIS MATRONALIS (sweet rocket)
Sow 6 mm (¼ in) deep in a seed bed.

PAPAVER ALPINUM (alpine poppy)
Sow 6 mm (¼ in) deep in a seed bed.

PAPAVER NUDICAULE (Iceland poppy)
Sow 6 mm (¼ in) deep in a seed bed.

PAPAVER ORIENTALE (oriental poppy)
Sow 6 mm (¼ in) deep in a seed bed.

BORDER BRIGHTENERS IN FLOWER THIS MONTH

◇

Dimorphotheca aurantiaca
(star of the veldt)

Echium lycopsis;
syn. *E. plantagineum*
(viper's bugloss)

Eschscholzia californica
(Californian poppy)

Felicia bergeriana
(kingfisher daisy)

Gilia lutea
(stardust)

Godetia grandiflora

Gypsophila elegans

Heliotropium × hybridum
(cherry pie)

Iberis umbellata
(candytuft)

Limnanthes douglasii
(poached egg plant)

Linaria maroccana
(toadflax)

Linum grandiflorum
(scarlet flax)

Lobelia erinus

Lychnis viscaria

Malcolmia maritima
(Virginian stock)

Mesembryanthemum criniflorum
(Livingstone daisy)

Nemophila menziesii
(baby blue eyes)

Nicotiana alata
(tobacco plant)

Nigella damascena
(love-in-a-mist)

Papaver rhoeas
(field poppy/Shirley poppy)

Petunia × hybrida

Phlox drummondii

Reseda odorata
(mignonette)

Tagetes patula
(French marigold)

Thunbergia alata
(black-eyed Susan)

Verbena × hybrida

Viola × wittrockiana
(pansy)

◇

Left: The sweetly-scented bright yellow flowers of Genista
cinerea *create a dominant display during June and July.
The colour often dominates near-by plants.*

JUNE

BULBS IN FLOWER THIS MONTH

◇

Allium aflatuensis

Allium ablopilosum

Allium giganteum

Allium moly
(golden garlic/lily leek)

Camassia quamash;
syn. *C. esculenta*
(common camass)

Gladiolus byzantinus
(Byzantine gladiolus)

Lilium candidum
(madonna lily/Bourbon lily)

Scilla peruviana
(Cuban lily)

◇

Right: Paeonia suffruticosa
*'Rock's Variety' develops
large white flowers with
maroon-crimson blotches at
the bases of the petals.*

FLOWERS

♦ Rock garden plants that have finished flowering can be trimmed back.

♦ Prune shrubs that have flowered earlier in the year, such as weigelas, deutzias and philadelphus to encourage the development of fresh shoots for flowering the following year.

FRUIT

♦ Pick strawberries only when the weather is dry, removing the fruits with the stalks still attached. Early fruits are picked in June, but some varieties will be producing crops until late summer.

♦ Pick early cherries as soon as they are ripe.

VEGETABLES

♦ Plant outdoor tomato plants and support them with stakes.

♦ Harvest summer lettuce when ready.

♦ Plant celery in a trench (*see* page 70).

♦ Thoroughly water all bean crops.

♦ Earth-up potatoes as necessary.

♦ Sow beetroot in small groups 13 cm (5 in) apart in drills 5 cm (2 in) deep and 30 cm (1 ft) apart.

♦ Sow garden peas 10 cm (4 in) apart in drills 5 cm (2 in) deep.

♦ Nip out the tops of broad beans to minimize the risk of black bean aphid attack and encourage the uniform development of pods.

Left: Helianthemum nummularium, *the well-known
Rock Rose, is ideal for both rock gardens and cascading over
low walls.*

*Right: Tomato plants in heated greenhouses will now be
producing fruits. Here, the variety 'Alicante' is being grown
in grow-bags with an automatic watering system to keep the
compost moist.*

LAWNS

♦ Cut grass regularly. Less grass is taken off the lawn throughout the year if it is cut each week rather than left until several inches high. The longer the grass, the quicker it grows. Feed the lawn with a quick-acting lawn fertilizer at 70 grams a square metre (2 oz a square yard). Use a fertilizer mixture with equal parts of nitrogen, phosphate and potash.

♦ Use a selective weedkiller if necessary. The grass should be growing strongly, with the application made on a day when the weather is neither dry nor wet. Follow the maker's instructions exactly. Do not cut the grass for three or four days after applying the weedkiller, and do not place the mowings on the compost heap.

GREENHOUSES

♦ Hydrangea cuttings that have made growth will need stopping. Nip out the growing points above the third pair of leaves to encourage sideshoots and so create a bushy and balanced plant.

♦ Stand pots of arum lilies outdoors to give them a rest. They can be placed on their sides in the shelter of a south- or west-facing wall.

♦ Fertilize melons by removing male flowers and dusting the pollen on to female flowers.

♦ Water all greenhouse plants as soon as they become dry. This is now a daily job – often twice a day during the height of summer – and needs to be done with great care. More plants are killed by being continually and excessively watered than by any other way. Allow the compost to become dry before giving it any water, and then soak the soil thoroughly. Each plant will need individual attention.

*Trees with attractive barks bring added interest to gardens.
Top:* Trachycarpus fortunei, *known as the Fan Palm or
Chusan Palm, is not hardy throughout the British Isles. Its
coarse and hairy trunk is a continuing interest in any
garden. Centre:* Betula papyrifera occidentalis, *a form of
the Paper Birch or Canoe Birch, reveals gleaming white
papery bark. Bottom:* Salix lucida, *the Shining Willow.*

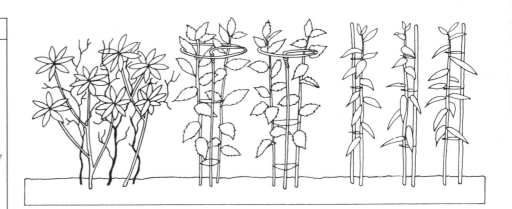

IN FLOWER THIS MONTH

YELLOW AND ORANGE

TREES
LABURNUM × WATERERI: see May

SHRUBS
BERBERIS CANDIDULA: see May

BUDDLEIA GLOBOSA (orange-ball shrub)
H: 3–3·5 m (10–12 ft) S: 2·4–3 m (8–10 ft)
Tender semi-evergreen with scented orange-yellow
globular heads in loose terminal clusters.

COLUTEA ARBORESCENS (bladder senna)
H: 1·8–2·4 m (6–8 ft) S: 1·8–2·4 m (6–8 ft)
Bushy lax deciduous, with pea-shaped 18 mm (¾ in)
long yellow flowers followed by 7·5 cm (3 in) red-
flushed pods.

COROKIA COTONEASTER: see May

CORONILLA GLAUCA: see May

CYTISUS BATTANDIERI
H: 3–4·5 m (10–15 ft) S: 2·4–3·5 m (8–12 ft)
Tree-like deciduous, with pineapple-scented
upright spikes of pea-shaped golden-yellow
flowers.

CYTISUS × BEANII, C. SCOPARIUS 'Golden Sunlight',
GENISTA HISPANICA, G. LYDIA, G. PILOSA: see May

GENISTA TINCTORIA 'Royal Gold' (Dyer's greenweed)
H: 75–90 cm (2 ft 6 in–3 ft) S: 1·2–1·5 m (4–5 ft)
Deciduous with rich golden-yellow pea-shaped
flowers.

HYPERICUM CALYCINUM (rose of Sharon/Aaron's
beard)
H: 30–45 cm (12–18 in) S: 1·2–1·5 m (4–5 ft)
Ground-covering evergreen with 7·5 cm (3 in) wide
cup-shaped golden-yellow flowers.

PHLOMIS FRUTICOSA (Jerusalem sage)
H: 90 cm–1·2 m (3–4 ft) S: 60–75 cm (2 ft–2 ft 6 in)
Shrubby evergreen with whorls of bright yellow
stalkless flowers up the stems.

PIPTANTHUS LABURNIFOLIUS, POTENTILLA FRUTICOSA
'Farreri': see May

SANTOLINA CHAMAECYPARISSUS
H: 45–60 cm (18–24 in) S: 75–90 cm (30–36 in)
Hardy evergreen with finely divided silvery leaves
and bright lemon-yellow button-like flowers.

SPARTIUM JUNCEUM (Spanish broom)
H: 2·1–2·7 m (7–9 ft) S: 1·8–2·4 m (6–8 ft)
Deciduous with evergreen appearance, and
fragrant pea-like golden-yellow flowers.

*Top right: Many herbaceous perennials need staking. This
must be done carefully, so that the border appears to be full
of flowers and not canes and other supports. Twiggy sticks
are useful for pushing into the soil around young plants so
that the growth rises through them. Others can be supported
with proprietary supports with looped tops, while some have
stems that need individual supports.*

*Right: Iris sibirica 'Tropic Night' is very distinctive when
its early to mid-June flowers are seen against an old, well-
weathered wall.*

IN FLOWER THIS MONTH

RED AND PINK

SHRUBS

BUDDLEIA COLVILEI
H: 3–5·4 m (10–18 ft) S: 1·8–3 m (6–10 ft)
Spreading half-hardy semi-evergreen with rose-pink flowers in drooping 15–20 cm (6–8 in) long terminal clusters.

CALYCANTHUS FLORIDUS (Carolina allspice)
H: 1·5–2·4 m (5–8 ft) S: 1·8–2·4 m (6–8 ft)
Deciduous with reddish-purple fragrant flowers.

CISTUS × PURPUREUS: see May

CISTUS 'Silver Pink'
H: 60–90 cm (2–3 ft) S: 60–90 cm (2–3 ft)
Evergreen with 7·5 cm (3 in) wide clear pink flowers and central bosses of yellow stamens.

CISTUS × SKANBERGII
H: 90 cm–1·2 m (3–4 ft) S: 90 cm–1·2 m (3–4 ft)
Evergreen with small soft pink flowers.

CORNUS FLORIDA 'Rubra' (flowering dogwood)
H: 3–4·5 m (10–15 ft) S: 4·5–5·4 m (15–18 ft)
Spreading and well-branched deciduous, with pink bracts.

CRINODENDRON HOOKERIANUM, CYTISUS SCOPARIUS 'Burkwoodii', *DAPHNE × BURKWOODII* 'Somerset': see May

DEUTZIA 'Magician'
H: 1·8 m (6 ft) S: 1·2 m (4 ft)
Very floriferous deciduous, with white-edged pink-tinted flowers with purple streakings on their reverses.

DEUTZIA × ROSEA
H: 90 cm (3 ft) S: 60–75 cm (24–30 in)
Compact deciduous with bell-shaped clear pink flowers. 'Carminea' has rose-carmine flushed flowers.

EMBOTHRIUM LANCEOLATUM: see May

ESCALLONIA 'C. F. Ball'
H: 1·8–2·4 m (6–8 ft) S: 1·5 m (5 ft)
Semi-evergreen with dark green leaves and red tubular flowers.

ESCALLONIA 'Donard Radiance'
H: 1·8 m (6 ft) S: 1·5 m (5 ft)
Semi-evergreen with large chalice-shaped rich pink flowers.

ESCALLONIA 'Donard Star'
H: 1·5–1·8 m (5–6 ft) S: 1·5 m (5 ft)
Semi-evergreen with glossy dark green leaves and rose-pink flowers.

ESCALLONIA 'Peach Blossom'
H: 1·8–2·4 m (6–8 ft) S: 1·5–1·8 m (5–6 ft)
Semi-evergreen with peach-pink flowers.

ESCALLONIA 'Slieve Donard'
H: 1·8 m (6 ft) S: 1·5 m (5 ft)
Evergreen with apple-blossom pink flowers.

INDIGOFERA GERARDIANA
H: 1·5–1·8 m (5–6 ft) S: 1·2–1·5 m (4–5 ft)
Deciduous and semi-hardy with rosy-purple pea-shaped flowers.

KALMIA LATIFOLIA (calico bush/mountain laurel)
H: 1·8–3 m (6–10 ft) S: 1·8–2·4 m (6–8 ft)
Evergreen with clusters of bright pink saucer-shaped flowers. 'Clementine Churchill' is rich rose-red.

KOLKWITZIA AMABILIS 'Pink Cloud', *LEPTOSPERMUM SCOPARIUM* 'Chapmanii': see May

POTENTILLA FRUTICOSA 'Red Ace'
H: 1·2–1·5 m (4–5 ft) S: 1·2–1·5 m (4–5 ft)
Shrubby and deciduous, with bright vermilion-flame flowers.

SYRINGA VULGARIS: see May

TAMARIX TETRANDRA
H: 3–4·5 m (10–15 ft) S: 3–3·5 m (10–12 ft)
Deciduous with bright pink flowers.

WEIGELA FLORIDA
H: 1·5–1·8 m (5–6 ft) S: 1·5–1·8 m (5–6 ft)
Deciduous with rose-pink foxglove-like flowers. 'Foliis Purpureis' has purple leaves and pink flowers.

WEIGELA 'Abel Carriere', *W.* 'Bristol Ruby', *W.* 'Newport Red': see May

CLIMBERS

CLEMATIS 'Comtesse de Bouchard'
H: 3–4 m (10–13 ft) S: 3 m (10 ft)
Deciduous with cyclamen-pink flowers with a hint of mauve.

CLEMATIS 'Hagley Hybrid'
H: 1·8–2·4 m (6–8 ft) S: 1·8 m (6 ft)
Deciduous with shell-pink flowers with brown anthers.

CLEMATIS 'Nelly Moser'
H: 3–4 m (10–13 ft) S: 3 m (10 ft)
Deciduous with blush-white flowers with carmine-red bars.

CLEMATIS MONTANA 'Rubens': see May

Right: Saintpauliae *can be increased by leaf cuttings from June to September. Select strong and healthy leaves and detach them from the parent plant with about 5 cm (2 in) of stalk. Insert the stalks, with the leaf still attached, into equal parts peat and sharp sand and place in 18°C/64°F. When rooted, pot up singly into small pots of peat-based compost or a lime-free loam-based type formed of equal parts loam, peat and sharp sand.*

FLOWERS

♦ Spray plants against pests and diseases as soon as they are seen.

♦ During dry weather water the soil thoroughly. It does more harm than good just to dampen the surface soil. If possible, use water from a sprinkler that gently applies water over a long period. Too much water applied suddenly will just run off the surface, probably taking some good top soil with it.

♦ Thin out seedlings in seed drills.

FRUIT

♦ Continue to tie new raspberry canes to supporting wires. No more than eight canes should be allowed to develop from each plant.

♦ Summer-prune gooseberries by shortening sideshoots to five leaves. This directs their vigour into the production of fruit buds.

♦ Spray fruit trees and bushes with fungicides and insecticides as necessary, according to the manufacturer's instructions.

♦ Continue to thin peach and nectarine fruits.

VEGETABLES

♦ Harvest kohlrabi when the roots are the size of a tennis ball.

♦ Lift early potatoes.

♦ Support asparagus peas.

♦ Thin summer spinach to 75 mm (3 in) apart, and later to 15 cm (6 in) apart.

♦ Sow summer spinach 12 mm ($\frac{1}{2}$ in) deep in drills 30 cm (1 ft) apart.

♦ Harvest leaf-type lettuces such as 'Salad Bowl'.

♦ Thin summer lettuce to 23–30 cm (9–12 in) apart.

♦ Harvest early garden peas.

Right above: The hardy evergreen North American Calico Bush, Kalmia latifolia, develops 7·5–10 cm (3–4 in) wide clusters of pink flowers during June.

Right: The Bridal Wreath or Foam of May, Spiraea × arguta, creates a mass of white flowers during April and May.

L A W N S

♦ Watering will be necessary in dry periods. Oscillatory or rotary sprinklers are excellent for saturating the lawn. Never apply water unless the equivalent of 6 mm (¼ in) of rainfall can be applied. Just dampening the surface does more harm than good. Also, check that you have a licence for the use of a lawn sprinkler.

IN FLOWER THIS MONTH

WHITE AND CREAM

TREES

CRATAEGUS × LAVALLEI: see May

ROBINIA PSEUDOACACIA (common acacia/false acacia/black locust)
H: 9–10·5 m (30–35 ft) S: 3–4·5 m (10–15 ft)
Light green deciduous leaflets and creamy-white fragrant flowers. Also 'Inermis' and 'Frisia'.

SHRUBS

CARPENTERIA CALIFORNICA
H: 2·4–3 m (8–10 ft) S: 1·8–2·4 m (6–8 ft)
Slightly tender evergreen with slightly scented glistening-white anemone-shaped 5–7·5 cm (2–3 in) wide flowers.

CHOISYA TERNATA, CISTUS × ANGUILARI, CISTUS × CYPRIUS: see May

CISTUS × CORBARIENSIS
H: 90 cm–1·2 m (3–4 ft) S: 1·8–2·4 m (6–8 ft)
Spreading deciduous, with 4 cm (1½ in) wide yellow-stained white flowers.

CONVOLVULUS CNEORUM
H: 60–90 cm (2–3 ft) S: 60–90 cm (2–3 ft)
Compact evergreen with pink-budded funnel-shaped white flowers.

CORNUS KOUSA
H: 2·4–3 m (8–10 ft) S: 2·4–3 m (8–10 ft)
Shrubby deciduous, with petal-like white bracts. Strawberry-like fruits in autumn.

CYTISUS ALBUS: see May

DABOECIA CANTABRICA 'Alba'
H: 60–90 cm (2–3 ft) S: 60–90 cm (2–3 ft)
Evergreen with bell-like white flowers.

DEUTZIA × ROSEA 'Campanulata'
H: 90 cm (3 ft) S: 90 cm (3 ft)
Deciduous with bell-shaped white flowers displaying purple calyces.

DEUTZIA SCABRA 'Pride of Rochester'
H: 1·8–2·4 m (6–8 ft) S: 1·2–1·8 m (4–6 ft)
Deciduous with peeling brown bark and cup-shaped double white flowers tinted pink.

ESCALLONIA × IVEYI
H: 1·8–3 m (6–10 ft) S: 1·8–2·4 m (6–8 ft)
Slightly tender evergreen with white flowers.

HEBE ARMSTRONGII
H: 90 cm (3 ft) S: 60–90 cm (2–3 ft)
Evergreen with deep golden-green leaves and white flowers in 2·5 cm (1 in) long terminal clusters.

HEBE 'Pagei'; syn. *Hebe pinguifolia* 'Pagei'
H: 15–23 cm (6–9 in) S: 75–90 cm (30–36 in)
Low evergreen with 2·5 cm (1 in) long spikes of white flowers.

MAGNOLIA SIEBOLDII: see May

Left: The Shrimp Plant, Justicia brandegeana, *is a greenhouse plant better known by its former name* Beloperone guttata. *From April to December it reveals shrimp-like flowers formed of overlapping brownish-pink bracts.*

IN FLOWER THIS MONTH

WHITE AND CREAM

OLEARIA × SCILLONIENSIS
H: 1·2–1·5 m (4–5 ft) S: 1·2–1·5 m (4–5 ft)
Slightly tender evergreen with grey-green leaves
and brilliant white daisy-like flowers.

PHILADELPHUS 'Beauclerk'
H: 1·8–2·4 m (6–8 ft) S: 1·5–1·8 m (5–6 ft)
Deciduous with highly scented white flowers
flushed cerise pink.

PHILADELPHUS 'Belle Etoile'
H: 2·4–3 m (8–10 ft) S: 3–3·5 m (10–12 ft)
Deciduous with scented large, single white flowers
flushed pink.

PHILADELPHUS 'Virginal'
H: 2·4–2·7 m (8–9 ft) S: 1·8–2·4 m (6–8 ft)
Deciduous with double or semi-double scented
white flowers.

POTENTILLA ARBUSCULA 'Abbotswood'
H: 60–75 cm (2–2½ ft) S: 1·2–1·5 m (4–5 ft)
Deciduous with white flowers above greyish-green
leaves.

PYRACANTHA ATALANTIOIDES
H: 3–4·5 m (10–15 ft) S: 3–3·5 m (10–12 ft)
Evergreen with white hawthorn-like flowers
followed by crimson berries.

PYRACANTHA CRENULATA
H: 2·4–3 m (8–10 ft) S: 2·4–3·5 m (8–12 ft)
Evergreen with clusters of white flowers followed
by bright orange-red berries.

STRANVAESIA DAVIDIANA
H: 3·5–4·5 m (12–15 ft) S: 3·5–4·5 m (12–15 ft)
Hardy evergreen with white hawthorn-like white
flowers followed by crimson berries.

SYRINGA VULGARIS 'Maud Notcutt': see May

VIBURNUM OPULUS (guelder rose)
H: 3–3·5 m (10–12 ft) S: 3–3·5 m (10–12 ft)
Deciduous with heavily scented flat heads of white
flowers followed by translucent red berries. 'Sterile'
is the Snowball Bush with round flower heads.

VIBURNUM PLICATUM, V. RHYTIDOPHYLLUM: see May

CLIMBERS

CLEMATIS MONTANA: see May

HYDRANGEA PETIOLARIS (Japanese climbing
hydrangea)
H: 6–7·5 m (20–25 ft) S: 6–7.5 m (20–25 ft)
Vigorous deciduous, with creamy-white flat flower
heads up to 25 cm (10 in) wide.

LONICERA JAPONICA 'Halliana'
H: 4·5–6 m (15–20 ft) S: 4·5–6 m (15–20 ft)
Strong-growing evergreen or semi-evergreen with
highly fragrant white flowers changing to yellow.

WISTERIA VENUSTA: see May

GREENHOUSES

♦ Stop cucumber plants at the desired height.

♦ Thin bunches of grapes by about a third if not
already completed.

♦ Water and feed tomato plants regularly. Also
remove all sideshoots.

♦ Support and stake achimenes using twiggy
sticks at the outside edges of the pots. Split canes
and green string can also be used.

♦ Spray chrysanthemums regularly to control
aphids and capsid bugs.

♦ Tomatoes will be ripening and are best picked
regularly, each morning.

♦ Carnations are often badly attacked at this time
of year by aphids, thrips and red spider mites.
Spray immediately they are seen. A damp atmosphere helps to reduce the risk of an infestation of
red spider mites.

♦ Water all plants as necessary, and dampen the
floor and staging to create a buoyant atmosphere.

*Right: The Butterfly Flower, Schizanthus pinnatus, is
also known as the Poor Man's Orchid. It is ideal for a frost-
proof greenhouse or in an annual border. The showy flowers
appear from June to autumn outdoors, or during spring in a
greenhouse.*

ROCK PLANTS IN FLOWER THIS MONTH
◇

Aethionema grandiflorum
(Persian candytuft)

Alyssum saxatile 'Flore-pleno'
(gold dust)

Androsace carnea
(rock jasmine)

Androsace lanuginosa
(Himalayan androsace)

Antennaria dioica

Aquilegia flabellata 'Nana Alba'

Armeria maritima 'Alba'
(thrift)

Armeria maritima 'Vindictive'
(thrift)

Aubrieta deltoidea

Campanula portenschlagiana;
syn. C. muralis

Campanula poscharskyana

Dianthus deltoides
(maiden pink)

Dimorphotheca barberiae
'Compacta'

Erinus alpinus

Gentiana verna
(spring gentian)

Geranium cinereum

Geranium farreri;
syn. G. napuligerum

Geranium subcaulescens

Gypsophila repens

Gypsophila repens 'Fratensis'

Helianthemum nummularium;
syn. H. chamaecistus

Helichrysum milfordiae;
syn. H. marginatum

Iberis sempervirens

Lewisia cotyledon

Lithospermum diffusum;
now Lithodora diffusa

Polygonum affine 'Donald
Lowndes'

Potentilla aurea chrysocraspeda

Saxifraga paniculata;
syn. S. aizoon

Sedum dasyphyllum

Sedum spathulifolium

Sempervivum octopodes

Silene acaulis

Thymus doerfleri;
now T. hirsutus doerfleri

Thymus nitidus

Thymus serpyllum
(wild thyme)

Veronica cinerea

Veronica prostrata
◇

FLOWERS

♦ Flag irises that are crowded can be lifted and divided. This usually needs doing every three years. Discard the old central parts and use only the younger parts from the outside.

♦ Cut out sucker growths from roses. Sever them as near to the rootstock as possible to prevent further growths.

♦ When cutting roses use sharp secateurs to sever the stems just above a healthy bud. This will prevent dead spurs arising later.

FRUIT

♦ Summer-prune both red and white currants, shortening laterals to five leaves, but do not prune the leader shoots.

♦ If too many fruits have developed on apples and pears, thin them out after the natural 'June drop' that normally occurs this month and early July.

♦ Tie the new shoots of cane fruits to their supporting wires.

VEGETABLES

♦ Summer lettuce can still be sown, until late July or early August.

♦ Harvest cauliflowers maturing from seed sown under glass in gentle heat in January.

♦ Stop the stems of ridge cucumbers.

♦ Sow radishes 12 mm (½ in) deep.

♦ Thin beetroot to one seedling every 13 cm (5 in).

♦ Sow kohlrabi thinly in drills 12 mm (½ in) deep and 38 cm (15 in) apart.

♦ Support garden peas with pea-sticks or wire-netting.

♦ Water broad beans.

♦ Pick broad beans before the pods become tough.

Right: Lavatera trimestris *is a stunningly attractive hardy annual also known as* Lavatera rosea. *It looks superb when against a wall and combined with the woolly-grey leaves of* Ballota pseudodictamnus *(seen at the front of the picture).*

LAWNS

♦ Bare areas can be seeded. Loosen the surface with a fork, apply lawn seed at 70 grams a square metre (2 oz a square yard) and gently firm the surface. Place a sheet of clear plastic over the site until the seeds germinate, then remove.

GREENHOUSES

♦ Ensure begonias are now allowed to become dry at their roots as this rapidly induces the flower buds to drop off.
♦ White fly is often a nuisance, especially where cinerarias and tomatoes are being grown. Spray or fumigate the plants immediately an attack is seen. Repeat about 10 days later to kill young adults.
♦ Water and feed all plants as necessary.

Below: Water-lilies will now be brightening garden pools. Most of them start flowering between May and July and continue to bring colour to the garden until mid to late September.

IN FLOWER THIS MONTH

BLUE AND MAUVE

SHRUBS

BUDDLEIA ALTERNIFOLIA
H: 3·5–4·5 m (12–15 ft) S: 2·4–3·5 m (8–12 ft)
Hardy deciduous, often grown as a tree with arching branches displaying scented lavender-blue flowers in clusters 2·5 cm (1 in) wide.

CEANOTHUS DENTATUS: see May

CEANOTHUS 'Gloire de Versailles'
H: 1·8–2·4 m (6–8 ft) S: 1·5–2·1 m (5–7 ft)
Deciduous with terminal heads of fragrant, soft powder-blue flowers.

CEANOTHUS THYRSIFLORUS: see May

DABOECIA CANTABRICA 'Atropurpurea'
H: 60–90 cm (2–3 ft) S: 75–90 cm (2 ft 6 in–3 ft)
Ground-covering evergreen with rich purple bell-shaped flowers.

HEBE 'Carl Teschner'
H: 23–30 cm (9–12 in) S: 60–75 cm (24–30 in)
Dense spreading evergreen with violet-blue flowers in 2·5 cm (1 in) long spikes.

HEBE × FRANCISCANA 'Blue Gem'
H: 90 cm–1·2 m (3–4 ft) S: 90 cm–1·2 m (3–4 ft)
Neat evergreen with 5–7·5 cm (2–3 in) long spikes of violet flowers.

ROSMARINUS OFFICINALIS, SYRINGA VULGARIS: see May

TEUCRIUM FRUTICANS
H: 1·2–1·5 m (4–5 ft) S: 90 cm–1·2 m (3–4 ft)
Half-hardy evergreen with aromatic grey-green leaves and two-lipped pale lavender flowers.

VINCA MAJOR: see April

VINCA MINOR: see March

CLIMBERS

ABUTILON VITIFOLIUM, CLEMATIS 'Barbara Jackman': see May

CLEMATIS 'Jackmanii Superba'
H: 3·5–4·5 m (12–15 ft) S: 3–3·5 m (10–12 ft)
Deciduous with violet-purple flowers.

CLEMATIS 'Lasurstern', *CLEMATIS* 'Mrs. Cholmondeley': see May

CLEMATIS 'President'
H: 3·5–4·5 m (12–15 ft) S: 3–3·5 m (10–12 ft)
Deciduous with 15 cm (6 in) wide purple flowers suffused claret.

CLEMATIS 'W. E. Gladstone'
H: 3·5–4·5 m (12–15 ft) S: 3–3·5 m (10–12 ft)
Deciduous with large pale lavender flowers with lighter centres.

CLEMATIS MACROPETALA, WISTERIA FLORIBUNDA, W. SINENSIS: see May

Left: Acer griseum *is unforgettable for its buff-coloured bark that peels to reveal light orange-brown under bark. It has the bonus of mid-green leaves that turn scarlet and red in autumn.*

◇ J U L Y ◇

This is the season of the traditional herbaceous border, crowded with colour and promising more to come. Most of us have just one or two flower borders into which we have to pack all our garden brighteners. Mixed borders are therefore often the only means of providing a constant display of colour, using trees, shrubs, herbaceous and annual plants.

Officinados of herbaceous plants now often grow species and varieties that do not need support, and this makes growing them much easier. They are planted in borders set in a lawn. When grouped together, each perhaps the shape of a kidney, they can be fitted together like a jigsaw with grass paths between them. Each border need not be large, but 1·5 m (5 ft) is the minimum. And to keep the beds in proportion to their heights, the tallest plants should be about half the width of the border.

Those gardeners with room for just one border need not be dismayed, however, nor need their gardening be less exciting.

Walls, trellis-work and arbours are all candidates for colour, whether from flowers or attractive leaves. Large-flowered clematis are the epitome of a floriferous climber, but well worth growing for continuous summer colour is the golden-leaved hop *Humulus lupulus* 'Aureus', an herbaceous climber that each year creates a screen of soft yellow leaves.

Hydrangea petiolaris (climbing hydrangea) is also known for its wall-covering attributes, when it displays creamy-white flowers in heads up to 25 cm (10 in) wide. Another climber of the same family is *Hydrangea anomala* with 18–20 cm (7–8 in) wide flat heads of white flowers, but it needs a warm and sheltered position, perhaps against a west or south-facing wall. Wisterias are now past their best, but their blue can be replaced with the distinctively flowered *Passiflora caerulea* (common passion flower). It is not fully hardy and needs the protection of a warm wall, but when in flower this Brazilian climber with its 7·5 cm (3 in) wide white-petalled flowers with dominant and intricate centres always demands attention.

Delphiniums are now raising their well-known heads, and will continue to do so. *Delphinium elatum*, the parent of the many spire-like heads of colourful flowers, is seldom grown and most types that are now cultivated are derived from crosses. Specialist catalogues offer a wide range of colours and heights, and for success they need a sunny site, preferably sheltered from strong winds and deep well-cultivated rich soil. Don't neglect supporting the shoots, which is best done with bamboo canes and strong green string.

Towards the end of this month and into August is often the driest part of the year and plants need to be kept well watered.

Few gardeners are not captivated by the bright yellow daisy-like flowers of Rudbeckia fulgida *'Goldsturm'. They appear from July to September and create dominant displays in mixed and herbaceous borders.*

FLOWERS

♦ Continue to sow seeds, as indicated.

♦ Feed outdoor chrysanthemums with a fertilizer high in potash. Scatter it around the plants, hoe it in and water the soil if the weather is dry.

♦ Trim hedges regularly, especially privet. If left unclipped hedges not only look untidy but eventually become bare at their bases.

♦ Feed roses to encourage a further flush of blooms. Use a general fertilizer high in potash.

♦ Dead-head flowers to encourage the formation of further blooms. It also helps to keep the garden tidy.

♦ Increase garden pinks by taking 75 mm (3 in) long cuttings and inserting them in small pots of peat and sharp sand. Place them in a cold frame.

FRUIT

♦ Protect fruits from birds by spreading nets over them, supported on metal or wooden stakes, or preferably invest in a wire fruit cage that will protect the fruits throughout the year.

♦ Continue to hoe shallowly between soft fruits, taking care not to damage the roots of the plants. Any perennial weeds must be removed completely. If just their tops are hoed off, the weeds will appear later.

VEGETABLES

♦ Transplant winter cabbages from the seedbed to their cropping positions, 45 cm (18 in) apart in rows 45 cm (18 in) apart.

♦ Harvest summer spinach.

♦ Sow endive 12 mm (½ in) deep in rows 25–30 cm (10–12 in) apart.

♦ Sow spring cabbage in seedbeds between now and August, 18 mm (¾ in) deep in drills 15–20 cm (6–8 in) apart.

♦ Harvest summer spinach.

♦ Lift potatoes when their tops are dying down.

♦ Remove sideshoots from tomato plants.

Right: The vegetable garden will now be crowded with crops. Ensure that they are given plenty of water, preferably through a sprinkler that creates small droplets of water that do not damage the crops or the structure of the soil. Just dampening the surface soil does more harm than good, and the sprinkler needs to be left in one position for several hours.

FLOWERS TO SOW THIS MONTH

ANNUALS AND BIENNIALS

MATTHIOLA INCANA (Brompton stocks)
Sow 6 mm (¼ in) deep in a seed bed.

MYOSOTIS SYLVATICA (forget-me-not)
Sow 6 mm (¼ in) deep in a seed bed.

VIOLA × WITTROCKIANA (pansy)
Sow 6 mm (¼ in) deep in a seed bed.

PERENNIALS

DELPHINIUM ELATUM
Sow 6 mm (¼ in) deep in a seed bed.

GEUM CHILOENSE
Sow 6 mm (¼ in) deep in a cold frame.

PAPAVER ALPINUM (alpine poppy)
Sow 6 mm (¼ in) deep in a seed bed.

PAPAVER NUDICAULE (Iceland poppy)
Sow 6 mm (¼ in) deep in a seed bed.

PAPAVER ORIENTALE (oriental poppy)
Sow 6 mm (¼ in) deep in a seed bed.

Below: Hose-reels can be bought from most garden centres or hardware shops, but the do-it-yourself enthusiast can construct a home-made reel from pieces of wood and metal. All that is needed is a wooden surround, with a metal handle through the centre.

IN FLOWER THIS MONTH

YELLOW AND ORANGE

SHRUBS

COLUTEA ARBORESCENS, CYTISUS BATTANDIERI: see June

GENISTA HISPANICA, G. PILOSA: see May

GENISTA TINCTORIA 'Royal Gold', *HYPERICUM CALYCINUM:* see June

HYPERICUM PATULUM 'Hidcote'
H: 90 cm–1·5 m (3–5 ft) S: 1·2–1·5 m (4–5 ft)
Semi-evergreen or deciduous with large shallow saucer-shaped golden-yellow flowers.

PHLOMIS FRUTICOSA: see June

POTENTILLA FRUTICOSA 'Farreri': see May

SANTOLINA CHAMAECYPARISSUS: see June

SENECIO 'Sunshine'
H: 90 cm–1·2 m (3–4 ft) S: 1·2–1·8 m (4–6 ft)
Hardy evergreen with loose clusters of bright yellow daisy-like 2·5 cm (1 in) wide flowers.

SPARTIUM JUNCEUM: see June

Below: Erigeron speciosus 'Strahlenmeer' is one of the Fleabanes, flowering from June to August and creating a dominant splash of colour in a mixed or herbaceous border.

LAWNS

♦ Grass beneath children's garden swings soon wears out during summer – but do not replace it with concrete, which is painful to fall on. Rather, either re-sow the areas with seed, move the swing or put a large rubber mat under it.

♦ Continue to cut the lawn. Do not allow the grass to become long before cutting it. Also trim the edges regularly.

GREENHOUSES

♦ Continue to remove sideshoots from tomato plants, bending them sideways so that they snap off cleanly. Also, pick all fruits that are ripe. When the plants reach the desired height cut off the growing points just above a leaf joint above a flowering truss. The leading stems are usually too tough to be snapped sideways without damaging the plant, and are best cut out with a sharp knife.

♦ Pick cucumbers as they mature.

♦ Water and feed cucumber plants regularly, and syringe the plants daily with water.

♦ Move perpetual-flowering carnations into a garden frame. At this time of year the greenhouse becomes too hot.

♦ Increase *Begonia rex* from leaf cuttings. Slit well-developed leaves and lay them on the surface of a mixture of peat and sharp sand in a propagating frame with some bottom heat.

♦ Pot on young plants of winter- and spring-flowering types raised from seed sown earlier in the year.

♦ Water and ventilate all plants. The temperature quickly rises in the greenhouse at this time of year and the plants rapidly dry out.

Left: Hypericum patulum *'Hidcote', often called Aaron's Beard or Rose of Sharon, produces golden-yellow flowers up to 7·5 cm (3 in) wide from June to September.*

FLOWERS

FRUIT

♦ Late-flowering chrysanthemums in pots outdoors will need to have their supporting canes tied to wires to prevent strong winds blowing them over.

♦ Keep gladioli and lilies well watered. They must not be allowed to dry out.

♦ Support border plants, tying in new shoots to canes or by using twiggy sticks.

♦ Keep borders free from weeds by hand-weeding or by using a hoe.

♦ Continue to remove rose suckers clearly at their point of origin.

♦ Tulips heeled-in when the ground was needed for summer bedding plants can be lifted, cleaned and placed in a cool, dark, dry and vermin-proof place until replanted in autumn.

♦ Strawberries can be planted from now to mid-August, as well as in early spring. Obtain plants from a reputable source, certified free of diseases. Rake the surface level and apply a fertilizer with a high potash content. Set the plants 38–45 cm (15–18 in) apart in rows 75 cm (30 in) apart. If the weather is dry thoroughly water them to settle soil around the roots.

♦ Summer-prune pear trees, cutting all lateral and leading shoots (except the main one) to six leaves of growth.

♦ During late summer and into autumn apples and pears will be ready for picking and storing. Now is the time to clean out the fruit store thoroughly and to check that it is dry and vermin proof. It should be well ventilated.

Right: Hakonechloa macro *'Aureola' is a stunningly attractive golden-leaved grass, ideal for softening the edges of a low wall. It creates colour over many months.*

IN FLOWER THIS MONTH

RED AND PINK

SHRUBS

BUDDLEIA DAVIDII 'Fortune' (butterfly bush)
H:2·4–2·7 m (8–9 ft) S: 2·3–2·7 m (8–9 ft)
Deciduous with lilac flowers with orange eyes.
'Royal Red' has rich red-purple flowers.

CISTUS × PURPUREUS: see May

C. 'Silver Pink', *C. × SKANBERGII, CORNUS FLORIDA*
'Rubra', *DEUTZIA* 'Magician', *D. × ROSEA:* see June

ERICA CINEREA 'C. D. Eason' (bell heather)
H: 23–30 cm (9–12 in) S: 23–30 cm (9–12 in)
Evergreen with rose-red flowers. 'Coccinea' reaches
15 cm (6 in) high and has carmine-red flowers.

ERICA VAGANS 'Mrs. D. F. Maxwell' (Cornish heath)
H: 90 cm–1·2 m (3–4 ft) S: 1·2–1·8 m (4–6 ft)
Evergreen with deep cerise flowers. 'St. Keverne'
has rose-pink flowers.

ESCALLONIA 'C. F. Ball', *E.* 'Donard Radiance', *E.*
'Donard Star', *E.* 'Peach Blossom', *E.* 'Slieve
Donard': see June

HEBE 'Great Orme'
H: 90 cm–1·2 m (3–4 ft) S: 90 cm–1·2 m (3–4 ft)
Evergreen with 10 cm (4 in) long spikes of pink
flowers.

HEBE SPECIOSA 'La Seduisante'
H: 1·2–1·5 m (4–5 ft) S: 1·2–1·5 m (4–5 ft)
Evergreen with 10 cm (4 in) long spikes of bright
crimson flowers. 'Gloriosa' is bright pink and
'Simon Deleaux' rich red.

HYDRANGEA MACROPHYLLA 'Hamburg'
H: 1·2–1·8 m (4–6 ft) S: 1·5–1·8 m (5–6 ft)
Deciduous with deep rose mop-headed flowers in
acid soil. 'Kluis Superba' has rose-red, and
'Westfalen' rich crimson-red flowers.

INDIGOFERA GERARDIANA: see June

PHYGELIUS CAPENSIS
H: 75–90 cm (2 ft 6 in–3 ft) S: 60 cm (2 ft)
Evergreen with scarlet hunting horn-shaped
flowers.

POTENTILLA FRUTICOSA 'Red Ace': see June

CLIMBERS

CLEMATIS 'Comtesse de Bouchard', *C.* 'Hagley
Hybrid', *C.* 'Nelly Moser': see June

CLEMATIS MONTANA 'Rubens': see May

Left: Cacti can be raised from seed sown in spring and summer. Place broken crocks in the base of a pot and add a handful of peat (top picture). Then, top-up the pot with a sandy seed compost and level the surface. Sow the seeds thinly and use the tip of a pencil to separate any that are touching (centre picture). Only the lightest sieving of soil is needed over them. If a sieve is not available, gently sprinkle compost over them by rubbing a handful between your hands (lower picture).
Water the compost by standing the container in a bowl of water until moisture percolates through to the surface. Then place the pot in 15°C/59°F and cover with a pane of glass. Turn the glass daily to get rid of the condensation that builds up on the lower surface.

Far left: Heel cuttings can be taken by pulling off a small sideshoot so that a small piece of stem comes away with it. Use a sharp knife to trim up the heel, and remove the lower pair of leaves. The cutting can then be inserted in a rooting compost.

BORDER BRIGHTENERS IN FLOWER THIS MONTH
◇

Adonis aestivalis
(pheasant's eye)

Ageratum houstonianum

Alonsoa warscewiczii
(mask flower)

Althaea rosea;
now *Alcea rosea*

Alyssum maritimum;
now *Lobularia maritima*

Amaranthus caudatus
(love-lies bleeding)

Anchusa azurea;
syn. *A. italica*

Anchusa capensis

Anemone coronaria
(poppy anemone)

Antirrhinum majus
(snapdragon)

Aquilegia vulgaris
(granny's bonnet)

Arctotis × hybrida
(African daisy)

Asperula orientalis;
syn. *A. azurea/A. setosa*
(annual woodruff)

Begonia semperflorens

Bellis perennis
(daisy)

Brachycome iberidifolia
(Swan River daisy)

Calceolaria integrifolia;
syn. *C. rugosa*

Calendula officinalis
(pot marigold/English
marigold)

Callistephus chinensis
(China aster)

Campanula medium
(Canterbury bell)

Celosia argentea plumosa
(Prince of Wales' feather)

Centaurea cyanus
(cornflower)

Centaurea moschata
(sweet sultan)

Cheiranthus × allionii
(Siberian wallflower)

Chrysanthemum carinatum;
syn. *C. tricolor*

Clarkia elegans

Clarkia pulchella

VEGETABLES

◆ Tie up the leaves of endive and place a large pot over them to blanch the stems.
◆ Water summer lettuce when the weather is dry.
◆ Harvest summer lettuce when ready.
◆ Thin kohlrabi to 15 cm (6 in) apart.
◆ Harvest French beans when the pods are 15 cm (6 in) long.
◆ Harvest shallots.
◆ Mulch and water runner beans.
◆ Harvest globe artichokes when the scales are still tight.
◆ Tie celery stems together and mound up soil around them.

LAWNS

◆ Ants can be a nuisance on a lawn, although they do little harm. They do, however, remove soil from around grass roots which in dry weather causes distress to the plants. If they do become a problem use an ant killer – but ensure it is safe to use on lawns.
◆ Dogs usually do little damage to lawns, although urine from bitches will cause yellowing and eventually kill grass. Buckets of water can be promptly applied when visiting bitches perform on your lawn, but if it is your own animal there is no real solution to this problem other than fencing off an area for her.

Right: Alchemilla mollis, the Lady's Mantle, displays its star-shaped yellow-green flowers from June to August. It is ideal for softening the edges of a path.

GREENHOUSES

♦ Do not allow coleus plants to flower, picking off all flowers as soon as they appear. The plant is grown solely for its attractive leaves.

♦ Cyclamen in garden frames as well as in a greenhouse will need syringing with clean water every morning and evening. Do not do this job when the sun is shining strongly.

♦ Water and feed plants in their final pots.

♦ If you are planning to go away on holiday within the next month arrange for someone to water the plants and ventilate the greenhouse.

♦ Shade plants when the sun is shining strongly. Damp-down the greenhouse daily to create a buoyant atmosphere.

♦ Propagate such plants as saintpaulias, busy Lizzies, ivies and *Hoya carnosa*.

♦ Cut back sideshoots to two leaves beyond each melon fruit. Also, remove some of the leaves.

♦ In unheated greenhouses grapes will need a final thinning.

BORDER BRIGHTENERS IN FLOWER THIS MONTH
◇

Cleome spinosa
(spider flower)

Consolida ajacis
(larkspur)

Convolvulus tricolor;
syn. *C. minor*

Cotula barbata
(pincushion plant)

Dianthus barbatus
(sweet William)

Left: The fragrant bright white flowers of the Tree Poppy, Romneya trichocalyx, *appear from June to September.*

Below: Catananche caerulea, *Cupid's Dart, displays its 4 cm (1½ in) wide cornflower-like purple-blue flowers during June and July.*

JULY

BORDER BRIGHTENERS IN FLOWER THIS MONTH

◇

Didiscus caeruleus;
now *Trachymene caeruleus*
(blue lace flower)

Dimorphotheca aurantiaca
(star of the veldt)

Echium lycopsis;
syn. *E. plantagineum*
(viper's bugloss)

Emilia flammea
(tassel flower)

Eschscholzia californica
(Californian poppy)

Felicia bergeriana
(kingfisher daisy)

Gaillardia pulchella

Gilia lutea
(stardust)

Godetia grandiflora

Gypsophila elegans

Helianthus annuus
(sunflower)

Heliotropium × hybridum
(cherry pie)

Iberis umbellata
(candytuft)

Lavatera trimestris

Limnanthes douglasii
(poached egg plant)

Linaria maroccana
(toadflax)

Linum grandiflorum
(scarlet flax)

Lobelia erinus

Lychnis viscaria

IN FLOWER THIS MONTH

WHITE AND CREAM

TREES

CATALPA BIGNONIOIDES (Indian bean tree)
H: 4·5–6 m (15–20 ft) S: 5·4–6 m (18–20 ft)
Deciduous bright green large heart-shaped leaves and foxglove-like white flowers with yellow and purple markings.

SHRUBS

ABELIA CHINENSIS
H: 1·2 m (4 ft) S: 1·2 m (4 ft)
Deciduous with clusters of scented tubular white flowers flushed pink.

BUDDLEIA DAVIDII 'Peace' (butterfly bush)
H: 2·1–2·7 m (7–9 ft) S: 2·1–2·4 m (7–8 ft)
Deciduous strong-growing shrub with 25–50 cm (10–20 in) long plumes of white flowers. Other white forms include 'White Cloud' and 'White Profusion'.

BUDDLEIA FALLOWIANA 'Alba'
H: 1·8–3 m (6–10 ft) S: 1·2–1·8 m (4–6 ft)
Deciduous and bushy, with sweetly scented creamy-white flowers.

CISTUS × ANGUILARI, C. × CYPRIUS: see May

CONVOLVULUS CNEORUM, CORNUS KOUSA, DABOECIA CANTABRICA 'Alba', *DEUTZIA × ROSEA* 'Campanulata', *D. SCABRA* 'Pride of Rochester', *ESCALLONIA × IVEYI:* see June

GAULTHERIA PROCUMBENS (partridge-berry/wintergreen/checkerberry)
H: 10–15 cm (4–6 in) S: 75 cm–1 m (2 ft 6 in–3 ft 6 in)
Ground-hugging evergreen with white urn-shaped flowers and red berries.

HEBE ARMSTRONGII: see June

HEBE BRACHYSIPHON
H: 1·5–1·8 m (5–6 ft) S: 1·2–1·8 m (4–6 ft)
Bushy evergreen with white flowers in 5 cm (2 in) long clusters.

HOHERIA GLABRATA
H: 3–4·5 m (10–15 ft) S: 2·4–3 m (8–10 ft)
Upright deciduous, with sweetly scented pure white flowers in clusters 5 cm (2 in) wide.

HYDRANGEA HORTENSIA 'Madame E. Mouillière'
H: 1·2–1·8 m (4–6 ft) S: 1·5–2·1 m (5–7 ft)
Deciduous, mop-headed pink-tinted white flowers.

HYDRANGEA PANICULATA
H: 3–3·5 m (10–12 ft) S: 3–3·5 m (10–12 ft)
Deciduous with 15–20 cm (6–8 in) long pyramidal heads of white flowers that age to pink.

MAGNOLIA GRANDIFLORA
H: 3–4·5 m (10–15 ft) S: 1·8–3 m (8–10 ft)
Evergreen with creamy-white bowl-shaped fragrant flowers up to 20 cm (8 in) wide.

OLEARIA × HAASTII
H: 1·8–2·4 m (6–8 ft) S: 2·4–3 m (8–10 ft)
Evergreen with white daisy-like flowers in terminal clusters.

OLEARIA × SCILLONIENSIS: see June

OLEARIA MACRODONTA
H: 2·4–3 m (8–10 ft) S: 1·8–2·4 m (6–8 ft)
Evergreen with prickly holly-like leaves and daisy-like small white flowers in clusters 15 cm (6 in) wide.

PHILADELPHUS 'Beauclerk', *P.* 'Belle Etoile', *P.* 'Virginal', *POTENTILLA ARBUSCULA* 'Abbotswood': see June

ROMNEYA COULTERI
H: 1·2–1·8 m (4–6 ft) S: 1·2–1·8 m (4–6 ft)
Herbaceous sub-shrub with 10–13 cm (4–5 in) wide white flowers with golden stamens.

CLIMBERS

ACTINIDIA CHINENSIS (Chinese gooseberry)
H: 7·5–9 m (25–30 ft) S: 4·5–6 m (15–20 ft)
Deciduous with cup-shaped cream-coloured flowers that become buff-yellow.

HYDRANGEA PETIOLARIS, LONICERA JAPONICA 'Halliana': see June

POLYGONUM (correctly *Fallopia*) *BALDSCHUANICUM* (mile-a-minute vine/Russian vine)
H: 7·5–9 m (25–30 ft) S: 7·5 m (25 ft)
Deciduous with white or pale pink flowers.

TRACHELOSPERMUM JASMINOIDES
H: 3–3·5 m (10–12 ft) S: 1·8–3 m (6–10 ft)
Evergreen with fragrant white jasmine-like flowers. Not fully hardy.

FLOWERS

♦ Start planting autumn-flowering bulbs such as colchicums and sternbergias.
♦ Layer stems of border carnation to produce new plants.
♦ Feed dahlia plants, hoeing and watering it into the soil. Also, mulch the plants to conserve moisture in the soil. Do not mulch dry soil.

FRUIT

♦ Hoe between newly planted strawberry plants and remove runners to assist in building up strong plants for fruiting the following year.
♦ In dry seasons it will be necessary to water soft fruits, especially recently planted strawberry plants. Ensure that the soil is thoroughly soaked, and not just the surface moistened.

Left: Stone sinks are ideal
places for many rock garden
plants. Here, a dwarf
African Daisy,
Dimorphotheca ecklonis
'Prostrata', nestles in a sink,
with aquilegias below. The
shrub on the wall is the
Chilean Potato Tree,
Solanum crispum.

BORDER BRIGHTENERS
IN FLOWER
THIS MONTH

Malcolmia maritima
(Virginian stock)

Matthiola bicornis
(night-scented stock)

Mesembryanthemum criniflorum
(Livingstone daisy)

Nemophila menziesii
(baby blue eyes)

Nicotiana alata
(tobacco plant)

Nigella damascena
(love-in-a-mist)

Papaver rhoeas
(field poppy/Shirley poppy)

Petunia × hybrida

Phlox drummondii

Reseda odorata
(mignonette)

Salvia splendens

Scabiosa atropurpurea
(sweet scabious)

Tagetes erecta
(African marigold)

Tagetes patula
(French marigold)

Tagetes tenuifolia
(marigold)

Thunbergia alata
(black-eyed Susan)

Verbena × hybrida

Viola × wittrockiana
(pansy)

Zinnia elegans

Right: Red Hot Pokers, or Torch Lilies as they are sometimes called, create a spectacular blast of colour and shape in a border from June to October.

VEGETABLES

♦ Sow turnips and swedes thinly in drills 12 mm ($\frac{1}{2}$ in) deep and 30 cm (1 ft) apart, watering the drills first.
♦ Harvest ridge cucumbers.
♦ Mulch haricot beans.
♦ Harvest garden peas.
♦ Harvest salad onions.
♦ Thin summer lettuces to 23–30 cm (9–12 in) apart.
♦ Thin endive to 23–30 cm (9–12 in) apart.
♦ Harvest asparagus spears when 15 cm (6 in) high.
♦ Pick broad beans before the pods become tough.

LAWNS

♦ Water the lawn before it dries out totally. Use an oscillatory or rotary sprinkler and apply at least 6 mm ($\frac{1}{4}$ in) of water at each application. Just dampening the surface does more harm than good.
♦ Earthworms can be a problem, producing worm casts that if trodden upon create a mess. Also, the casts often contain weed seeds brought up from lower levels. Worms are essential to a lawn, but if they become a problem dissolve 25 grams of potassium permanganate in 5 litres of water (1 oz in a gallon) and sprinkle it over the surface.

GREENHOUSES

♦ Crotons and dracaenas too large for the greenhouse can be air layered, which will reduce their height and make them easier to accommodate.
♦ Re-pot the previous year's cyclamen and start them into growth.
♦ Ventilate and damp-down the greenhouse as necessary.
♦ Cucumbers must be picked regularly to encourage the development of further fruits.
♦ Pot on rooted pelargonium cuttings.

IN FLOWER THIS MONTH

BLUE AND MAUVE

SHRUBS

BUDDLEIA DAVIDII 'Empire Blue' (butterfly bush)
H: 2·1–2·7 m (7–9 ft) S: 2·1–2·7 m (7–9 ft)
Deciduous with large tapering heads of blue
flowers with orange eyes.

CEANOTHUS 'Gloire de Versailles': see June

CEANOTHUS 'Topaz'
H: 1·2–1·5 m (4–5 ft) S: 1·2–1·5 m (4–5 ft)
Deciduous with 10–15 cm (4–6 in) heads of rich
indigo-blue flowers.

CERATOSTIGMA WILLMOTTIANUM (hardy plumbago)
H: 75–90 cm (2 ft 6 in–3 ft) S: 90 cm (3 ft)
Half-hardy deciduous, with diamond-shaped
leaves and terminal clusters of rich blue flowers.

DABOECIA CANTABRICA 'Atropurpurea': see June

HEBE 'Autumn Glory'
H: 60–90 cm (2–3 ft) S: 75–90 cm (2 ft 6 in–3 ft)
Evergreen with 25–40 mm (1–1½ in) long spikes of
violet-blue flowers.

HEBE 'Carl Teschner' and *HEBE × FRANCISCANA* 'Blue
Gem': see June

HYDRANGEA MACROPHYLLA 'Blue Wave'
H: 1·2–1·8 m (4–6 ft) S: 1·5–1·8 m (5–6 ft)
Lacecap type with blue heads in acid soil.
'Générale Vicomtesse de Vibraye' is mop-headed.

LAVANDULA SPICA; syn. *L. officinalis* (Old English
lavender)
H: 90 cm–1·2 m (3–4 ft) S: 90 cm–1·2 m (3–4 ft)
Hardy evergreen with silver-grey narrow leaves
and 6·5 cm (2½ in) long spikes of grey-blue flowers.

LAVANDULA 'Hidcote'; syn. *L. nana atropurpurea*
H: 30–60 cm (1–2 ft) S: 45–60 cm (18–24 in)
Hardy compact evergreen with 5 cm (2 in) long
spikes of deep purple-blue flowers.

LAVANDULA STOECHAS (French lavender)
H: 45–60 cm (18–24 in) S: 45–60 cm (18–24 in)
Hardy evergreen with grey-green leaves and 5 cm
(2 in) long flower spikes with distinctive purple
bracts at their tops.

TEUCRIUM FRUTICANS: see June

VINCA MAJOR: see April   *VINCA MINOR:* see March

CLIMBERS

ABUTILON VITIFOLIUM: see May

CLEMATIS 'Elsa Spath'
H: 3·5–4·5 m (12–15 ft) S: 3–3·5 m (10–12 ft)
Deciduous with deep violet-blue 10 cm (4 in) wide
flowers with purple shading.

CLEMATIS 'Gipsy Queen'
H: 3·5–4·5 m (12–15 ft) S: 3–3·5 m (10–12 ft)
Deciduous with 10 cm (4 in) wide rich velvety
violet-purple flowers.

CLEMATIS 'Jackmanii Superba': see June

CLEMATIS 'Mrs. Cholmondeley': see May

CLEMATIS 'President', *C.* 'W. E. Gladstone': see June

SOLANUM CRISPUM (Chilean potato tree)
H: 4·5–6 m (15–20 ft) S: 3–4·5 m (10–15 ft)
Bushy scrambling semi-evergreen with star-shaped
2·5 cm (1 in) wide purple-blue flowers borne in 7·5–
15 cm (3–6 in) wide clusters. Not hardy in all areas.

BULBS IN FLOWER THIS MONTH

Allium moly
(golden garlic/lily leek)

Camassia quamash;
syn. *C. esculenta*
(common camass)

Crinum × powellii

Cyclamen purpurascens;
syn. *C. europaeum*

Galtonia candicans;
syn. *Hyacinthus candicans*
(summer hyacinth)

Gladiolus
– large-flowered hybrids,
butterfly, primulinus, and
miniature types

Lilium candidum
(madonna lily/Bourbon lily)

Lilium regale

◇

FLOWERS

♦ Transplant wallflowers, sweet Williams and Canterbury bells into a nursery bed, so that they can grow ready for planting out into their flowering positions in autumn. To ensure the plants transplant well water the soil the previous day.

♦ Disbud chrysanthemums that are not being grown as spray varieties. Leave the terminal bud and remove the small buds from around it. Bend them sideways so that they snap off.

♦ Increase shrubs such as deutzias, escallonias and weigelas by taking half-ripe cuttings.

FRUIT

♦ Clear strawberry beds that have finished fruiting: remove the straw, cut off all runners and old leaves. Hoe lightly between the rows.

♦ Increase blackberries and hybrid berries by layering long shoots.

Right: Half-ripe cuttings can be taken now. Trim the cutting just below a leaf-joint and remove the lower leaves. They can then be inserted in a mixture of peat and sharp sand.

ROCK PLANTS IN FLOWER THIS MONTH

◇

Achillea tomentosa
(woolly yarrow)

Aethionema grandiflorum
(Persian candytuft)

Androsace carnea
(rock jasmine)

Androsace lanuginosa
(Himalayan androsace)

Aquilegia flabellata 'Nana Alba'

Armeria maritima 'Alba'
(thrift)

Armeria maritima 'Vindictive'
(thrift)

Aster alpinus

Campanula carpatica

Campanula cochleariifolia
(fairy thimbles)

Campanula portenschlagiana;
syn. *C. muralis*

Campanula poscharskyana

Crepis incana

Dianthus deltoides
(maiden pink)

Dimorphotheca barberiae
'Compacta'

Erinus alpinus

Geranium cinereum

Geranium farreri;
syn. *G. napuligerum*

Geranium subcaulescens

Gypsophila repens

Gypsophila repens 'Fratensis'

Helianthemum nummularium;
syn. *H. chamaecistus*

Hypericum polyphyllum
'Sulphureum'

Lithospermum diffusum;
now *Lithodora diffusa*

Potentilla aurea chrysocraspeda

Saxifraga paniculata;
syn. *S. aizoon*

Sedum spurium

Sempervivum octopodes

Silene schafta

Thymus doerfleri;
now *T. hirsutus doerfleri*

Thymus serphyllum
(wild thyme)

Veronica cinerea

Veronica prostrata

◇

Left: Silver-leaved herbaceous perennials introduce a new colour theme to both mixed and herbaceous borders. Here, the White Sage, Artemisia ludoviciana, *blends well with a border edging of sedums.*

Right: **Hydrangea aspera aspera** *creates a rounded form, with pale porcelain-blue flowers during June and July. It is a shrub that is soon damaged by late spring frosts and therefore best grown in the south or west. It does well under a protective canopy of tall pines.*

VEGETABLES

♦ Stop tomato plants two leaves above the fourth truss.
♦ Sow radishes 12 mm ($\frac{1}{2}$ in) deep.
♦ Summer lettuce can still be sown.
♦ Harvest endive, severing the plant at soil-level.
♦ Harvest cauliflowers.
♦ Pick asparagus peas when 25 mm (1 in) long, before they become tough.
♦ Harvest kohlrabi when the size of tennis balls.
♦ Earth-up celery planted in trenches.
♦ Harvest runner beans while they are still young and tender.

LAWNS

♦ Roller mowers are essential to produce 'striped' lawns. These are those attractive lawns where the lawns appear patterned. Hover mowers and rotaries without rollers will not create stripes. Hover-types, however, can be used on damp or even wet grass without any fear of skidding, and are ideal for steep slopes and banks.

GREENHOUSES

♦ Top-dress chrysanthemums in pots outdoors, and ensure that there is no risk of them toppling over.
♦ Continue to water, feed and pick tomatoes.
♦ By this time in the season the greenhouse is showing signs of wear and tear. Make a note of all repairs that will be necessary before the onset of winter.
♦ Check that greenhouse shading painted on the glass has not been washed off. Replace as necessary.
♦ Make further sowings of primulas, calceolarias, cinerarias and gloxinias for flowers during spring. Sow the seeds thinly.
♦ Check for any infestation of pests and diseases, and spray as soon as they are seen.

Above: Lawn weeds will be very much in evidence now. In a small lawn they are best removed by using a small fork and digging them out, roots as well. On a large lawn, however, it will be easier to use a lawn weedkiller. Follow the maker's directions exactly.

◇ AUGUST ◇

Late-summer flowering shrubs are most welcome now, when they help to create further interest and to create a theme that will continue until the onset of frosts. *Hydrangea macrophylla* (common hydrangea) creates large colour splashes through to September, mainly in blues but also reds, pinks and purples. There are two main types: those with large mop heads up to 20 cm (8 in) wide, and the lacecaps with 10–15 cm (4–6 in) wide flat heads. In neutral or acid soils pink-flowered varieties may become blue or purple, while in soils which are alkaline (with lime in them) blue varieties become reddish-purple or pink.

Another shrub, related to the common hydrangea, is *Hydrangea paniculata* 'Grandiflora' which during August and September reveals 38–45 cm (15–18 in) long pyramidal heads of white flowers that slowly turn pink. It flowers on the current season's growth and to produce the necessary growth the plant must be pruned severely during early spring. Cut back the previous year's flowering shoots by half.

The outstandingly attractive July to October flowers of *Hibiscus syriacus* from Syria are a certain eye-catching feature for late summer and into autumn. Many varieties are widely grown, in colours including white, blue, red and pink. *H. rosa-sinensis* flowers in a greenhouse at this time of year, with 13 cm (5 in) wide flowers in crimson, pink, salmon and yellow from June to September. Interestingly, the flowers contain a quantity of astringent juice which was used at one time by Chinese women to dye their hair and eyebrows, while in Java it was known as the shoe-black plant and used to clean black shoes.

Romneya coulteri and *Romneya trichocalyx* (tree poppies) flower up to September, revealing 10–13 cm (4–5 in) wide white flowers with beautiful central yellow bosses. They do not grow well in cold easterly or northern areas. *Hebe* 'Autumn Glory' cannot be left out of a short list of late summer- and autumn-flowering shrubs. With a height of 60–90 cm (2–3 ft) and dark green leaves on purple stems it produces spikes of violet-blue flowers from July until autumn. Ardent admirers of variegated plants might consider *Hebe × andersonii* 'Variegata' with cream variegated mid-green leaves and lavender-coloured flowers from July to October although it is not suitable for very cold areas.

Few climbing plants are as well known as *Fallopia baldschuanicum*, better known and sold as *Polygonum baldschuanicum* (mile-a-minute or Russian vine). It has many other common names, including Siberian vine and Bukhara fleece, indicating its place of origin. From July to October it displays white or pale pink flowers in fleece-like tapering spires. It can grow 4·5 m (15 ft) each year.

Many hostas will now be producing flowers, but for most of them it is the leaves that are the chief attraction. There are some exceptionally variegated forms, such as *Hosta fortunei* 'Albopicta' with pale green and buff-yellow leaves, and *H. f.* 'Aureo-marginata' with gold-edged leaves. *Hosta undulata* 'Variegata' also has colourful foliage, variegated gold on green. Others, such as *H. elata* with glossy dark green leaves are plainer, but nevertheless attractive.

Astilbes will also be at their best now and look superb at the edge of an informal pond. *Astilbe × arendsii* is a hybrid with many distinctive forms, such as clear pink 'Bressingham Beauty', rosy-red 'Federsee', brick-red 'Red Sentinel', and the exceptionally beautiful white 'White Gloria'.

The beautiful herbaceous *Salvia nemorosa*, better known as *S. × superba*, is in flower now and into next month and is especially attractive when planted in front of the tall, 1·8–2·4 m (6–8 ft) *Lilium henryi*. The rich bluish-purple flowers of the salvia contrast against the pale apricot-yellow heads of the lily.

The bright summer days of August soon shorten into the early autumn days of September, but not before dahlias and chrysanthemums have brightened our gardens. There is still plenty of colour left in the year.

Mixed borders, with a medley of herbaceous perennials, shrubs, annuals, bulbous and tuberous plants, are an attractive garden feature. Such borders create interest over a long period, right up to the frosts of autumn.

FLOWERS

♦ Trim hedges to keep them neat and tidy.

♦ Continue to plant autumn-flowering bulbs for naturalizing in grass and among shrubs.

♦ Pick sweet peas regularly to encourage the development of further flowers.

♦ Increase pansies and violas by inserting cuttings in boxes of sandy compost.

♦ Start planting bulbs in bowls for flowering indoors during winter. Place them in a cool, dark place.

♦ Keep the flower beds free from weeds. Hoe and mulch as necessary.

FRUIT

♦ Summer-prune apples, completing by early September.

♦ Pick apples as soon as they are ready. The stalks should still be attached to the fruits. Gently lift up the fruits and if the stalks come away from the fruiting spur the fruit is ready for picking.

♦ Pick plums and gages as soon as they are ripe. They are best eaten straight away.

♦ If plum trees are heavily laden with fruits support the branches with wooden props.

FLOWERS TO SOW THIS MONTH

PERENNIALS

PAPAVER ALPINUM (alpine poppy)
Sow 6 mm (¼ in) deep in a seed bed.

PAPAVER NUDICAULE (Iceland poppy)
Sow 6 mm (¼ in) deep in a seed bed.

PAPAVER ORIENTALE (oriental poppy)
Sow 6 mm (¼ in) deep in a seed bed.

Right: Delphinium consolida *'Stock Flowered' is an outstanding Larkspur, with spires of cottage-garden flowers from June to August.*

Far right top: The ornamental grass Carex stricta *'Aurea' creates a loose fountain-like mound of bright leaves.*

Far right below: Anthemis cupaniana *creates a mass of bright daisy-like flowers with golden centres from June to August. They appear among grey, finely-divided and aromatic leaves.*

Right: Sweet corn can be raised by sowing seeds in the open soil as soon as all risk of frost has passed. It must be grown in blocks of plants, rather than single lines, as it is pollinated by wind.

IN FLOWER THIS MONTH

YELLOW AND ORANGE

TREES

KOELREUTERIA PANICULATA (golden rain tree/pride of India/China tree)
H: 3–5·4 m (10–18 ft) S: 3–4·5 m (10–15 ft)
Deciduous with yellow flowers in large terminal clusters.

SHRUBS

COLUTEA ARBORESCENS: see June

CYTISUS NIGRANS
H: 60 cm–1·2 m (3–4 ft) S: 90 cm (3 ft)
Erect deciduous, with 2·5 cm (1 in) long pea-shaped yellow flowers.

GENISTA AETNENSIS (Mount Etna broom)
H: 4·5–6 m (15–20 ft) S: 4·5–5·4 m (15–18 ft)
Large tree-like deciduous, with rush-like stems and golden-yellow pea-like flowers.

GENISTA TINCTORIA 'Royal Gold', *HYPERICUM CALYCINUM:* see June

HYPERICUM PATULUM 'Hidcote': see July

POTENTILLA FRUTICOSA 'Farreri': see May

SANTOLINA CHAMAECYPARISSUS: see June

SENECIO 'Sunshine': see July

SPARTIUM JUNCEUM: see June

CLIMBERS

CLEMATIS ORIENTALIS (orange-peel clematis)
H: 4·5–6 m (15–20 ft) S: 3–4·5 m (10–15 ft)
Well-branched deciduous, with scented, nodding, star-like 4 cm (1½ in) wide yellow flowers.

CLEMATIS TANGUTICA
H: 4·5–5·4 m (15–18 ft) S: 2·4–3·5 m (8–12 ft)
Deciduous with rich yellow nodding lantern-like flowers.

Below: Onions need careful ripening if they are to last long when stored. The first task is to gently fork the bulbs loose from the soil, breaking their roots. A week or so later lift them by hand and place them in rows, as illustrated.

VEGETABLES

♦ Blanch cardoons, wrapping light-proof material around each plant.
♦ Harvest French beans when 15 cm (6 in) long.
♦ Remove sideshoots from tomato plants.
♦ Harvest globe artichokes when the scales are still tight.
♦ Thin summer spinach to 75 mm (3 in) apart, and later to 15 cm (6 in) apart.

LAWNS

♦ Feed the lawn with a slow-acting lawn fertilizer at about 70 grams a square metre (2 oz a square yard). Use a fertilizer mixture with a low nitrogen, fairly high phosphate and medium potash content to encourage root development.
♦ Water the lawn during dry spells, thoroughly saturating it.

GREENHOUSES

♦ Prick off seedlings as soon as they have germinated and can be handled. When setting them in boxes or pots, hold them only by their leaves. The delicate stems are easily crushed if held too firmly.
♦ Cinerarias are susceptible to attack from a pest that burrows beneath the surface of leaves. As soon as they are seen spray with a suitable insecticide, repeating as necessary. Follow the maker's instructions exactly when using any insecticide.
♦ Remove some of the lower leaves from tomato plants to allow better air circulation as well as more light to reach the fruits.
♦ Continue to pick tomatoes as they ripen. This encourages later fruits to reach maturity quicker.
♦ Grapes will be ready for picking. When all the bunches have been cut spray the plant with clean water to deter red spider mites.
♦ Pick cucumbers as they mature.

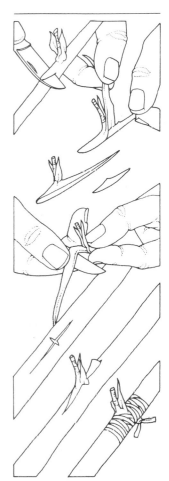

Above: Roses can be budded during July and August, when the rootstocks are in full leaf. The buds of the variety to be budded should be strong and healthy. To prepare the bud, which is in the angle of a leaf joint, use a sharp knife to cut 12 mm (½ in) below the bud and draw it slantwise beneath the bud to a point 2·5 cm (1 in) above the bud. The sliver of wood underneath the bud is best removed. On the rootstock make a T-cut 4 cm (1½ in) long and 18 mm (¾ in) wide. Slip the bud into this cut and tie it in place with a piece of raffia. Proprietary ties are available for this job. After about three weeks the leaf stalk on the bud will fall off when lightly touched, and eventually the raffia will need to be carefully cut away to prevent constriction of the stem. During the following February, cut off the growth on the rootstock, about 2·5 cm (1 in) above the bud.

**BORDER BRIGHTENERS
IN FLOWER
THIS MONTH**
◇

Adonis aestivalis
(pheasant's eye)

Ageratum houstonianum

Althaea rosea;
now *Alcea rosea*

Alyssum maritimum;
now *Lobularia maritima*

Amaranthus caudatus
(love-lies-bleeding)

Amaranthus hypochondriacus
(prince's feather/pygmy
torch)

Anchusa azurea;
syn. *A. italica*

Anchusa capensis

Antirrhinum majus
(snapdragon)

Arctotis × hybrida
(African daisy)

Begonia semperflorens

Bellis perennis
(daisy)

Brachycome iberidifolia
(Swan River daisy)

Calceolaria integrifolia;
syn. *C. rugosa*

Calendula officinalis
(pot marigold/English
marigold)

Callistephus chinensis
(China aster)

Celosia argentea plumosa
(Prince of Wales' feather)

Centaurea cyanus
(cornflower)

Centaurea moschata
(sweet sultan)

Chrysanthemum carinatum;
syn. *C. tricolor*

Clarkia elegans

Clarkia pulchella

Cleome spinosa
(spider flower)

Consolida ajacis
(larkspur)

Convolvulus tricolor;
syn. *C. minor*

Cosmea bipinnatus

Cotula barbata
(pincushion flower)

Didiscus caeruleus;
now *Trachymene caeruleus*
(blue lace flower)

Dimorphotheca aurantiaca
(star of the veldt)

Echium lycopsis;
syn. *E. plantagineum*
(viper's bugloss)

FLOWERS

♦ Cordon-grown sweet peas which have reached the tops of their supports can be untied and lowered and trained up supports further down the row.
♦ Continue to sow seeds, as indicated.
♦ Remove dead flower heads to tidy up the border and encourage the development of fresh blooms.
♦ Plant bulbs of *Amaryllis belladonna* (belladonna lily) and *Fritillaria imperialis* (crown imperial).

FRUIT

♦ Strawberries can still be planted (*see* page 106).
♦ Pick apples when they are ready to be detached from the tree.

VEGETABLES

♦ Sow turnips and swedes thinly in drills 12 mm ($\frac{1}{2}$ in) deep and 30 cm (1 ft) apart. Water the drills first.
♦ Harvest beetroot.
♦ Harvest sweet corn when the 'silks' have withered.
♦ Thin summer lettuce to 23–30 cm (9–12 in) apart.
♦ Harvest summer lettuce when ready.
♦ Sow spring cabbage in seedbeds between now and August, 18 mm ($\frac{3}{4}$ in) deep in drills 15–20 cm (6–8 in) apart.

Right: Pinus strobus 'Nana', *a form of the Weymouth Pine, develops into a dense bush ideal for a large rock garden or in a conifer collection.*

Below: Ceanothus × 'Gloire de Versailles' *is an ideal shrub for a mixed border, where its fragrant flowers create colour from June to October.*

BORDER BRIGHTENERS IN FLOWER THIS MONTH
◇

Emilia flammea
(tassel flower)

Eschscholzia californica
(Californian poppy)

Felicia bergeriana
(kingfisher daisy)

Gaillardia pulchella

Gilia lutea
(stardust)

Godetia grandiflora

Gypsophila elegans

Helianthus annuus
(sunflower)

Heliotropium × hybridum
(cherry pie)

Hibiscus trionum
(flower-of-an-hour)

Iberis umbellata
(candytuft)

Lavatera trimestris

Limnanthes douglasii
(poached egg plant)

Linum grandiflorum
(scarlet flax)

Lobelia erinus

Malcolmia maritima
(Virginian stock)

Matthiola bicornis
(night-scented stock)

Nemophila menziesii
(Baby blue eyes)

Nicotiana alata
(tobacco plant)

Nigella damascena
(love-in-a-mist)

Papaver rhoeas
(field poppy/Shirley poppy)

Petunia × hybrida

Phlox drummondii

Reseda odorata
(mignonette)

Rudbeckia hirta
(black-eyed Susan)

Salvia patens

Salvia splendens

Scabiosa atropurpurea
(sweet scabious)

Tagetes erecta
(African marigold)

Tagetes patula
(French marigold)

Tagetes tenuifolia
(marigold)

Thunbergia alata
(black-eyed Susan)

Verbena × hybrida

Zinnia elegans
◇

Left: Agrostemma githago *'Milas', a form of our native corn-cockle, is a spectacular hardy annual. The pale lilac flowers blend well with red-flowered annuals.*

IN FLOWER THIS MONTH

RED AND PINK

SHRUBS

BUDDLEIA DAVIDII 'Fortune', *ERICA CINEREA* 'C. D. Eason', *E. VAGANS* 'Mrs. D. F. Maxwell': see July

CALLUNA VULGARIS 'County Wicklow'
H: 30–45 cm (12–18 in) S: 30–45 cm (12–18 in)
Evergreen with double shell-pink flowers.

CALLUNA VULGARIS 'Darkness'
H: 30–45 cm (12–18 in) S: 30–45 cm (12–18 in)
Evergreen with deep, rose-purple flowers and bright green foliage.

CALLUNA VULGARIS 'J. H. Hamilton'
H: 15–20 cm (6–8 in) S: 20–25 cm (8–10 in)
Evergreen with large pink double flowers.

CALLUNA VULGARIS 'Peter Sparkes'
H: 30 cm (12 in) S: 30–45 cm (12–18 in)
Evergreen with double pink flowers.

CALLUNA VULGARIS 'Tib'
H: 30–45 cm (12–18 in) S: 30–45 cm (12–18 in)
Evergreen with double rosy-red flowers.

ESCALLONIA 'C. F. Ball', *E.* 'Donard Radiance', *E.* 'Donard Star', *E.* 'Peach Blossom', *E.* 'Slieve Donard': see June

FUCHSIA MAGELLANICA
H: 1·2–1·5 m (4–5 ft) S: 90 cm–1 m (3 ft–3 ft 6 in)
Deciduous with scarlet and purple flowers.

HEBE 'Great Orme', *HEBE SPECIOSA* 'La Seduisante'
HYDRANGEA MACROPHYLLA 'Hamburg': see July

INDIGOFERA GERARDIANA: See June

PHYGELIUS CAPENSIS: see July

POTENTILLA FRUTICOSA 'Red Ace': see June

CLIMBERS

CLEMATIS 'Ernest Markham'
H: 4 m (13 ft) S: 3–4 m (10–13 ft)
Deciduous with large, glowing, petunia-red flowers.

CLEMATIS 'Hagley Hybrid': see June

CLEMATIS 'Ville de Lyon'
H: 3–4 m (10–13 ft) S: 3–4 m (10–13 ft)
Deciduous with bright carmine-red flowers shading to crimson at the edges.

LAWNS

♦ Lawn edges that have been encroached on by herbaceous plants can either be cut back or edged with two or three rows of house bricks to prevent the grass at the edge of the border being killed and becoming an eye-sore. Alternatively, paving slabs can be set along the edge.

♦ Continue to cut the lawn regularly, as well as the edges.

GREENHOUSES

♦ Arum lilies stood outside earlier in the year can be re-potted.

♦ Plant winter- and spring-flowering plants such as freesias and lachenalias.

♦ Continue to pick tomatoes and cucumbers. Take cuttings of heliotrope, pelargoniums and fuchsias.

♦ Shade all plants from strong sunlight.

♦ Water all plants regularly, ensuring that they are not given excessive water.

♦ If you are going away on holiday arrange for someone to look after the greenhouse or fit automatic ventilator openers, which are not expensive and can be used the year through. If you are going away for just a few days either pack moist peat around the pots, stand them in large bowls shallowly filled with water, or fit up an automatic watering device such as wicks inserted into the pots and trailed into a large bowl of water. Proprietary wick-watering systems are available.

Below: Sweet peppers can be grown under cloches or in a greenhouse. This banana-looking variety is useful for salads and cooking.

Right: The Curry Plant,
Helichrysum
angustifolium, *is covered*
with a down that emits a
strong smell of curry. From
June to August it is ablaze
with mustard-yellow flowers.

FLOWERS

♦ Check chrysanthemums and dahlias for attack from earwigs.

♦ Remove suckers from rose bushes. Cut them off close to the rootstock to prevent further ones developing.

♦ Before going away on holiday, hoe off all weeds and mulch the soil. Thoroughly water the soil before applying the mulch.

♦ Trim hedges to keep them neat.

FRUIT

♦ Blackcurrants planted the previous autumn or early in the year will have developed young shoots from their bases. Cut out at soil-level the weakest of these. The shoots that are left are the ones that will bear fruit the following year.

VEGETABLES

♦ Water summer lettuce if the weather is dry

♦ Earth-up celery planted in trenches.

♦ Harvest runner beans while still young and tender.

♦ Bend over the tops of onions in preparation for lifting them.

♦ Thin swedes and parsnips to 15 cm (6 in) apart.

♦ Harvest ridge cucumbers.

♦ During dry summers the whole vegetable plot will need regular watering.

LAWNS

♦ Continue to water the lawn during dry spells. Thoroughly soak the lawn each time, as just dampening the surface does more harm than good.

BULBS IN FLOWER THIS MONTH

◇

Acidanthera bicolor

Crinum × powellii

Cyclamen purpurascens;
syn. *C. europaeum*

Cyclamen hederifolium;
syn. *C. neapolitanum*

Galtonia candicans;
syn. *Hyacinthus candicans*
(summer hyacinth)

Gladiolus
– large-flowered, butterfly,
primulinus, and miniature
types

Lilium auratum
(golden-rayed lily)

Lilium henryi

Lilium speciosum

Lilium tigrinum
(tiger lily)

◇

IN FLOWER THIS MONTH

WHITE AND CREAM

SHRUBS

ABELIA CHINENSIS: see July

AESCULUS PARVIFLORA
H: 2·1–2·4 m (7–8 ft) S: 2·1–2·7 m (7–9 ft)
Bushy deciduous, with 20–30 cm (8–12 in) erect candles of white flowers revealing pink stamens.

ARALIA ELATA (Japanese angelica tree)
H: 3–4·8 m (10–16 ft) S: 2·1–2·7 m (7–9 ft)
Suckering deciduous, with large leaves and small flowers in large branched heads.

BUDDLEIA DAVIDII 'Peace', *B. FALLOWIANA* 'Alba': see July

CLERODENDRON TRICHOTOMUM
H: 3–4·5 m (10–15 ft) S: 3–3·5 m (10–12 ft)
Slow-growing deciduous, with fragrant star-like white flowers.

CALLUNA VULGARIS 'Alba Plena' (heather/ling)
H: 30–38 cm (12–15 in) S: 38–45 cm (15–18 in)
Evergreen with double white flowers.

CALLUNA VULGARIS 'Beoley Gold' (heather/ling)
H: 30–38 cm (12–15 in) S: 38–45 cm (15–18 in)
Evergreen with yellow foliage and white flowers.

CALLUNA VULGARIS 'Gold Haze' (heather/ling)
H: 60 cm (2 ft) S: 60–75 cm (24–30 in)
Evergreen with masses of white flowers.

CALLUNA VULGARIS 'Serlei' (heather/ling)
H: 45–60 cm (18–24 in) S: 60–75 cm (24–30 in)
Evergreen, with dark green foliage and white flowers.

CLETHRA ALNIFOLIA (sweet pepper bush)
H: 1·8–2·1 m (6–7 ft) S: 1·5–1·8 m (5–6 ft)
Deciduous with creamy-white bell-shaped and fragrant flowers in terminal clusters.

CONVOLVULUS CNEORUM, DABOECIA CANTABRICA 'Alba': see June

ERICA VAGANS 'Lyonesse' (Cornish heath)
H: 75 cm–1·2 m (2 ft 6 in–4 ft) S: 1·5–1·8 m (5–6 ft)
Mid-green evergreen with pure white flowers.

ESCALLONIA × IVEYI: see June

EUCRYPHIA × NYMENSENSIS
H: 3·5–4·5 m (12–15 ft) S: 1·8–2·4 m (6–8 ft)
Quick-growing evergreen with 6·5 cm (2.5 in) wide cream flowers.

GAULTHERIA PROCUMBENS: see July

HIBISCUS SYRIACUS 'Dorothy Crane'
H: 1·8–2·7 m (6–9 ft) S: 1·2–1·8 m (4–6 ft)
Deciduous with 7·5 cm (3 in) wide pure white flowers displaying crimson centres. 'Jeanne d'Arc' has double white flowers, 'Monstrosus' white flowers with maroon centres, and 'Snowdrift' pure white.

HOHERIA GLABRATA, HYDRANGEA MACROPHYLLA 'Madame E. Mouillière', *H. PANICULATA:* see July

ITEA ILICIFOLIA
H: 3·5–5·4 m (12–18 ft) S: 2·4–3·5 m (8–12 ft)
Holly-like evergreen with long drooping tassels of greenish-white flowers.

MAGNOLIA GRANDIFLORA: see July

MYRTUS COMMUNIS (common myrtus)
H: 2·5–3 m (8–10 ft) S: 1·8–2·4 m (6–8 ft)
Evergreen with small fragrant white flowers with fluffy stamens.

OLEARIA × HAASTII, O. MACRODONTA, POTENTILLA ARBUSCULA 'Abbotswood', *ROMNEYA COULTERI:* see July

CLIMBERS

ACTINIDIA CHINENSIS: see July

CLEMATIS FLAMMULA
H: 3 m (10 ft) S: 1·8–2·4 m (6–8 ft)
Tangled deciduous, with sweetly scented white flowers.

LONICERA JAPONICA 'Halliana': see June

POLYGONUM BALDSCHUANICUM, TRACHELOSPERMUM JASMINOIDES: see July

Below: Greenhouse plants need protection from strong sunlight. The simplest method is to paint the outside with a layer of whitewash, but this also reduces the amount of light on dull days. The best method is to install blinds. Localized areas in alpine houses, as well as greenhouse, can be specifically shaded by muslin.

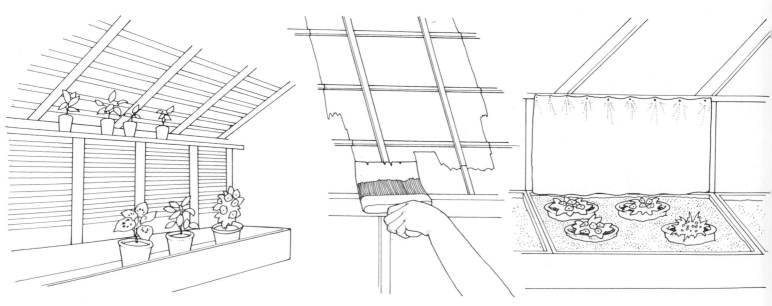

GREENHOUSES

♦ Bulbs for Christmas flowering should be ordered now. Specially treated bulbs are needed if they are to flower at Christmas.

♦ Cyclamen can be sown now, producing flowering plants in about 15 months' time.

♦ Be alert for signs of damping off on soft tissues such as many leaves and flowers. Keeping the atmosphere dry will assist in controlling its spread. Remove and burn all infected tissue.

♦ Continue to remove bottom leaves from tomato plants to assist fruit ripening.

♦ Pick cucumbers and tomatoes as they begin to ripen.

♦ Many annuals can be sown in a greenhouse to produce flowering plants during early spring. These include clarkia, cornflowers, godetia and nemesia.

♦ Check for infestations of pests and spray as necessary.

Left: Zinnia *'Persian Carpet'* creates a sea of small, double and semi-double flowers in bicoloured and tricoloured shades from July to September.

Below: Cistus × crispus *'Sunset' forms a compact shrub, with sage-green leaves and vivid cerise flowers from July to October. Here it blends well with Ballota* pseudodictamnus.

FLOWERS

♦ Border carnations layered earlier will now have rooted and can be moved to their flowering positions.

♦ Prune rambler roses as they finish flowering. Untie them from their supports, lay them on the ground and cut out at ground-level all stems that have borne flowers. Retain all the stems made during the current season and tie them back to their supports.

♦ Spray with pesticides and insecticides as necessary, especially against aphids that can soon increase to devastating proportions if neglected.

♦ Check the stakes and ties supporting dahlias and chrysanthemums.

FRUIT

♦ Prune established blackcurrant bushes. Cut out at ground level all shoots that bore fruit earlier in the year. Do not prune the young shoots produced during the current year which will bear fruit the following one.

♦ Further summer-prune pears, shortening lateral shoots not previously pruned.

♦ Use pesticides and fungicides as necessary.

VEGETABLES

♦ Sow kohlrabi thinly in drills 12 mm ($\frac{1}{2}$ in) deep and 38 cm (15 in) apart.

♦ Sow radishes 12 mm ($\frac{1}{2}$ in) deep.

♦ Harvest salad onions.

♦ Sow lettuce for cutting in spring. Sow seeds 12 mm ($\frac{1}{2}$ in) deep in drills 25 cm (10 in) apart.

Right: Solidago 'Crown of Rays' *is a hardy herbaceous perennial that creates a strong colour impact from July to October. It blends well with the small, white, starry flowers of* Gypsophila paniculata, *which flowers from June to August.*

ROCK PLANTS IN
FLOWER
THIS MONTH
◇

Achillea tomentosa
(woolly yarrow)

Androsace lanuginosa
(Himalayan androsace)

Campanula carpatica

Campanula cohleariifolia
(fairy thimbles)

Campanula portenschlagiana

Campanula poscharskyana

Crepis incana

Dianthus deltoides
(maiden pink)

Dimorphotheca barberiae
'Compacta'

Erinus alpinus

Geranium cinereum

Geranium farreri;
syn. *G. napuligerum*

Geranium subcaulescens

Hypericum polyphyllum
'Sulphureum'

Lithospermum diffusum;
now *Lithodora diffusa*

Potentilla aurea chrysocraspeda

Sedum cauticolum

Sedum spurium

Silene schafta

Thymus serphyllum
(wild thume)

Veronica cinerea
◇

IN FLOWER THIS MONTH

BLUE AND MAUVE

SHRUBS

BUDDLEIA DAVIDII 'Empire Blue': see July

CARYOPTERIS × CLANDONENSIS
H: 60 cm–1 m (2 ft–3 ft 6 in) S: 75 cm–1·2 m (2 ft 6 in–4 ft)
Bushy deciduous, with 2·5–5 cm (1–2 in) wide clusters of blue tubular flowers. 'Arthur Simmonds' bears bright blue flowers, 'Heavenly Blue' is compact with deep blue flowers, and 'Kew Blue' has rich blue flowers.

CEANOTHUS 'Gloire de Versailles': see June

CEANOTHUS 'Topaz', *CERATOSTIGMA WILLMOTTIANUM*: see July

DABOECIA CANTABRICA 'Atropurpurea': see June

HEBE 'Autumn Glory': see July

HEBE × FRANCISCANA 'Blue Gem': see June

HIBISCUS SYRIACUS 'Blue Bird'
H: 1·8–2·4 m (6–8 ft) S: 1·2–1·8 m (4–6 ft)
Deciduous with 7·5 cm (3 in) wide hollyhock-like mid-blue flowers with red centres. 'Coeleste' has deep blue flowers.

HYDRANGEA MACROPHYLLA 'Blue Wave', *LAVANDULA SPICA, L.* 'Hidcote', *L. STOECHAS*: see July

LIPPIA CITRIODORA; syn. *Aloysia triphylla* (lemon-scented verbena)
H: 1·2–1·5 m (4–5 ft) S: 1·2 m (4 ft)
Deciduous with lemon-scented leaves and tubular pale mauve flowers. Not hardy in all areas.

TEUCRIUM FRUITICANS: see June

CLIMBERS

CLEMATIS 'Elsa Spath', *C.* 'Gipsy Queen': see July

CLEMATIS 'Jackmanii Superba': see June

CLEMATIS 'Mrs. Cholmondeley': see May

CLEMATIS 'W. E. Gladstone': see June

SOLANUM CRISPUM: see July

Above: The evergreen shrub Eucryphia × nymanensis *develops 6·5 cm (2½ in) wide white flowers during August and September.*

Right: The hardy herbaceous perennial Lychnis flos-jovis *is awash with purple or red flowers from June to August.*

Centre: Automatic ventilators are invaluable for a home gardener, rapidly reacting to changes in temperature. Damping down a greenhouse helps to create a bouyant atmosphere.

Far right: Runner beans will now be producing an abundance of beans. Pick them regularly to encourage the development of further ones.

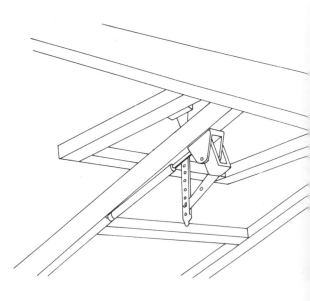

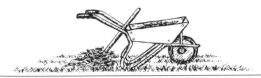

LAWNS

♦ Lawn alternatives include chamomile (*Anthemis nobilis*), a small fern-like and prostrate plant with a sweet scent. Plants are best spaced 10–13 cm (4–5 in) apart, nipping out their tips when 75 mm (3 in) high and slowly reducing the height to 18 mm ($\frac{3}{4}$ in) as other shoots develop.

♦ Continue to cut lawns regularly. If left to grow high the grass will soon be difficult to cut for some lawn mowers.

GREENHOUSES

♦ Pot up cinerarias into their final pots. If leaf miners are seen in the leaves dip the foliage into an insecticide. This will also help to control other pests such as aphids.

♦ Sinningia (gloxinias) will finish flowering about now. Place the pots on their sides in a dry and cool part of the greenhouse. Alternatively, place them in a cold frame for a few weeks before bringing them into a cool and dry position in the greenhouse.

♦ Take cuttings of a range of plants such as coleus, begonias, pilea, tradescantia, zebrina and impatiens. They do not require a high temperature.

♦ Gather up all fallen leaves – they look unsightly and encourage pests and diseases.

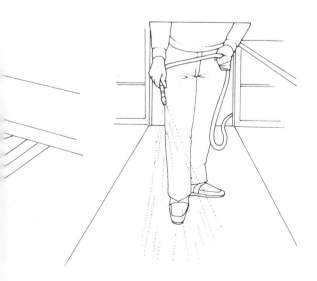

◇ SEPTEMBER ◇

The weather and changing seasons are taking a toll of many border plants, but there are still plenty of climbers providing a colourful array of flowers. The large-flowered clematis such as *Clematis* 'Ernest Markham' with large petunia-red flowers, *C.* 'Ville de Lyon' displaying carmine-red heads shading to crimson at their edges, and *C.* 'Mrs. Cholmondeley' bearing lavender-blue flowers are just a few to delight us now: others are mentioned under plants in flower this month.

Solanum crispum (Chilean potato tree), which started flowering in June is still bearing 2·5 cm (1 in) wide star-shaped purplish-blue flowers with distinctive yellow anthers. The best form is *S. c.* 'Glasnevin' (also known as 'Autumnale') which is hardier and has a longer flowering period.

Bulbs are very much in evidence now. *Colchicum autumnale* (naked boys) flowers from August to October and is frequently erroneously called autumn crocus or meadow saffron. It has 15 cm (6 in) high flowers that look bare without the 20–25 cm (8–10 in) long leaves that appear in late winter. Incidentally the leaves tend to swamp near-by plants and therefore this colchicum is best given plenty of room.

Galtonia candicans (summer hyacinth) gains its common name from its late summer flowers and its former name, *Hyacinthus candicans*. It is a distinctive bulbous plant, creating interest in a border when most other plants are past their best. It rises to 1·2 m (4 ft) with spire-like heads of pendulous bell-shaped white flowers, each 4 cm (1½ in) long.

Several lilies are still creating strong colour impact: *Lilium auratum* (golden-rayed lily) rises to 1·5–2·1 m (5–7 ft) and reveals fragrant bowl-shaped flowers, brilliant white and with raised golden bands, while *Lilium tigrinum* (tiger lily) is up to 1·8 m (6 ft) high with orange-red Turk's-cap-like flowers spotted purple-black. The bulbs of this species were eaten at one time in China and Japan. *Lilium speciosum* is also in flower during August and September with 7·5–13 cm (3–5 in) wide fragrant white flowers shaded crimson.

Gladioli are superb for their long display, from July to September, of upright sword-like leaves and spikes crowded with florets in a range of colours. The large-flowered hybrids rise to 60 cm–1·2 m (2–4 ft).

A really late-flowering bulbous plant is *Nerine bowdenii* with 10–15 cm (4–6 in) wide heads formed of up to eight pink flowers from September to November. It is only half-hardy and needs the protection of a warm wall facing south or west, and a covering of straw or bracken during winter.

Two cyclamen that delight gardens now are *Cyclamen hederifolium*, better known as *C. neapolitanum*, and *C. purpurascens*, better known as *C. europaeum. C. hederifolium* flowers from August to November with flowers ranging from mauve to pink, and *C. purpurascens* with rich carmine flowers from July to September. Both naturalize well in light woodland shade.

The autumn-flowering crocus *Crocus kotschyanus* is not spectacular, but makes a good underplanting for the August and September flowering shrub *Clerodendron trichotomum*. Its 7·5 cm (3 in) high rose-lilac flowers with deep orange blotches at their centres show off the scented star-like pink-white flowers of the clerodendron, borne in clusters 23 cm (9 in) wide. The clerodendron also has turquoise-blue berries.

One of the late-flowering joys of the herbaceous border is *Sedum* 'Autumn Joy'. During September its 13–20 cm (5–8 in) wide heads reveal pink flowers that during the following month deepen to orange-red and finally to a dark orange-brown. It grows to only 45–60 cm (1½–2 ft) and is ideal towards the front of the border, possibly near to a corner where it is even more apparent.

As this month draws to an end one of the great joys in the gardening year is the beautifully coloured leaves of many trees, and soon these will be very much in evidence.

The hardy shrubby perennial Perovskia atriplicifolia *develops a wispy but dominant display of violet-blue flowers amid finely-cut grey-green leaves during August and September. The leaves have a bonus of scent, resembling that of sage.*

**BORDER BRIGHTENERS
IN FLOWER
THIS MONTH**
◇

Adonis aestivalis
(pheasant's eye)

Ageratum houstonianum

Alonsoa warscewiczii
(mask flower)

Althaea rosea;
now *Alcea rosea*)

Alyssum maritimum;
now *Lobularia maritima*

Amaranthus caudatus
(love-lies-bleeding)

Amaranthus hypochondriacus
(prince's feather/pygmy
torch)

Antirrhinum majus
(snapdragon)

Arctotis × hybrida
(African daisy)

Begonia semperflorens

Bellis perennis
(daisy)

Calceolaria integrifolia,
syn. *C. rugosa*

Calendula officinalis
(pot marigold/English
marigold)

Callistephus chinensis
(China aster)

Centaurea cyanus
(cornflower)

Centaurea moschata
(sweet sultan)

Clarkia elegans

Clarkia pulchella

Convolvulus tricolor;
syn. *C. minor*

Cosmos bipinnatus

Dimorphotheca aurantiaca
(star of the veldt)

FLOWERS

♦ Continue to tie late-flowering herbaceous plants to their stakes.

♦ Remove dead flower heads from herbaceous plants.

♦ Continue to prune rambler roses (*see* page 132).

FRUIT

♦ Continue to pick apples as soon as the stalks part easily from the fruiting spur. The stalk should remain attached to the fruit.

♦ Pick pears as soon as they can be removed stalk-intact from the tree.

Right: Sedum × *'Autumn Joy' is an essential part of any herbaceous or mixed border. Initially the flower heads are pink when first opening in September. They become orange-red and by October are orange-brown.*

VEGETABLES

♦ Harvest summer spinach.
♦ Harvest globe artichokes while the scales are still tight.
♦ Blanch cardoons, wrapping light-proof material around them.

LAWNS

♦ Leatherjackets and chafer grubs can be a problem in autumn. To check for them place a wet sack on the lawn's surface in the evening. Any present will be seen beneath the sack in the morning. Use a insecticides to kill them.

**BORDER BRIGHTENERS
IN FLOWER
THIS MONTH**
◇

Eschscholzia californica
(Californian poppy)

Felicia bergeriana
(kingfisher daisy)

Gaillardia pulchella

Gilia lutea
(stardust)

Gypsophila elegans

Helianthus annuus
(sunflower)

Heliotropium × hybridum
(cherry pie)

Hibiscus trionum
(flower-of-an-hour)

Iberis umbellata
(candytuft)

Lavatera trimestris

Lobelia erinus

Nicotiana alata
(tobacco plant)

Petunia × hybrida

Reseda odorata
(mignonette)

Rudbeckia hirta
(black-eyed Susan)

Salvia patens

Salvia splendens

Scabiosa atropurpurea
(sweet scabious)

Tagetes erecta
(African marigold)

Tagetes patula
(French marigold)

Tagetes tenuifolia
(marigold)

Thunbergia alata
(black-eyed Susan)

Verbena × hybrida

Zinnia elegans
◇

Left: Filipendula purpurea *is an elegant hardy herbaceous perennial sometimes still listed as* Spiraea palmata. *During mid to late summer it reveals carmine-rose flowers amid large-lobed leaves.*

GREENHOUSES

♦ Cyclamen sown the previous year will now be producing early flowers. Pick these off, removing the stems as well as the flowers. If stems, or pieces of them, are left it encourages diseases. The removal of these early flowers helps the plant to build up a better display later on.

♦ Disbud chrysanthemums unless they are being grown as spray types.

♦ Take cuttings of heliotrope. They root rapidly in a propagating frame.

♦ Prick out cyclamen sown in August.

♦ Remove shading from the glass if the weather is becoming dull. However, during Indian summers it is best left in place until the end of this month.

♦ Winter- and spring-flowering plants can be brought indoors from cold frames. Give them a cool position in slight shade.

♦ Water all plants, taking care that the compost is not continually soaked with water.

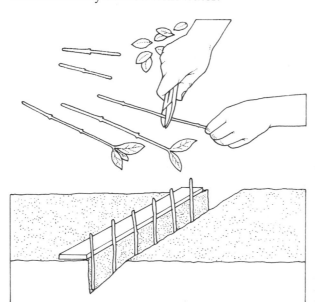

Many shrubs and soft fruits can be increased from hardwood cuttings in autumn. They root quite well when inserted in a trench in a sheltered part of the garden. Firm the soil well around them.

IN FLOWER THIS MONTH

YELLOW AND ORANGE

SHRUBS
COLUTEA ARBORESCENS, GENISTA TINCTORIA 'Royal Gold', *HYPERICUM CALYCINUM*: see June
HYPERICUM PATULUM 'Hidcote': see July
POTENTILLA FRUTICOSA 'Farreri': see May
SPARTIUM JUNCEUM: see June

CLIMBERS
CLEMATIS ORIENTALIS, C. TANGUTICA: see August

Left: Limonium sinuatum 'Blue River' is a perennial grown as a half-hardy annual. From late July to September it reveals strongly-coloured flowers. This species was previously known as Statice sinuata.

FLOWERS

♦ Cut down herbaceous plants that have flowered and look a mess. In cold areas leave the old stems on the plants to provide a small degree of protection from severe frost.
♦ Remove bedding plants that have finished flowering and prepare the soil for spring-flowering bedding plants and bulbs. Fork the soil and apply a dressing of bonemeal.
♦ Lift gladioli corms together with the stems. If the foliage and stems have withered they can be easily removed from the corms. If not, hang them up for a few weeks in a garden shed until the corms can be removed easily.

FRUIT

♦ Cut out all raspberry canes that bore fruits earlier in the year. Cut them out at soil-level and space out the new canes formed during the year which will bear fruits the following season.

VEGETABLES

♦ Water summer lettuces if the weather is dry.
♦ Place cloches over outdoor tomato plants to help ripen the last fruits. First cut the plants from their stakes and lay them along the row.
♦ Thin kohlrabi to 15 cm (6 in) apart.
♦ Harvest onions, first putting a garden fork under them to break the roots.
♦ Harvest cauliflowers.
♦ Harvest summer lettuce when ready.
♦ Plant spring cabbages 25–30 cm (10–12 in) apart in rows 30 cm (12 in) apart, dipping the young plants in calomel paste first.

Left above: The hardy Common Hydrangea, Hydrangea macrophylla, *seldom fails to create interest from July to September with its large flower heads.*

Left below: The hardy herbaceous perennial Echinacea purpurea, *the Purple Cone Flower, bears flowers from July to September.*

Above: Daffodil bulbs can be planted as soon as they are available, during August and September, and are best planted in irregular groups. The bulbs are graded according to the number of 'noses' or growing points they have. For example, a 'single-nosed' bulb has just one growing point and is unlikely to produce more than one flower. A 'double-nosed' type may produce two flowers, and a 'mother' bulb will have more than two growing points.

Left: Malus × robusta develops attractive fruits in autumn. Two excellent forms are 'Red Siberian' (red fruits) and 'Yellow Siberian' (yellow).

SEPTEMBER

BULBS IN FLOWER THIS MONTH

Acidanthera bicolor

Colchicum autumnale
(naked boys)

Colchicum speciosum

Crinum × powellii

Cyclamen purpurascens;
syn. *C. europaeum*

Cyclamen hederifolium;
syn. *C. neapolitanum*

Galtonia candicans;
syn. *Hyacinthus candicans*
(summer hyacinth)

Gladiolus – large-flowered
hybrids

Lilium auratum
(golden-rayed lily)

Lilium speciosum

Lilium tigrinum
(tiger lily)

Nerine bowdenii

◇

Right: The Chusan Palm,
Trachycarpus fortunei, *is
well worth growing in a
sheltered position in the
south or west. Its shiny fan-
like leaves always attract
attention. Its bark is
illustrated on page 90.*

IN FLOWER THIS MONTH

RED AND PINK

SHRUBS

ERICA CINEREA 'C. D. Eason', *E. VAGANS* 'Mrs. D. F. Maxwell': see July

CALLUNA VULGARIS 'County Wicklow', *C. V.* 'Darkness': see August

CALLUNA VULGARIS 'H. E. Beale'
H: 30–45 cm (12–18 in) S: 30–45 cm (12–18 in)
Evergreen with double pink flowers.

CALLUNA VULGARIS 'Peter Sparkes', *C. V.* 'Tib': see August

ESCALLONIA 'C. F. Ball', *E.* 'Donard Radiance', *E.* 'Donard Star', *E.* 'Peach Blossom', *E.* 'Slieve Donard': see June

FUCHSIA MAGELLANICA: see August

HEBE 'Great Orme', *H. SPECIOSA* 'La Seduisante': see July

HIBISCUS SYRIACUS 'Hamabo'
H: 1·8–2·4 m (6–8 ft) S: 1·2–1·8 m (4–6 ft)
Deciduous with three-lobed leaves and crimson-centred blush-white 7·5 cm (3 in) wide flowers. 'Woodbridge' has large single rose-pink flowers with carmine eyes.

HYDRANGEA MACROPHYLLA 'Hamburg': see July

INDIGOFERA GERARDIANA: see June

PHYGELIUS CAPENSIS: see July

POTENTILLA FRUTICOSA 'Red Ace': see June

CLIMBERS

CLEMATIS 'Ernest Markham', *C.* 'Ville de Lyon': see August

LAWNS

♦ New lawns can be created in late summer and early autumn from seed or turves (*see* pages 59 and 72).

GREENHOUSES

♦ Continue to pot up seedling cyclamen into small pots. Do not bury the corms, but leave them just resting on the surface.

♦ Pot up hyacinths and narcissi for flowering indoors at Christmas. After planting, plunge them outdoors under sand so that they develop strong root systems before being brought into heat later in the year and gently forced into flower.

♦ Continue to re-pot arum lilies.

♦ Sow suitable varieties of lettuces, carrots and radishes for maturing under cloches or cold frames.

♦ Complete the harvesting of melons and clear away the plants.

Left: Variegated hostas are superb value-for-money plants, creating colour and interest over a long period in a mixed or herbaceous border. Here, Hosta fortunei *'Obscura Marginata' brings colour right up to the frosts of autumn.*

FLOWERS

♦ Daffodils to be naturalized in grass can be planted now. Scatter the bulbs on the grass and plant them where they fall to produce a natural-looking arrangement.

♦ Protect late-flowering chrysanthemums with small 'hats' to keep water off the blooms.

♦ Cut off red hot poker heads when they have faded.

♦ Cut off and dry seed-heads from such plants as honesty, Chinese lanterns and poppies for decoration indoors during winter.

♦ Plant further bowls of forced bulbs for flowering indoors during winter. Put the planted bowls in a cool and dark position.

♦ Prepare the ground for the autumn-planting of herbaceous plants.

♦ Plant outdoor bulbs such as crocuses, muscari, daffodils, species narcissus, snowdrops and winter aconites.

FRUIT

♦ Plant peaches and nectarines. Nectarines are a variety of peach with smooth skin and a less hardy constitution. They are best grown as wall-trained trees, protected from cold winds.

VEGETABLES

♦ Tie up the leaves of endive and place a large pot over them to blanch the stems.

♦ Thin lettuce for cutting in spring to 75 mm (3 in) apart.

♦ Harvest kohlrabi when the roots are the size of tennis balls.

♦ As soon as crops are harvested remove all the remaining debris so that the soil's surface is bare. Rubbish left on the soil from crops encourages pests and diseases to linger and spread. Any material that is known to be contaminated with pests is best burned, rather than putting it on the compost heap.

Above: Herbaceous perennials can be divided in autumn or spring. Spring is the best time in extremely cold areas. Some clumps can be split up by hand, pulling the plant into several pieces. Others need to be prised apart with two garden forks, and it may be necessary to trim back some of the roots. When splitting up large clumps, discard the old central part, replanting only the younger pieces from around the outside.

Left: Acer cappadocicum is well known for its rich yellow leaves in autumn. Many other acers display rich autumn colouring.

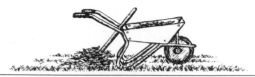

LAWNS

♦ Aeration is best tackled in autumn and early winter. Machines can be used to take out cores of soil, but a home gardener often has to rely on a garden fork, inserting it as far as possible into the soil. Hollow-tined foot-operated tools and other mechanical aerators make the job much easier. After forking the lawn brush off all rubbish. Then brush a mixture of sharp sand and fine compost into the holes.

♦ Electric-powered lawn rakes are ideal for removing moss and dead grasses from a lawn. It is amazing how much material they do remove – all to the lawn's advantage. In fact, when the amount of material removed by a powered machine is compared to that when using a hand rake there is no comparison. And such machines turn a laborious job into one of great satisfaction and pleasure.

GREENHOUSES

♦ Pick all tomatoes and clear away the plants. Also remove all supporting wires and canes, clean them and store until next year.

♦ Pick all cucumbers and clear away the plants.

♦ Carefully water all plants started into growth.

♦ Many greenhouse plants are taken indoors to flower during winter and spring months. Do not place them on cold window-sills, especially where curtains could knock off flowers.

♦ Take large exhibition chrysanthemums into the greenhouse for subsequent flowering.

♦ Cyclamen kept in frames during summer will now have to be placed in a greenhouse, as they may be damaged by early frost.

♦ Tuberous-rooted begonias and gloxinias that have flowered can be placed on their sides in a cool and dry part of the greenhouse.

♦ Pots of achimenes can be treated in the same manner as gloxinias and tuberous-rooted begonias.

♦ Continue to pot up bulbs for flowering during winter and early spring indoors. After being potted plunge the pots under sand for a few weeks so that they build up a strong root system.

IN FLOWER THIS MONTH

WHITE AND CREAM

TREE

SOPHORA JAPONICA (Japanese pagoda tree)
H: 3·5–4·5 m (12–15 ft) S: 3–4·5 m (10–15 ft)
Slow-growing deciduous, with pea-like creamy-white flowers in clusters 15–25 cm (6–10 in) long.

SHRUBS

ABELIA CHINENSIS: see July

ARALIA ELATA, CALLUNA VULGARIS 'Alba Plena', *C. v.*
'Beoley Gold', *C. v.* 'Gold Haze', *C. v.* 'Serlei',
CLETHRA ALNIFOLIA: see August

CONVOLVULUS CNEORUM, DABOECIA CANTABRICA
'Alba': see June

ERICA VAGANS 'Lyonesse', *ESCALLONIA × IVEYI,*
HIBISCUS SYRIACUS 'Dorothy Crane', *HYDRANGEA*
MACROPHYLLA 'Madame E. Mouillière', *H.*
PANICULATA: see August

MAGNOLIA GRANDIFLORA: see July

MYRTUS COMMUNIS: see August

OLEARIA × HAASTII, POTENTILLA ARBUSCULA
'Abbotswood', *ROMNEYA COULTERI:* see July

CLIMBERS

CLEMATIS FLAMMULA: see August

LONICERA JAPONICA 'Halliana': see June

POLYGONUM BALDSCHUANICUM: see July

Far left: Solidago 'Leraft' creates a display of bright golden-yellow flowers during August and September. Like many other hybrid solidagos it is ideal for late colour in a mixed or herbaceous border.

Below: Cannas are ideal for a mixed border, and can be seen here with antirrhinums and Goat's Rue, Galega officinalis.

FLOWERS

FRUIT

Below: Sedum spectabile *'Carmen' creates bright carmine flower heads, 7·5–13 cm (3–5 in) wide, during September and October.*

♦ If winter-flowering pansies have started to develop flowers pick them off to encourage stronger and larger flowers later in the season.

♦ Protect choice alpines from excessive wet weather with small panes of glass.

♦ Continue to remove bedding plants that have finished flowering and prepare the site for spring bedding plants.

♦ Plant blackberries and hybrid berries any time from now until late winter. Set the plants 1·8–3 m (6–10 ft) apart depending on the vigour of the variety. After planting cut the canes down to within 23 cm (9 in) of soil level. Supporting wires are needed at 30 cm (1 ft), 75 cm (30 in) and 1·5 m (5 ft) above the soil. The wires are strained between strong supports at either end of the row.

IN FLOWER THIS MONTH

BLUE AND MAUVE

SHRUBS

CARYOPTERIS × CLANDONENSIS: see August

CEANOTHUS 'Gloire de Versailles': see June

CEANOTHUS 'Topaz', CERATOSTIGMA
WILLMOTTIANUM: see July

DABOECIA CANTABRICA 'Atropurpurea': see June

HEBE 'Autumn Glory': see July

HEBE × FRANCISCANA 'Blue Gem': see June

HIBISCUS SYRIACUS 'Blue Bird': see August

LAVANDULA SPICA, L. 'Hidcote': see July

CLIMBERS

CLEMATIS 'Elsa Spath', C. 'Gipsy Queen': see July

CLEMATIS 'Jackmanii Superba': see June

CLEMATIS 'Mrs. Cholmondeley': see May

SOLANUM CRISPUM: see July

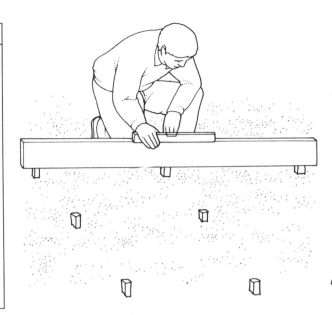

*Left: When levelling large
areas of garden the best way
is to put stout pegs in the
soil and to rest a straight-
edged board across them in
several directions. By placing
a spirit-level on top of the
board variations in level can
be seen and measured.*

*Below: The evergreen shrub
Hebe 'Autumn Glory'
develops spikes of violet-blue
flowers over a long period,
from July to autumn.*

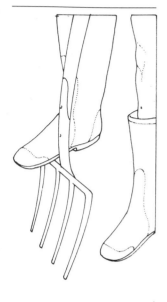

VEGETABLES

♦ Pick Brussels sprouts as soon as the buttons are firm. Pick only those that are ready on each plant, leaving the others to mature.

♦ Harvest haricot beans when the pods turn yellow.

♦ Asparagus crowns planted in April will have produced several stems bearing fern-like foliage. Cut this to soil-level and fork soil from between the rows on to the asparagus beds to leave a ridge.

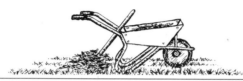

LAWNS

♦ Bumps and depressions in the lawn can be eradicated by slicing back the turf and either adding or removing soil.

♦ Repair broken lawn edges. Cut out a rectangular section and reverse the broken part so that it faces inwards.

♦ Garden swings that, together with young feet, have created bare patches on the lawn can be packed up for the winter and the area mentally recorded for re-sowing in spring.

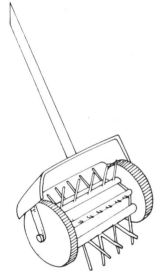

Above: Autumn is the time for aerating a lawn. A small area can be pierced by the prongs of a fork, but for large lawns the best way is with a mechanical aerator.

GREENHOUSES

♦ Freesias that have been in the cold frame are now taken into the greenhouse. Water the compost and give them plenty of light and air.

♦ Perpetual-flowering carnations that have been in a garden frame can also be taken into the greenhouse. They grow best in a dry, light and airy atmosphere.

♦ Pot up small bulbs such as crocuses, scillas and chionodoxas for early spring colour. Do not subject them to high temperatures.

♦ Heating may be necessary on cold, damp nights.

♦ Check that ventilators close properly. During summer wooden types often warp slightly in the strong sunlight and humid atmosphere in the greenhouse.

ROCK PLANTS IN FLOWER THIS MONTH
◇

Achillea tomentosa
(woolly achillea)

Androsace lanuginosa
(Himalayan androsace)

Campanula cochleariifolia
(fairy thimbles)

Campanula portenschlagiana;
syn. *C. muralis*

Campanula poscharskyana

Dianthus deltoides
(maiden pink)

Dimorphotheca barberiae
'Compacta'

Gentiana sino-ornata

Geranium cinereum

Geranium subcaulescens

Hypericum polyphyllum
'Sulphureum'

Lithospermum diffusum;
now *Lithodora diffusa*

Silene schafta
◇

Left: The graceful and hardy perennial ornamental grass Miscanthus sinensis *'Silver Feather' develops large and feathery heads that adorn borders. The flower heads can also be used for winter decoration indoors.*

◇ OCTOBER ◇

The fascination of plants and gardening is that no two seasons are ever exactly the same. For instance, leaves that one year change colour in early October will another year still be green in early November. But on average it is by the end of this month that at least some colour can be expected. *Prunus sargentii* is one of the first trees to produce autumn colouring with crimson and orange leaves, but it is the acers that are perhaps the best-known trees for their colourful leaves. *Acer campestre* (hedge maple) from Europe has leaves tinted red in spring, mid-green in summer and crimson in autumn. It is a large tree, reaching 9 m (30 ft) after 20 or so years and ultimately 10·5 m (35 ft) or more.

Acer cappodocicum is, ultimately, another large tree, with five- or seven-lobed green leaves that turn rich yellow in autumn. *Acer platanoides* (Norway maple) also has yellow leaves in autumn. *Acer japonicum* is a small tree with several forms that assume superb colouring in autumn. The form 'Aureum' has yellow leaves turning rich crimson, 'Vitifolium' rich crimson, and 'Aconitifolium' crimson.

Cercidiphyllum japonicum (Katsura tree) from Japan has rounded grey-green leaves which turn red and yellow. Perhaps the best-known autumn-colouring tree is *Liquidambar styraciflua* (sweet gum) from North America. The deeply lobed dark green leaves turn scarlet and orange. It is ideal as a specimen tree on a lawn in a large garden, when the tree's outline can be admired from a distance.

A modestly sized shrub at up to 2·4 m (8 ft) high, *Fothergilla monticola*, has sweetly scented flowers formed mainly of creamy-white stamens clustered at the tips of shoots like bright pipe cleaners during May before the leaves appear. During autumn the leaves assume rich red and orange-yellow tints. The coloured leaves blend well with an underplanting of autumn-flower crocuses or the mauve to pink-flowered *Cyclamen hederifolium*.

Few shrubs are as long flowering as the shrubby *Potentilla fruticosa* with flowers from May to August, but if yellow flowers into autumn are your fancy then try the June to October flowering *P. arbuscula*, frequently known as *P. fruticosa arbuscula*.

A spectacular late-flowering shrubby herbaceous perennial is *Ceratostigma plumbaginoides*. It rises to 30 cm (1 ft), produces small leaves that take on reddish tints in autumn and clusters of blue flowers from July to November. Few other plants have such outstanding qualities. Better known are *Aster novi-belgii* and *A. novae-angliae* (Michaelmas daisies) flowering on Michaelmas, the 29 September and a significant feast in the agricultural calendar. As well as being the feast in honour of archangel Michael, and instituted as far back as A.D. 487, it was the day on which wages for agricultural workers were reviewed. These daisies are in flower well into October on the near forgotten Old Michaelmas Day, 10 October.

If your eye likes contrasts in the garden then try the 50 cm (20 in) high *Kniphofia galpinii* (torch lily) with soft orange-yellow poker-like flower heads during September and October. They look especially fine against the beautiful *Cotinus coggygria* 'Foliis Purpureis' (smoke tree) with plum-purple rounded to pear-shaped leaves that in autumn assume soft red tints before falling.

If the weather is kind dahlias will still be creating a spectacular display in a wide range of colours and shapes. Each year many new varieties enter dahlia catalogues, while others fall out of commerce. There are, however, some that have been firm favourites for many years and if you are in doubt about the varieties to grow make these your first choices.

As this month draws to an end there will be masses of fruits ripening and changing colours, mainly on flowering crabs, sorbus, viburnum, euonymus and crataegus. Most of these will be dominating the garden with colour during November, and some into midwinter.

Apple trees will now be burgeoned with fruit that needs to be picked. As soon as each apple, together with its stalk, parts easily from the fruit spur it can be picked. Here, 'Spartan' is grown as a cordon, which allows it to be planted in a small garden.

FLOWERS

♦ Complete pruning rambler roses (*see* page 132).
♦ Cut down the stems of outdoor chrysanthemums that have flowered to 15 cm (6 in) of soil-level, fork up the roots and pack them in boxes. Store them in a cool, frost-proof place during winter.
♦ Complete the planting of spring bedding plants such as wallflowers, forget-me-nots and polyanthus.

FRUIT

♦ Mulch between strawberry rows with well-rotted compost or manure. Lightly hoe the soil first to remove all weeds.
♦ Plant blackcurrants between now and early spring. Set the plants 1·5–1·8 m (5–6 ft) apart in soil well prepared with manure and compost. Immediately after planting cut all shoots to within an inch or two of soil level.

VEGETABLES

♦ Harvest summer lettuce.
♦ Dig up chicory when the leaves are dying, cut off the roots and store them in a cool position in boxes of sand in a frost-proof shed.
♦ Harvest globe artichokes when the scales are still closed.
♦ Established asparagus beds should have their stems and foliage cut down to soil-level, and all the debris removed.

IN FLOWER THIS MONTH
YELLOW AND ORANGE

SHRUBS
HYPERICUM CALYCINUM: see June
HYPERICUM PATULUM 'Hidcote': see July
POTENTILLA FRUTICOSA 'Farreri': see May

CLIMBERS
CLEMATIS ORIENTALIS, C. TANGUTICA: see August

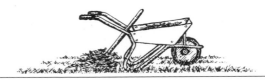

LAWNS

♦ Aerate the lawn if you have not already done so. Use either a garden fork or a hollow-tined lawn aerator. Brush off all rubbish before brushing in a mixture of sharp sand and compost.
♦ Electric-powered lawn rakes make easy work of removing dead moss and old grasses.
♦ Use a bulb-planter to plant naturalized bulbs in the lawn. Set them at the edges of the lawn and mark their positions with canes and string.

GREENHOUSES

♦ Chrysanthemums still outside must be brought into a greenhouse before they are damaged by frost.
♦ Ventilate the greenhouse whenever possible as stagnant conditions encourage diseases.
♦ Water plants carefully to avoid totally saturating the compost. This is vital at this time of the year.
♦ Arum lilies growing strongly will soon absorb plenty of water.
♦ Plants in frames must be watered carefully, and the frames covered during cold nights. Old sacking and hessian helps to keep out frost.
♦ Place gloxinias and tuberous begonias that have finished flowering under the greenhouse benching, in a dry and cool but frost-proof position.
♦ Scrub off all shading from the outside of the greenhouse. Also, take down and store any removable roller blinds.

IN FLOWER THIS MONTH

BLUE AND MAUVE

SHRUBS
CARYOPTERIS × CLANDONENSIS: see August
CEANOTHUS 'Gloire de Versailles', *C.* 'Topaz': see June
CERATOSTIGMA WILLMOTTIANUM: see July
DABOECIA CANTABRICA 'Atropurpurea': see June
HEBE 'Autumn Glory': see July
HIBISCUS SYRIACUS 'Blue Bird': see August

CLIMBERS
SOLANUM CRISPUM: see July

BORDER BRIGHTENERS IN FLOWER THIS MONTH
◇

Alonsoa warscewiczii (mask flower)

Amaranthus caudatus (love-lies-bleeding)

Antirrhinum majus (snapdragon)

Gaillardia pulchella

Rudbeckia hirta (black-eyed Susan)

Tagetes erecta (African marigold)
◇

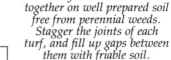

Above: When laying turf, always set them close together on well prepared soil free from perennial weeds. Stagger the joints of each turf, and fill up gaps between them with friable soil.

Left: Cercidiphyllum japonicum *displays slightly pendulous branches bearing bright green leaves. In autumn these assume red and yellow tints before falling.*

FLOWERS

♦ Half-ripe shrub cuttings taken in late summer will now have produced roots. Pot them up individually into small pots and replace in a cold frame during winter.

♦ Remove all stakes and supports not needed. Clean them and store for the winter.

FRUIT

♦ Raspberry canes can be planted from now until early spring. Prepare the ground thoroughly, incorporating plenty of well-rotted manure or compost. This is best done by taking out a trench 75 cm (30 in) wide and forking the compost into its base, then replacing the top-soil.

VEGETABLES

♦ Plant spring cabbages 25–30 cm (10–12 in) apart in rows 30 cm (12 in) apart. First dip the young plants in calomel dust.

♦ Harvest garden peas.

♦ Lift trench celery.

♦ Harvest winter cabbage as they mature.

♦ Sow lettuce 12 mm ($\frac{1}{2}$ in) deep and thinly under cloches.

LAWNS

♦ Bad drainage, noticeable during the previous autumn and winter, can be corrected now by installing drains. Tile drains are best, but expensive. Drains formed of rubble are cheaper but less effective as a long-term solution. Set them in a herring-bone fashion, sloping down to an outlet or soakaway. If it is a soakaway it should be a large hole filled with rubble.

GREENHOUSES

♦ Azaleas still outside in a cold frame must be taken indoors now.

♦ Check cyclamen plants for any sign of disease. Decaying flowers must be picked off immediately, together with the flower's stem.

♦ Do not heat the greenhouse excessively. Provide slight heat that will keep the atmosphere dry. Feed cyclamen plants with a diluted feed every two weeks.

IN FLOWER THIS MONTH

RED AND PINK

SHRUBS

ERICA VAGANS 'Mrs. D. F. Maxwell': see July

CALLUNA VULGARIS 'H. E. Beale': see September

CALLUNA VULGARIS 'Peter Sparkes', *C. V.* 'Tib',
FUCHSIA MAGELLANICA: see August

HEBE 'Great Orme', *H. SPECIOSA* 'La Seduisante': see July

HIBISCUS SYRIACUS 'Hamabo': see August

INDIGOFERA GERARDIANA: see June

CLIMBERS

CLEMATIS 'Ernest Markham', *C.* 'Ville de Lyon': see August

Far left above: Blueberry 'Colville', a variety of the north American high-bush blueberry (Vaccinium Corymbosum) grows best in moist, peaty and acid soil. Blueberries are excellent for pie-fillings and jams, and ripen during late summer and autumn.

Far left below: Plums are ready for picking from mid-summer to mid-autumn. Cooking plums are best picked when under-ripe, while dessert varieties when fully coloured just before full maturity. Plums need to be eaten, bottled or made into jam soon after being picked. The variety illustrated here is Edwards, but the most widely grown one is Victoria, a double-purpose cooking and dessert variety.

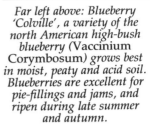

Left: Autumn is the time to rake out dead grasses from the lawn. Powered lawn rakes are available and make large lawns much easier to tackle.

ROCK PLANTS IN FLOWER THIS MONTH

◇

Androsace lanuginosa (Himalayan androsace)

Gentiana sino-ornata

Geranium cinereum

Geranium subcaulescens

Lithospermum diffusum; now Lithodora diffusa

Silene schafta

◇

FLOWERS

♦ Lift dahlias as soon as their tops have been damaged by frost. Cut the stems off at 10–13 cm (4–5 in) above soil-level. Dig up the tubers carefully and place them upside down in boxes to dry out. Place in a frost-proof position. Ensure that each tuber has been correctly labelled.

FRUIT

♦ Plant red and white currants from now until early spring. Set the plants 1·5 m (5 ft) apart. When grown as cordons set them 38 cm (15 in) apart.
♦ Increase blackcurrants by taking 20 cm (8 in) long cuttings from the current season's shoots and inserting them 15 cm (6 in) deep in a nursery bed.

Right: Parrotia persica *is a slow-growing and wide-spreading deciduous tree with mid-green leaves. In autumn they assume rich amber, gold and crimson tints.*

VEGETABLES

♦ Harvest kohlrabi roots when the size of tennis balls.

♦ Harvest parsnips.

♦ Winter spinach can be produced by placing cloches over late sowings of spinach. Place sheets of glass over the ends.

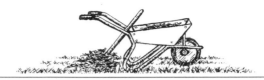

LAWNS

♦ For new lawns dig the soil thoroughly to a spade's depth and remove all perennial weeds. Leave the surface with large lumps of soil exposed to the action of winter weather. By spring this will have been broken down to a fine tilth. Prepare an area several yards larger than you intend to form into a lawn to allow the edges to become well established before being cut back.

GREENHOUSES

♦ Pot up winter-flowering houseplants into larger pots if they become pot-bound.

♦ Ventilate the greenhouse carefully to avoid cold draughts.

♦ Keep the atmosphere dry to minimize the risk of diseases. If puddles form in the base of the greenhouse, use a cane to make holes for draining.

Below: In autumn the vegetable garden starts to look bare, but Brussels Sprouts are still waiting to be picked. As soon as the buttons on the stems are firm, pick them. Start at the bottom of the stem and work upwards as they become ready to pick.

**BULBS IN FLOWER
THIS MONTH**

Colchicum autumnale
(naked boys)

Colchicum speciosum

Cyclamen hederifolium;
syn. *C. neapolitanum*

Nerine bowdenii

◇

FLOWERS

♦ Clean up herbaceous borders.
♦ Clean up garden ponds, removing all dead plants as well as leaves that have fallen in it during autumn. If there are still large numbers of leaves to fall – possibly into the pond – place a net over the pool.

LAWNS

♦ Sweep away leaves as soon as they fall. If left they soon create a mess when worms try to bury them. Sweep the leaves into a heap and use two boards to collect and lift the leaves into a barrow.
♦ Herbaceous and bedding plants that have fallen on to the lawn should be cut back to prevent lawn edges becoming damaged. Lawn edges covered with plants encourage slugs.

GREENHOUSES

♦ Water chrysanthemums as they become dry. If they are in very large clay pots knock the pot with a cotton reel spiked on a bamboo cane: if it sounds hollow, the plant needs watering, but if there is a dull, solid sound it does not.
♦ Keep water off the foliage of all plants, and if possible water in the morning so that any splashes can dry before night-fall.
♦ It is a good idea to put plants on shelves high up in the roof of the greenhouse, so that they have the maximum amount of light. However, such places are often the coldest parts of a greenhouse and plants there may be damaged by frost.
♦ If one side of your greenhouse is subjected to very cold north and east winds place a sheet of clear polythene over it. Also, check that all ventilators and the door fit their frames.
♦ In exposed areas, long-term protection can be achieved by planting a row of conifers on the north and east side of the greenhouse, but not too close.

Far right: The Hare's Tail Grass, Lagurus ovatus, *creates interest in mixed and herbaceous borders from June to autumn. It displays fluffy white heads on slender stems.*

FRUIT

♦ Fruited blackberry and hybrid berry canes can be cut back at soil-level. Tie in and spread out the young canes made during the current season.
♦ Increase both red and white currants by taking 30 cm (1 ft) long cuttings. Remove all but the top three or four buds and insert the cuttings 15 cm (6 in) deep in a nursery bed. Gooseberries can be increased in the same way.

VEGETABLES

♦ Thin lettuces sown under cloches earlier in the month to 7·5–10 cm (3–4 in) apart.

IN FLOWER THIS MONTH

WHITE AND CREAM

SHRUBS

ABELIA CHINENSIS: see July

ARBUTUS UNEDO
H: 4·5–5·4 m (15–18 ft) S: 3–3·5 m (10–12 ft)
Evergreen with peeling and shredding bark, ivory-coloured pendent flowers and orange-red strawberry-like fruits.

CALLUNA VULGARIS 'Alba Plena', *C. v.* 'Serlei': see August

DABOECIA CANTABRICA 'Alba': see June

ERICA VAGANS 'Lyonesse': see August

ELAEAGNUS × EBBINGEI
H: 3–4·5 m (10–15 ft) S: 2·7–3·5 m (9–12 ft)
Fast-growing evergreen with small, fragrant, silvery flowers on mature plants.

ELAEAGNUS MACROPHYLLA
H: 1·8–3 m (6–10 ft) S: 1·8–3 m (6–10 ft)
Spreading evergreen with small, silvery fragrant flowers.

ELAEAGNUS PUNGENS 'Maculata'
H: 2·4–3·5 m (8–12 ft) S: 2·4–3 m (8–10 ft)
Slow-growing evergreen with leathery glossy green leaves splashed gold and silvery flowers.

HIBISCUS SYRIACUS 'Dorothy Crane': see August

OSMANTHUS HETEROPHYLLUS
H: 1·8–3 m (6–10 ft) S: 1·8–2·4 m (6–8 ft)
Rounded evergreen with small white, scented, flowers in clusters.

CLIMBERS

LONICERA JAPONICA 'Halliana': see June
POLYGONUM BALDSCHUANICUM: see July

◇ NOVEMBER ◇

Leaves ablaze with autumn tints are still appearing, on climbers as well as trees and shrubs. *Parthenocissus quinquefolia* (true Virginia creeper) is one of the most vigorous of all climbers, growing up to 20 m (65 ft) or so high, and best when climbing in a tall tree: it is too strong-growing for the average house wall. During autumn its three or five coarsely serrated leaflets turn brilliant orange and scarlet. *Parthenocissus tricuspidata* (Boston ivy) is not quite so vigorous and ideal for covering old walls where it produces rich crimson and scarlet leaves in autumn. It is often erroneously called the Virginia creeper, but it is *P. inserta* that is the common Virginia creeper. It can be distinguished from the true creeper by its non-adhesive tendrils: the true version is self-clinging with adhesive discs.

The beautiful *P. henryana* (Chinese Virginia creeper) is better suited to small areas, although even this species often reaches 7·5 m (25 ft). It is self-clinging, with leaves formed of three to five leaflets with silvery-white lines along the main veins. In autumn the leaves turn from green to brilliant red.

The grape family, *Vitis*, produces a wealth of colourful leaves in autumn, perhaps the best-known one being *V. coignetiae* (Japanese crimson glory vine). However, it grows up to 26 m (85 ft) and is too vigorous for most houses. Smaller types are *V. labrusca* (fox grape) with growth of 4·5–6 m (15–20 ft) and brown-red leaves in autumn, and *V. vinifera* 'Purpurea' (Teinturier grape) with claret-red leaves throughout summer, changing to rich purple in autumn.

Many trees and shrubs still have beautiful berries in November and occasionally into the New Year. These include several members of the hawthorn family, *Crataegus × grignonensis* with long-lasting large red berries, and *C. prunifolia* displaying round, rich red fruits. Flowering crabs are also to the fore with attractive fruits. *Malus* 'Golden Hornet', well suited to moderately sized gardens with its 4·5–5·4 m (15–18 ft) height after 20 or so years, bears gloriously bright yellow fruits that remain long after the leaves have fallen. *M.* 'Red Sentinel', certainly small garden-sized at 3–4·5 m (10–15 ft) high, produces large cardinal-red fruits that often persist through to March. *M.* 'Yellow Siberian', at about the same height, creates a mass of bright yellow cherry-like fruits that persist well into winter.

A noted late-berrying member of the *Sorbus* genus is *S. hupehensis* with bunches of white berries mainly in August and September but often remaining into early winter. Another berrying member of the genus *Rosaceae* is *Cotoneaster*. Here again there are several superb late-berrying types, such as *C. distichus* with large bright scarlet berries until spring, *C. lacteus* with dense clusters of red berries well into winter, and *C. × watereri* with red round berries lasting into winter.

The densely branched deciduous *Corylus avellana* 'Contorta' (Harry Lauder's walking stick), although at its best in late winter when bearing yellow male catkins, is nevertheless attractive during early winter with its curled and twisted twigs. Also called the corkscrew hazel, it was discovered in a hedgerow in Gloucestershire in about 1863.

This is the time of year when evergreen shrubs are especially treasured, with year through attractive foliage. Those with variegations are particularly valuable, such as *Elaeagnus pungens* 'Maculata' with leaves splashed with gold, *Euonymus fortunei* 'Emerald 'n Gold' with golden variegated leaves, *E. fortunei* 'Silver Queen' displaying creamy-white and cream variegations, and the many variegated forms of holly. These include *Ilex × altaclarensis* 'Golden King' with golden-edged wide leaves, *I. aquifolium* 'Golden Queen' with crinkled and spiny leaves edged bright yellow, and *I. aquifolium* 'Silver Queen' with silver-edged leaves.

Variegated wall fillers such as the ivies are also ideal for winter colour. One of the best is a form of the Persian ivy, *Hedera colchica* 'Variegata' with pale green and creamy-yellow leaves. *H. canariensis* 'Gloire de Marengo' (also known as *H. c.* 'Variegata') displays leaves with silver-grey to white edges.

Brilliantly-coloured leaves in autumn are a bonus feature in any garden. Here, the True Virginia Creeper, Parthenocissus quinquefolia *(previously known as* Vitis hederacea*) created a stunning display of three or five-lobed brilliant crimson leaves.*

FLOWERS

♦ Check that bulbs being forced for flowering indoors are not becoming dry. When the shoots are about 25 mm (1 in) high the bowls can be moved into a cool position in the greenhouse or home. Do not place them in a high temperature.

♦ Where new borders are being prepared, dig the soil deeply and incorporate plenty of well-rotted compost or manure. Remove and burn all perennial weeds.

♦ Spring-flowering bedding plants that have not been planted in formal schemes can be set among shrubs to provide additional colour in spring.

FRUIT

♦ Plant gooseberries, 1·5 m (5 ft) apart, between now and late winter.

♦ Plant apples and pears between now and early spring, whenever the soil is not frozen or too wet. Stake the tree at the same time, taking care not to damage the roots. Select dwarf rootstocks for the small garden, creating a small, early-fruiting tree that can be picked easily.

♦ Prune apple trees as soon as they are planted. Maiden trees are cut back to 50 cm (20 in) high; older trees that have developed sideshoots can have these cut back by one-half to two-thirds.

Below: Erica vagans *'Lyonesse', one of the Cornish Heaths, produces a mass of pure-white flowers from July to winter.*

VEGETABLES

♦ Cut globe artichokes down to soil-level and cover the roots with straw to protect them from severe frost.

♦ Lift trench celery.

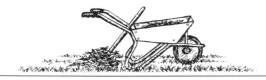

LAWNS

♦ Lawn-mowing is coming to an end in even the mildest of areas. After the last cut thoroughly clean the machine. Wash off all mud and grass, and cover all bright-metal parts with a thin layer of oil or grease.

GREENHOUSES

♦ Plants that are being rested need to be checked from time to time to ensure that their corms or tubers are not shrivelling through lack of moisture.

♦ Ventilate the greenhouse on fine days, but avoid draughts on the plants.

♦ Protect plants in cold frames by covering them with sacking or hessian on frosty nights.

♦ *Convallaria majalis* (lily of the valley) can be encouraged to flower early by potting up a few crowns in a 15 cm (6 in) pot. Use a loam-based compost with plenty of sharp sand added to it. Lightly cover the crowns with the compost and stand the pots in a cool position. Ensure that the compost does not dry out.

♦ Reduce the amount of water given to foliage plants. Just keep the compost damp.

IN FLOWER THIS MONTH

YELLOW AND ORANGE

SHRUBS
HAMAMELIS VIRGINIANA (common witch hazel)
H: 2·4–3 m (8–10 ft) S: 1·8–2·7 m (6–9 ft)
Spreading deciduous shrub or small tree with spider-like yellow flowers, 18–25 mm (¾–1 in) wide.
MAHONIA 'Charity': see January

Deciduous shrubs or trees sold as bare-rooted subjects can be planted during their dormant period, from late autumn to late winter. However, the soil must not be frozen or waterlogged. Dig out a hole large enough to accommodate the roots and fork over the bottom (top picture). Add a sprinkling of bonemeal. Use a straight stick to check that the old soil mark on the stem will be an inch or so below the surface when planted and firmed (bottom picture). Ensure that friable soil is worked between the roots and use your heel to firm the soil. A secure stake will be necessary until the plant is established.

FLOWERS

♦ Agapanthus in cold areas will need protection from severe frost. Cover the plants with straw.
♦ Shrubs and trees in large tubs may become too wet in high rainfall areas. Therefore, tie a piece of plastic sheeting over the soil.
♦ Periodically check the soil to ensure that it is not too dry.
♦ Rake up all leaves and place on a compost heap for subsequent digging into the soil.

FRUIT

♦ Plant raspberry canes in soil already prepared (*see* page 158). Ensure the soil is firm and sprinkle a light dressing of bonemeal over the area. Set the canes 45 cm (18 in) apart. If two rows are to be planted set them 1·8 m (6 ft) apart. Plant the canes 7·5 cm (3 in) deep, thoroughly firming the soil over them. Wires spaced 75 cm (30 in) and 1·3 m (4 ft 6 in) high and secured to posts are needed for support.

VEGETABLES

♦ Plant chicory roots in large pots containing sand, water and place in a dark position at 7°C/45°F or slightly higher.
♦ Harvest leeks. Trim off roots and excessive leaves.

LAWNS

♦ Check the lawn for firework debris from Guy Fawkes festivities. Long pieces of wood attached to rockets soon become embedded in wet lawns and may during early spring damage mowing machines.

GREENHOUSES

♦ Successful greenhouse gardening in winter very much depends on carefully watering the plants. If you are undecided as to whether a plant needs water, err on the side of keeping the compost dry rather than flooding it with water.

♦ Pots of bulbs that have been plunged outside under sand for six to eight weeks can now be brought into the light. At first they must not be given high temperatures. With hyacinths and other forced bulbs the flower buds must be well developed and apparent before the bulbs are forced.

♦ Azaleas and solanums need to be checked to ensure that the compost is not dry.

♦ Chrysanthemums that have finished flowering can be cut down to 30 cm (1 ft) above the pot and the old stems put on the rubbish heap for burning.

IN FLOWER THIS MONTH

RED AND PINK

TREES
PRUNUS SUBHIRTELLA 'Autumnalis Rosea'
H: 6–7·5 m (20–25 ft) S: 6–7·5 m (20–25 ft)
Deciduous cherry tree with pink flowers.

SHRUBS
ERICA × DARLEYENSIS 'Jack H. Brummage',
E. HERBACEA 'Foxhollow', *E. H.* 'Myretoun Ruby',
E. H. 'Praecox Rubra', *E. H.* 'Ruby Glow', *E. H.*
'Vivellii', *E. H.* 'Winter Beauty': see January

Left: Raspberry canes need secure supports. Every year check that the straining posts at the ends of the rows are firmly placed, with three rows of wires stretched between them.

FLOWERS

♦ Plant bare-rooted deciduous shrubs and trees between now and early spring, whenever the soil is not too wet or frozen. Container-grown plants can be planted at any time when the soil is not too wet or frozen.

♦ Plant deciduous hedges from bare-rooted plants.

FRUIT

♦ Established apple trees can be pruned between now and late winter.

♦ Plant plums and gages between now and late winter whenever the soil is workable. Two- or three-year-old trees are best.

VEGETABLES

♦ Pick Brussels sprouts as soon as the buttons are firm.

♦ Harvest parsnips.

♦ Harvest kohlrabi when the roots are the size of a tennis ball.

IN FLOWER THIS MONTH
WHITE AND CREAM

SHRUBS
ARBUTUS UNEDO, ELAEAGNUS × EBBINGEI,
E. MACROPHYLLA, E. PUNGENS 'Maculata': see October

Left top: The purpose of pruning fruit trees is to shape them during their formative years, to maintain the tree's shape during later years, and to maintain a balance between growth and the production of fruits. Apples can be pruned at any time between the fall of their leaves and when the buds burst in spring.

Left: As well as being grown as bushes, gooseberries can be formed into standards. This variety is 'Leveller'.

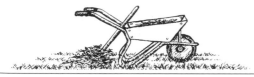

LAWNS

♦ When digging alongside lawns place a plank parallel to the lawn edge. This will help to protect the edge. Also, when running a wheelbarrow over the lawn use a series of planks. Any damage caused to the lawn now cannot be repaired until spring. Therefore, remove planks from the surface.

GREENHOUSES

♦ This month is notorious for damp weather and extra care must be taken to keep the atmosphere dry. Avoid splashing water on the floor.
♦ Bulbs recently brought into the greenhouse from a plunge bed in the garden can now be given a higher temperature.

Below: In many areas birds soon destroy growth and fruiting buds, which eventually may result in the death of the plant. The long-term solution to this problem is to construct a permanent cage in which to grow soft fruits and dwarf-sized trees.

FLOWERS

♦ Fork lightly between shrubs. Remove all weeds, especially perennial types that last from one season to another.

♦ Place cloches or small panes of glass over Christmas roses to keep the flowers free from mud splashes.

FRUIT

♦ Root pruning is nearly a job of the past, but if you have inherited an exceptionally vigorous apple tree now is the time to prune the roots.

♦ Store apples and pears that have been picked but are not yet ready for eating. Place in a cool, vermin-proof shed.

Right: The South African Nerine bowdenii *is a bulbous plant that creates colour from September to November. However, it does need a warm south or west-facing wall.*

VEGETABLES

♦ Harvest winter cabbage as they mature.
♦ Dig the vegetable plot as soon as crops have been cleared. Leave the surface 'rough' so that the action of frost and rain will break it down to a fine surface by spring. If the surface is left fine now, it will compact by spring.

LAWNS

♦ All lawn equipment such as edging irons and shears will need to be thoroughly cleaned, dried and given a coating of oil or grease. Hang up in a dry shed until needed next year.

GREENHOUSES

♦ Continue to transfer bulbs from their plunge bed in the garden to a cool temperature in the greenhouse, but not before they are showing shoots. If taken into a greenhouse too early, failure is certain when they are given a higher temperature.
♦ Check all plants that are being rested during the winter to ensure that the tubers or corms are not shrivelled through being too dry.

BULBS IN FLOWER THIS MONTH

◇

Cyclamen hederifolium
syn. *C. neapolitanum*

Nerine bowdenii

◇

Below: Cyclamen hederifolium, *better known as* Cyclamen neapolitanum, *creates a mass of flowers from August to November. It is ideal for planting on a bank, even under coniferous trees, where it soon produces a carpet of colour.*

◇ DECEMBER ◇

Few flowering plants, except the ever-reliable *Jasminum nudiflorum* (winter-flowering jasmine) and *Prunus subhirtella* 'Autumnalis' (autumn-flowering cherry) with its semi-double November to March white flowers are very much in evidence. However, several distinctive plants have coloured stems including *Cornus alba* (red-barked dogwood) with rich red stems during winter and *Cornus alba* 'Sibirica' (Westonbirt dogwood) with brilliant crimson stems. To produce the young stems each year the shrub must be severely pruned in late winter or early spring. Of a similar nature, *Salix alba* 'Vitellina' (golden willow) develops yellow stems, while *Salix alba* 'Chermesina' (scarlet willow) bears orange-scarlet shoots. All these plants look superb when positioned where they reflect in still water or even ice.

Cortaderia selloana, also known as *C. argentea* (pampas grass) is a useful perennial evergreen which produces large, fluffy, silvery heads on long stems. These look especially attractive when covered with a light fall of snow, although heavy falls tend to weigh down the heads and stems, flattening the display.

Conifers, and especially golden types, are a further treat during the dull season. There are many to choose from, including the dwarf and slow-growing types as well as the ones that create imposing focal points throughout summer as well as when covered by snow. Some of the large ones are *Chamaecyparis lawsoniana* 'Winston Churchill' which reaches 7·5 cm (25 ft) high and up to 2·4 m (8 ft) wide after 20 years, and *C. l.* 'Lutea' with a height of 9 m (30 ft) and width of 1·8 m (6 ft) after the same period. The foliage is bright golden-yellow. *C. l.* 'Stewartii' and *C. l.* 'Lanei' also display golden foliage. Dwarf types, suitable for even the smallest gardens, include *C. l.* 'Minima Aurea' with vertically arranged golden-yellow scale-like leaves and a total height after 10 years of 50 cm (20 in) and width of 40 cm (16 in), and *C. l.* 'Aurea Densa' with golden foliage and similar dimensions. *Cedrus deodara* 'Aurea' (golden Himalayan cedar) has a drooping nature with long golden needles and reaches 3 m (10 ft) high after 10 years with an ultimate height of 12 m (40 ft). However, for a golden semi-prostrate form, 75 cm (2½ ft) high and up to 1·5 m (5 ft) wide, select *Cedrus deodara* 'Golden Horizon'. Another somewhat fluffy-looking golden conifer is the thread-like *Chamaecyparis pisifera* 'Filifera Aurea'. It has a domed outline, 1 m (3½ ft) high and 1·2 m (4 ft) wide after 10 years, ultimately 4·5 m (15 ft) high. There are, therefore, golden conifers to suit gardens of all shapes and sizes.

Both frost and snow help to enrich the garden with colour contrasts. Conifers and other evergreens take on further attractive qualities during winter. The variegated elaeagnus and the grey-leaved *Senecio* 'Sunshine' look especially radiant when covered by frost. Light falls of snow also enrich them, but heavy layers soon break branches or flatten the plant. If possible, brush off gently before it freezes into position. Large conifers with a neat and symmetrical outline usually escape damage in all but the heaviest of falls, but those with several leading stems such as some junipers can be damaged when the weight bends them outwards.

As the year draws to a close there is often a sense of anticipation in the garden, looking forward to another season of freshness and the chance to create further colour as eventually spring arrives, with summer not far behind. It is a season of armchair gardening, planning and close anticipation of the year ahead.

December frosts and early winter snow bring extra interest to many evergreen shrubs. Here, the silver-grey leaved New Zealand shrub Senecio greyi *sparkles under a light covering of snow. During June and July it bears daisy-like yellow flowers.*

FLOWERS

◆ Cover tender-rooted herbaceous plants with straw or bracken to prevent frost damage.

◆ Check bulbs being forced for flowering indoors. If the compost is dry water it, and when the shoots are about 25 mm (1 in) high move the containers to a cool position indoors or in a greenhouse.

◆ Do not tread on the soil unnecessarily as it will quickly compact when wet.

◆ It is worthwhile visiting a botanical or National Trust Garden during winter to see the wide range of plants in flower and to make notes. There are trees, shrubs and bulbs that bring life to gardens in winter, and are an essential part of any balanced collection of plants for year through colour.

FRUIT

◆ Apply simazine to established strawberry beds to control weeds, following the manufacturer's directions.

◆ Check all posts and ties supporting trees. Ties that are constricting trunks must be removed immediately and replaced.

VEGETABLES

◆ Harvest leeks, trimming off the roots and excessive leaves.

◆ Harvest parsnips.

LAWNS

◆ Leaves may still be falling from trees and shrubs and blowing about on the lawn. Sweep them up as soon as possible along with any needles from conifers, which should be burnt.

GREENHOUSES

♦ Move flowering plants from the greenhouse indoors. Take care not to move them into a high temperature or draughts, where they may lose their flowers.

♦ Keep the glass on the outside of the greenhouse clean. By now it is probably smeared and dirty. Use soapy water to wash off the dirt, and then plenty of water to get rid of the soap. Remember to close all ventilators when doing this job. Also, avoid squirting water into the greenhouse through the overlapping panes of glass that do not fit perfectly.

♦ Keep the leaves of foliage plants clean so that they can use all the light available at this dull time of the year.

♦ Continue to water the plants carefully, not splashing any on the greenhouse floor.

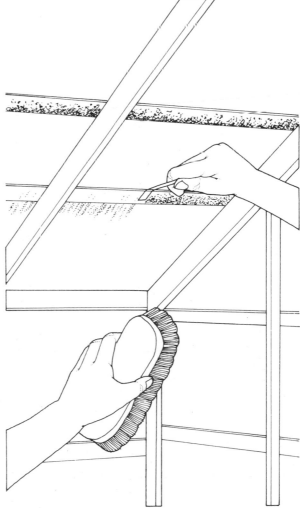

Left: Winter is the time to clean up the greenhouse. Use plenty of hot soapy water to wash away all dirt, especially from between the panes of glass. Remove all debris from the floor and soil area, and clean the staging.

FLOWERS

♦ Continue to prepare borders for planting in spring. Remove all perennial weeds and leave the surface rough so that a large area of soil is exposed to the action of frost and rain.
♦ When cutting evergreens for Christmas decorations, use a sharp pair of secateurs.

FRUIT

♦ Inspect all fruits in store and remove any showing signs of disease.
♦ Check all apple and pear trees for canker and treat when seen.

VEGETABLES

♦ Young shoots developed from chicory roots can be harvested now.
♦ Harvest turnips and swedes.
♦ Harvest kohlrabi when the roots are the size of a tennis ball.

LAWNS

♦ Brush lawns with a besom or rubber lawn rake to scatter worm casts and remove dead grass. However, if the surface is wet or frosty wait until the weather improves.

IN FLOWER THIS MONTH

RED AND PINK

SHRUBS
ERICA × DARLEYENSIS 'Arthur Johnson', *E. × D.* 'Jack H. Brummage', *E. HERBACEA* 'Foxhollow', *E. H.* 'Myretoun Ruby', *E. H.* 'Praecox Rubra', *E. H.* 'Ruby Glow', *E. H.* 'Vivellii', *E. H.* 'Winter Beauty': see January

GREENHOUSES

♦ Keep the compost in bowls of bulbs well watered.

♦ Carefully water cyclamen and remove all faded flowers.

♦ Avoid draughts from ventilators, and check that plants on high shelving are not being kept too cold.

♦ Check that you have boxes, pots and compost ready for seed sowing and clean plastic or metal labels to avoid the confusion of seeds sown without clear labelling.

Left: Grafting is a way to join two plants together. It is the usual method of increasing apples and pears. Crown or rind grafting is used to rejuvenate old fruit trees and consists of uniting a new variety (called a scion) with an established root system. Main stems and branches are cut back during the dormant season. Actual grafting does not take place until March. Several scions are inserted into each cut branch. The scions, about 10 cm (4 in) long, are cut at one end so that they slip into slits cut in the branch. The grafts are bound with raffia or plastic tape and sealed with grafting wax.

Far left: The range of variegated hollies is wide, and here can be seen Ilex × altaclarensis 'Lawsoniana'. It eventually develops into a large shrub or tree, up to 7·5 m (25 ft) high and 3·5 m (12 ft) wide.

Left: Conifers are a continual delight throughout the year, but during winter their qualities are especially valued. The Chinese Fir, Cunninghamia lanceolata, bears emerald green leaves that resemble large centipedes.

FLOWERS

FRUIT

♦ Ensure all leaves are cleaned away from delicate plants in rock gardens. If left they soon cause the plants to rot and decay.
♦ When newly planted trees and shrubs have been loosened by frost, re-firm them.

♦ Continue to plant raspberry canes if the soil is workable – not wet or frosted (*see* page 158).
♦ Late ripening apples still in store will need to be checked regularly to ensure they are in good condition.

VEGETABLES

♦ Harvest winter cabbage as they mature.
♦ Harvest leeks, cutting off the roots and excessive leaves.
♦ Harvest parsnips.
♦ Browse through seed catalogues.

LAWNS

♦ Fusarium can be prevented by stiffly brushing the grass and applying a fungicide if there is risk of snowfalls. Fusarium attacks grass trapped in a humid atmosphere under snow.

GREENHOUSES

♦ Cut down the last of the chrysanthemums to flower to about 30 cm (1 ft) above the pot. Label the pots and place them close together in a cool part of the greenhouse to make room for seed sowing.
♦ Thoroughly clean all the glass, scraping away as much dirt as possible from between the panes of glass.
♦ Propagation frames are well worth buying, as they enable a relatively small area to be warmed for sowing and germinating seeds. It also enables the rest of the greenhouse to be kept at a temperature that suits the rest of the plants.

IN FLOWER THIS MONTH
WHITE AND CREAM
SHRUBS
ERICA × *DARLEYENSIS* 'Silver Bells', *E. HERBACEA* 'Springwood White', *E. LUSITANICA*, *VIBURNUM* × *BODNANTENSE*, *V. TINUS:* see January

Left: The Winter-flowering Jasmine, Jasminum nudiflorum, *reveals bright yellow flowers from November to April. It is not a climber, but one of nature's leaners and therefore needs a supporting framework to which it can be tied.*

GLOSSARY

Activator A chemical product, normally granular or powdered, that speeds up the decay of material in a compost heap.

Adventitious A plant organ, usually a shoot or root, that appears in an unexpected position. For example, the tips of branches and shoots of willows or forsythias when touching the ground will develop roots.

Aerial root A root that appears above soil-level, such as an adventitious root on a stem.

Alpine Generally any small plant suitable for a rock garden or alpine house, but strictly one that in its natural habitat grows on mountains, above the level at which trees thrive.

Air layering A method of increasing plants by encouraging roots to form on a stem by cutting the stem, ensuring it stays open by inserting a match-stick into it, and packing peat or moss around the cut. Wrapping the moss with plastic helps to keep the moss moist and encourage rapid rooting.

Alternate The arrangement of leaves on a stem, arising singly and on opposite sides.

Anaerobic Able to live without oxygen or air, usually referring to bacteria.

Annual A plant that grows from seed, flowers and dies within the same year. However, many plants that are not strictly annuals are treated as such. For instance, Lobelia erinus is a half-hardy perennial usually grown as a half-hardy annual, Mirabilis jalapa (marvel of Peru) is a perennial grown as a half-hardy annual, and Impatiens sultanii (busy Lizzie) is a greenhouse perennial treated as a half-hardy annual.

Anther The pollen-bearing male part of a flower. A small stem called a filament supports the anthers, which collectively are called the stamen.

Aphids The best-known and most widely-seen pests in a garden, breeding rapidly, sucking sap and transmitting virus diseases. Most common forms are blackfly and greenfly.

Aquatic Generally, a plant that grows in garden ponds, either totally or partially submerged, or growing at their edges, but strictly one that lives entirely in water.

Asexual Non-sexual; frequently used to refer to the propagation of plants through cuttings and other vegetative means or by division of the roots.

Auxin A substance that induces plants to form new growth, or effects its rate of development.

Axil The junction between a leaf and stem from where sideshoots or flowers may develop.

Axillary A bud that grows from an axil, forming a stem and flower or just a stem. Shoots growing from leaf-joints on tomato plants are removed; this is called side-shooting.

Bark ringing The cutting and removal of a section of bark around apple and pear trees to restrict growth and encourage fruiting.

Basal The lower leaves on a plant. Basal rot is a fungal disease infesting bulbs.

Bastard trenching A soil cultivation technique now seldom used: digging the soil down to two spade depths (also known as two spits deep).

Beard or bearded A tuft or area of hairs, usually on the petals of some flowers such as irises.

Bedding plant A plant raised and used as a temporary filler in a border. Spring bedding plants are planted in autumn for spring flowering and include wallflowers and tulips, while summer bedding plants are planted in spring for summer flowering. Usually half-hardy annuals raised under glass early in the year so that when set in the border they are – or nearly are – in flower.

Berry A fleshy fruit with small seeds such as currants, grapes, gooseberries and tomatoes.

Biennial A plant that makes its initial growth one year and flowers the following one, then dying. However, many plants not strictly biennial are treated as such. For

example, Bellis perennis (daisy) is a hardy perennial usually grown as a biennial, and Dianthus barbatus (sweet William) is a perennial usually grown as a hardy biennial.

Big Bud A swelling of buds on blackcurrants due to the big bud mite. Red currants are also attacked, but do not develop any swellings. Gooseberries can be infested and react in the same manner as red currants.

Bi-generic A hybrid between species of two different genera.

Black spot A fungal disease that attacks and disfigures roses.

Blanching The exclusion of light from the stems of some vegetables to whiten them and improve their flavour.

Blind A plant whose growing point has not developed properly.

Bog plant A plant that thrives in perpetually moist conditions.

Bole Loosely, the base of the trunk of a tree, but strictly the entire trunk.

Bolting The premature shooting up to flower of vegetables. Lettuces, beetroot, spinach and radishes are most susceptible.

Botrytis Also known as grey mould, a fungal disease chiefly found in badly ventilated, damp greenhouses. Soft-tissued plants such as lettuces and delicately flowered types like chrysanthemums are particularly prone to it.

Bonsai The growing of mature plants in a miniature form in a small container. It began in China more than 1000 years ago, quickly spreading to Japan.

Bordeaux mixture A fungicidal mixture of copper sulphate and lime.

Bottle garden Gardening in a closed environment created by a large glass bottle or case.

Bottom heat The warming of a rooting mixture from below, rather than above. The warmth is usually provided by electric wiring buried under a layer of well-drained and aerated rooting compost. Cuttings inserted into this root rapidly and seeds in boxes or pots placed on top are often encouraged to germinate quickly. In early days this bottom heat was supplied by buried hot water pipes or the heat produced from 'maturing' manure.

Bract A modified leaf, usually looking very like a petal. The brightly-coloured flower-like heads on poinsettia, the white petal-like appendages around the flowers on Davidia involucrata (dove tree), and the white or pink-flushed petal-like appendages on Cornus florida are all bracts.

Brassica A vegetable member of the Cruciferae family, such as cabbage, cauliflower and Brussels sprouts.

Break The branching of shoots after the terminal bud has been removed, often done to induce early and better flowering. Breaking is also used to describe streaking and flaking of another colour in some flowers due to a virus.

Bud A tightly-packed and closed immature shoot or flower.

Budding A method of propagation, whereby a dormant bud is inserted into a T-cut in the stem of a root-stock. Roses and fruit trees are increased in this way.

Bulb A storage organ with a bud-like structure. It is formed of fleshy scales attached to a flattened stem called the basal plate. Onions and tulips are excellent examples of bulbs. Erroneously, the term is often used to also include tubers, rhizomes and corms, which have a different structure.

Bulbil An immature and miniature bulb at the base of a mother bulb.

Calcifuge A lime-hating plant.

Callus A corky tissue that forms over damaged or cut stems. Before rooting, cuttings produce a callus.

Calyx The sepals as a whole, the outer ring of a flower.

Cambium A layer just below the bark where active growth occurs.

Capillary The passage of water upwards through soil. The finer the soil the higher the rise. The same principle is used in self-watering systems for greenhouse plants in pots.

Capsule A dry pod which splits to discharge its seeds.

Carpel The female part of a flower containing the ovules.

Catch crop A crop – usually of a salad nature – that is sown, grown and harvested while growing between long-growing crops.

Catkin A dense, unisexual flowering arrangement. On hazels they are pendulous, but with willows erect.

Cheshunt compound A mixture of copper sulphate and ammonium carbonate to control some fungal diseases.

Chlorophyll The green colouring matter found in all plants, except for a few parasites and fungi. It absorbs energy from the sun and plays an important role in photosynthesis, the method by which plants grow.

Chlorosis A disorder mainly of leaves, with parts showing as whitish areas. It can be caused by viruses, mutation or by mineral deficiencies.

Cloche The French for a bell-glass, now widely used for glass and plastic tunnel-like structures used to protect early crops, usually vegetables.

Clone A plant raised vegetatively from another, and so identical with it, unlike most seed-raised plants.

Columnar Rising vertically, usually trees and conifers.

Compost The growing medium formed either mainly of peat, sharp sand and loam in which plants are cultivated or of recycled vegetable waste from the kitchen and plant material from the garden. This can be combined with chemicals to encourage it to rot quickly. When fully decayed it makes an ideal substitute for farmyard manure.

Compositae A group of plants known as the daisy family, with about 15,000 members, ranging from daisies to chrysanthemums and dahlias to lettuces.

Conifer A plant with tree- or shrub-like proportions that bears cones such as pines, firs and spruces.

Container-grown A plant grown in a container for subsequent transplanting to its permanent position in the garden. Such plants – trees, shrubs and rock garden plants – can be planted at any time when the soil is not too wet, dry or frozen. The plant experiences little root disturbance and soon establishes itself in the ground. Plants lifted from the open soil and having bare roots experience considerable disturbance and can only be transplanted during their dormant season (for deciduous specimens) or early autumn or late spring if evergreen.

Cordon A form of trained fruit tree. Some are as single-stemmed types, others with two or three mains stems.

Corm An underground storage organ formed of a stem base greatly swollen laterally. A good example is a gladiolus. Young corms – cormlets – will form around its base, and can be removed and grown in a nursery bed for several seasons before reaching flowering-sized corms.

Corona A development of petals in certain plants to form a cup or trumpet, as in a daffodil.

Cotyledon The first leaf or leaves that a seedling produces. They are present in the seed and emerge on germination. They should not be confused with true leaves.

Cristate Crested, often used to describe some ferns and cacti.

Crock A piece of broken clay pot put at the base of a pot to prevent the drainage holes being blocked by compost.

Cross A hybrid offspring of parents of different cultivars.

Crown buds The buds on chrysanthemums that appear after the plant has been initially stopped (having the first terminal bud nipped out).

Cruciferous A group of plants containing such members as wallflowers and cabbages.

Cultivar A variety raised in cultivation.

Cutting A method of vegetative propagation, by which a severed piece of the parent plant is encouraged to develop roots.

Damping down A method of increasing the humidity in a greenhouse. Use a fine-rosed watering-can to dampen down the floor and the staging, mainly in spring and summer, when the atmosphere can dry out before nightfall. In autumn and winter, take care that the atmosphere is not damp at night.

Damping off A disease that usually attacks seedlings soon after germination, as well as older plants such as tomatoes grown in greenhouses. It is encouraged by overcrowding, a stuffy atmosphere and bad drainage in the compost or soil.

Deciduous A plant that loses its leaves at the beginning of its dormant season. This usually applies to trees, shrubs and some conifers, such as Ginkgo biloba (maidenhair tree) and larix.

Dibber A rounded, blunt-pointed tool for making planting holes. Large types can be used for planting brassicas, and smaller ones for pricking off seedlings into boxes or pots of compost.

Dicotyledons A group of plants characterized by seedlings with two cotyledons.

Dieback The progressive death of a shoot or branch, from the tip back to the stem.

Disbudding The removal of buds from around the sides of a main and central bud to encourage one flower of exhibition size.

Disc The central mass of florets, forming a circle, in many members of the daisy family.

Division A vegetative method of propagation involving splitting up roots. It is done mainly with herbaceous plants with fibrous roots.

Dormancy The resting period of a plant or seed.

Dot plant A plant in a bedding scheme with a particular characteristic (size, shape or special colour) that makes it stand out among the other plants.

Downy mildew A fungal disease resulting from cool, damp conditions and especially affecting lettuces and onions.

Drawn Thin and spindly after being in crowded or dark conditions.

Drill A narrow depression made in the surface of the soil – usually with a small pointed stick or a hoe – in which seeds are sown. Most vegetable seeds are sown in this manner, but peas are often sown in flat-bottom drills so that three rows can be sown close together.

Dutch light A large piece of glass secured in a wooden frame and used to protect plants.

Earthing-up The drawing up of soil around the base of a plant to exclude light or to support it against wind buffeting. Chiefly used for potatoes and celery.

Epiphyte A plant that grows on another but does not feed on it.

Ericaceous A member of the heather family.

Espalier A form of training fruit trees whereby lateral branches are trained horizontally along tensioned wires.

Etiolated Being blanched, the result of growth in poor light.

Evergreen A plant that continuously sheds and grows leaves throughout the year and therefore at any time appears to have a complete array of leaves. Some trees, shrubs and conifers are evergreen.

Everlasting A flower which when cut and dried keeps its shape and colour for a long period – but not forever.

F1 The first filial generation: the result of a cross between two pure-bred parents. F1 hybrids are large and strong plants, but their seeds will not produce replicas of the parents.

F2 The second generation from the cross of F1 hybrids.

Falls The outer petals of irises; those that hang vertically.

Fan-trained A method of training fruit trees, with branches radiating out like the spokes of a fan.

Fasciation A freak physical condition when stems or flowers are fused and flattened. The affected stems are best cut out.

Fastigiate Erect, upright growth, with the branches close together, the term is normally used to describe the many trees and conifers that reveal this type of growth.

Fertilization The sexual union of the male cell (pollen) with the female cell (ovule). Fertilization may be the result of pollination, when pollen falls upon the stigma. However, not all pollen germinates after falling on the stigma.

Fertilize To encourage the development of a plant by feeding it with manure or chemicals.

Filament The slender stalk that supports the anthers of a flower. Collectively, the anthers and filaments are the stamen.

Fillis A type of soft string, usually green, used for tying up plants.

Fimbriated Fringed, usually applied to a flower or petal.

Flocculate To cause very fine soil particles to form lumps by adding lime to it, improving the drainage of clay soils.

Floret A small flower that is part of an entire flower.

Foliar feed A fertilizer applied to foliage. Not all fertilizers or plants are suitable.

Frame A low structure of brick or wood, with a glass covering of Dutch lights. An invaluable part of greenhouse gardening, enabling seedlings and plants to be hardened off before being planted in the garden. They can also be used to protect water-sensitive plants in winter.

Friable Soil that is light, crumbly and moist.

Fungicide A chemical to combat fungus diseases, such as black spot and mildew.

Gall An abnormal swelling, caused by fungi, bacteria or insects. It is usually quite small, no larger than a marble.

Genus A group of plants with similar botanical characteristics. Some genera contain many species, others just one, which are then called monotypic.

Germination The process that occurs within a seed when given adequate moisture, air and warmth. The coat of the seed ruptures and the seed leaf (or leaves) grow up towards the light. A root develops at the same time. However to most gardeners germination is when they see the seed leaves appearing through the surface of compost on pots and boxes, or through the soil in the open garden.

Glaucous Greyish-green or bluish-green in colour, usually applied to stems, leaves and fruits of ornamental trees and shrubs.

Graft A method of propagation, when the tissue of a chosen variety is united with a rootstock of a known vigour. It is used to increase fruit trees and, sometimes, roses.

Graft union The point at which a graft took place, usually noticeable by a slight swelling on the stem.

Green manuring The growing of a crop such as mustard that can be subsequently dug into the soil to improve its physical and nutritional nature.

Ground cover A low, ground-hugging plant that forms a mat of foliage. It is useful in discouraging weeds.

Half-hardy A plant that can withstand fairly low temperatures, but needs protection from frost. For example, half-hardy annuals raised in warmth in a greenhouse early in the year

and then planted out as soon as all risk of frost has passed.

Hardening off The gradual accustoming of protected plants to outside conditions. Garden frames are useful for this purpose.

Hardwood cuttings A method of vegetatively increasing shrubs and trees by severing pieces of stems when ripe and inserting them in a rooting medium. Usually, all that is needed is to insert them into a nursery bed in the garden.

Hardy A plant that does not need to be protected from the weather.

Haulm The top growth on some vegetables, such as peas, beans and potatoes.

Heel A hardy, corky layer of bark and stem torn off when a sideshoot is pulled away from the main stem. Some cuttings root quickly if this is slightly trimmed and left in place.

Heeling-in The temporary planting of trees, shrubs and conifers while awaiting transfer to their permanent quarters, often because the final planting position has not been prepared or is too wet.

Herbaceous A plant that dies down to soil level after the completion of each season's growth. Usually refers to the hardy border plants that die down to ground level each autumn and develop fresh shoots in spring.

Herbicide A chemical formulation that kills plants, and generally known as a weedkiller.

Hermaphrodite Having both male and female organs in the same flower.

Honey fungus A fungus also known as bootlace that attacks a range of shrubs. Its presence is indicated by honey-coloured toadstools.

Hormone A growth-regulating substance which occurs naturally in both plant and animal tissue. Additional and synthetic amounts are used to induce plants to root rapidly. Others are used to stimulate the growth of weeds so that they 'burn' themselves out.

Hotbed The use of manure to help create bottom heat. As it ferments it heats up and encourages plants above it to grow rapidly.

Humus Microscopic dark brown decayed vegetable material.

Hybrid The progeny from parents of different species or genera. An F1 cultivar may be the result of a cross between cultivars of the same species.

Hybridization The crossing of one or more generations to improve a wide range of characteristics, such as flower size, time of flowering, sturdiness, fruit size or plant size.

Hydroponics The growing of plants without soil.

Incurved Flowers that curl inwards, mainly of some chrysanthemums.

Inflorescence The part of a plant which bears the flowers.

Insecticide A chemical for killing insects.

Internode The part on a stem or shoot between two leaf-joints (nodes).

Joint The junction between a shoot or stem and a leaf or leaf stalk. Also known as a node.

Juvenile leaf An early leaf which differs markedly from an adult leaf, especially on conifers.

Lanceolate Lance-shaped, of leaves.

Lateral A side-shoot growing from a main stem of a tree or shrub, normally used when discussing the fruiting and pruning of fruit trees.

Layering A vegetative method of increasing plants by lowering stems and slightly burying them in the ground. By twisting, bending or slitting the stem at the point where it is buried, the flow of sap is restricted and roots induced to develop. Rooting may take up to eighteen months before the new plant can be severed from its parent.

Leaching The draining away of nutrients

from the soil. It is most apparent in sandy soil. The fine particles in clay soils tend to retain nutrients.

Leader The terminal shoot or branch that will extend growth.

Leafmould Decayed leaves. It can either be spread over the surface as a mulch, or dug into the soil during winter.

Leguminous A member of the pea family.

Lime An alkaline substance used for countering acidity in the soil and improving clay soils by flocculation.

Linear Long and narrow, of leaves.

Loam A mixture of fertile soil, formed of sand, clay, silt and organic material.

Maiden The first year of a fruit tree after being budded or grafted.

Microclimate The climate within a very restricted area.

Mildew A fungus disease that attacks soft-tissued plants. There are two main types: downy mildew chiefly affects lettuces and onions; while powder mildew mainly effects fruit, roses and chrysanthemums.

Mist propagation A mechanical device that monitors the presence of water on a leaf, spraying them automatically if it becomes dry. Soft-leaved cuttings are placed under the misting unit, which because the loss of moisture from cuttings is being controlled can be kept at a slightly higher temperature to encourage rapid rooting.

Monoecious A plant which has separate male and female flowers on the same plant.

Mulch A surface dressing of bulky organic material. It conserves moisture in the soil, smothers weeds and increases the nutrient value of the soil.

Mutation A part of a plant – usually the flower – that differs from the plant's inherited characteristics.

Naturalize The planting of bulbs in a natural informal display.

Neutral Neither acid nor alkaline, of soil. On the pH scale this would be between 6·5 and 7·0.

Node A leaf joint or point where another stem branches out from the main one.

NPK A formula for the percentages of nitrogen, phosphate and potash in compound fertilizers.

Organic The cultivation of plants without chemical fertilizers or pesticides.

Pan A compacted and impervious layer in the soil that restricts the flow of water and air.

Peat Partly decayed vegetable material, usually acid.

Pelleted Coated, of seeds that have been treated to aid sowing and germination.

Perennial Usually used of herbaceous plants but also any plant that lives for several years, including trees, shrubs and climbers.

Pesticide A chemical compound for killing insects and other pests.

Photosynthesis The food-building process by which chlorophyll in the leaves is activated by sunlight. It reacts with moisture absorbed by the roots and carbon dioxide gained from the atmosphere to create growth.

pH A logarithmical scale used to define the acidity or alkalinity of a soil–water solution. Neutral is 7·0, with figures above indicating increasing alkalinity, and below increasing acidity. Most plants grow well in 6·5–7·0, frequently taken to be the practical neutral, rather than the scientific neutral at 7·0.

Pinching out The removal of the tip of a shoot or a terminal bud to encourage the development of sideshoots.

Pollen The male fertilizing agent from anthers.

Pollination When pollen from the anthers falls on the stigma.

Potting-on The transfer of an established plant into a larger pot.

Potting-up The transplant of a young plant

from a large container into a pot.

Pricking-out The removal of seedlings from a seedbox or seed pan into another box where they can be given more space.

Propagation The raising of new plants.

Pruning The removal with a knife or secateurs of unwanted parts of woody plants. With fruit trees it is done to encourage better and more regular fruiting. Shrubs are pruned to encourage better flowering.

Rhizome An underground or partly buried horizontal stem. They can be slender or fleshy.

Ridging A method of winter digging that leaves a large surface area of soil exposed to the elements. Long, mounded ridges are left on the surface.

Ring culture A method of growing tomatoes in bottomless pots on a base of well-drained gravel.

Rotation The division of a vegetable plot into three with no crop grown in the same plot in consecutive years.

Runner A shoot that grows along the ground, at intervals rooting into the soil. Strawberry runners are a good example.

Sapling A young tree before it develops a crown.

Saprophytic A plant that lives on decaying organic material.

Scion A shoot or bud that is grafted on to a rootstock.

Scree A freely-draining area of grit and small stones for alpine plants which need special drainage.

Seed leaf The first leaf (sometimes two) that appear after germination.

Self-fertile A plant with flowers that can be fertilized by its own pollen. This chiefly applies to fruit trees.

Self-sterile The opposite of self-fertile (see above).

Sequestrene A chemical compound enabling some plants to absorb minerals locked up in some soils.

Shrub A woody perennial with stems growing from soil-level and no trunk. Some plants can be grown as trees or shrubs.

Sideshoot A shoot growing out from the side of a main shoot.

Slip A heel cutting.

Softwood cutting A cutting of non-woody growth, a green shoot.

Soil block Compost that has been compressed into a block about the size of a 7·5cm (3in) flower pot. It is formed of peat and soil, and remains compact and firm until planted into the garden. Seeds can be sown in them, or young seedlings pricked off into them. They help to reduce root disturbance at planting time.

Species A group of plants that breed together and have the same characteristics.

Spit A depth of a spade's blade, usually about 30cm (1ft).

Sport An accidental change of shape, size or colour of a flower or plant.

Spur A short branch on a fruit tree.

Stamen The male part of a flower, formed of the anthers and filaments.

Stem The main stalk of a plant.

Sterilization The cleansing of soil, killing weed seeds, bacteria and fungi, by heat or chemicals.

Stigma The female part of a flower on which pollen alights.

Stipule A leaf-like sheath at the base of some flower stalks, such as in roses.

Stock The rooted part of a budded or grafted plant.

Stolon A runner.

Stomata A minute hole – usually in the undersides of leaves – that enables the exchange of gases. During respiration the plant absorbs air, retaining and using oxygen and giving off carbon dioxide. During photosynthesis the plant absorbs air, using the carbon dioxide and giving off oxygen. The plural is stoma.

Stool Of chrysanthemums, the plant when flowered and cut down to 15cm (6in) above soil-level.

Stop The removal of a growing tip to encourage the development of sideshoots.

Strain Seed-raised plants from a common ancestor.

Stratify A method of helping seeds with hard coats to germinate. The seeds are placed between layers of sand kept cold, usually the extent of one winter.

Striated Striped.

Strike The rooting of a cutting.

Style Part of the female reproductive organs of a flower, linked to stigma and ovary.

Sub-soil Soil below the normal depth at which the area is cultivated.

Sucker A basal shoot arising from the rootstock of a grafted plant.

Synonym A previous botanical name for a plant. It frequently happens that the plant is better known and sold under the earlier name by many nurseries.

Systemic Chemicals that penetrate a plant's tissue, attacking pests. The time they remain active within a plant depends on the type of plant and the temperature.

Tap-root A long, strong primary root on some plants, stretching deep down into the soil.

Tender A plant that is damaged by low temperatures.

Tendril A thread-like growth by which many climbers cling to their supports.

Thinning The removal of surplus shoots to allow others to develop properly.

Thong A root cutting, especially of seakale.

Tilth Soil which has been broken down in preparation for a seed-bed.

Tine A prong of a rake or fork.

Tip-bearing A fruit tree bearing flowers and fruit at the tips of the shoots.

Tomentose Having a hairy appearance.

Top-dress Spreading and lightly hoeing-in fertilizers around plants.

Topiary The clipping and shaping of densely-leaved shrubs and hedging plants into patterns and shapes.

Top-soil The top layer of soil, often taken to mean the top spit, 30cm (1ft) deep.

Transpiration The loss of moisture from a plant.

Truss A cluster of flowers or fruit, chiefly used with tomatoes.

Tuber An underground storage organ, such as a dahlia.

Variegated Multi-coloured, of leaves.

Variety A variant from the original species or hybrid.

Vegetative A method of propagation including division of roots, layering, grafting, budding and taking cuttings.

Venation The arrangement of veins in a leaf.

Watershoot A sappy, quick-growing growth that arises from buds on branches of old fruit trees.

Weeping Drooping branches, tree or conifer.

Windbreak A shrub, tree or conifer used to reduce the speed of the wind and to create shelter for cultivated plants.

Figures in italics refer to illustrations

Aaron's beard 91, *105*
Abelia chinensis 110, 130, 149, 162
  distichum 37
Abeliophyllium distichum 25
Abutilon vitifolium 81, 99, 113
Acacia
  Common 94
  False 94
  Rose 75
Acer campestri 154
  capillipes 8
  cappadocicum *147*, 154
  davidii 8
  griseum 99
  japonicum 154
  j. 'Aconitifolium' 154
  j. 'Aureum' 154
  j. 'Vitifolium' 154
  pensylvanicum 8
  platanoides 154
  saccharinum 18
Achillea, Woolly 115, 133, 153
Achillea filipendula 51, 71, 87
  f. 'Coronation Gold' *7*
  millefolium 51, 71, 87
  ptarmica 51, 71, 87
  tomentosa 115, 133, 153
Achimines 27, 95, 148
Acidanthera bicolor 129, 144
Actinidia chinensis 110, 130
Actotis x hybrida 86
Adonis aestivalis 31, 48, 68, 86,
  108, 124, 138
Aerators 148, *152*, 157
Aesculus x carnea 'Briottii' 74
  parviflora 130
Aethionema grandiflorum 81, 96, 115
  'Warley Rose' *50*, 81
Agapanthus 168
Ageratum houstonianum 31, 86,
  108, 124, 138
Agrimony eupatoria 51
Agrostemma githago 'Milas' *126*
Alcea rosea formerly *Althaea rosea*
  11, 22, 71, 87, 108, 124, 138
Alchemilla mollis 109
Allium ablopilosum 88
  aflatunensis 72, 88
  moly 81, 113
Allspice, Carolina 92
Almond 25, 37
  Common 37
Alonsoa warscewiczii 22, 33, 86,
  108, 138, 157
Alpines 38, 150
Alstroemeria ligtu 33
Althaea rosea see *Alcea rosea*
Alyssum maritimum see *Lobularia
  maritima*
  saxatile 33
  saxatile 'Flore-pleno' *50*, 81, 96
Amaranthus caudatus 31, 48, 68,
  108, 124, 138, 157
  hypochondriacus 31, 138
  tricolor 48
Amaryllis belladonna 124
Amelanchier lamarkii *44*, 61
Anchusa azurea; syn. 'A. *italica* 51,
  71, 86, 87, 108, 124
  capensis 48, 68, 108, 124
Androsace, Himalayan 96, 115,
  130, 153, 160
Androsace carnea 115
  lanuginosa 96, 115, 130, 153, 160
Anemone, Poppy 11, 22, 30, 33,
  51, 53, 68, 71, 86, 108
Anemone blanda 18, 22, 30, 53
  coronaria 11, 22, 30, 33, 51, 53,
    68, 71, 86, 108
Angel's tears 30, 55
Annuals 82, 100
  preparing ground 26, 30, *61*
  sowing *61*, 131
  thinning 67, 75
Antennaria dioica 81, 96
Anthemis cupaniana *120*
  nobilis 22, 33, 135
Antirrhinum (Snapdragon) 11, 22,
  33, 108, 124, 138, *149*, 157
Antirrhinum majus 11, 22, 33, 108,
  124, 138, 157
Ants 108
Aphids 75, 95, 132, 135
  black bean 88

Apple of Peru 49, 69
Apple trees, apples
  bark ringing 75
  diseases 14, 180
  feeding 24
  grafting *181*
  picking 106, 120, 124, 138, *154*
  planting 166
  pruning 120, 166, 170, *170*
  root pruning 172
  'Spartan' *154*
  spraying 38
  staking 166
  storage *14*, 106, 172, 182
  thinning fruits 96
Apricots 25, 38
Aquilegia alpina 51, 71, 81, 86
  flabellata 'Nana Alba' 81, 96, 115
  vulgaris 11, 22, 33, 51, 71, 86, 87,
    108
Arabis alpina 33, 51
  caucasica 'Flore Plena' 46
Aralia elata 130, 149
Arbours 100
Arbutus andrachne 39, 61
  x *andrachnoides* 8
  x *hybrida* 8
  unedo 8, 162, 170
Arctostaphylos uva-ursi 61
Arctotis x hybrida 31, 108, 124, 138
Arenaria montana 71, 87
Armeria maritima 'Alba' 81
  m. 'Vindictive' 81, 96, 115
Artemisia arborescens 82
  ludoviciana 115
Artichokes, Globe
  cutting down 167
  harvesting 108, 123, 139, 156
  planting 38
  protecting 166
  top-dressing 30
Asclepias curassavica 11, 22, 33
Ash, Mountain 78
Asparagus
  cutting foliage 152, 156
  feeding 27
  harvesting 56, 79, 112
  planting 56
  preparing ground 54
Asperula orientalis syn. *A. azurea/*
  A. setosa 31, 48, 68, 108
Aster, China 31, 108, 124, 138
Aster alpinus 115
  novae-angliae 154
  novi-belgii 33, 51, 71, 154
Astilbe x arendsii 118
  x a. 'Bressingham Beauty' 118
  x a. 'Federsee' 118
  x a. 'Red Sentinel' 118
  x a. 'White Gloria' 118
Aubreita deltoidea 32, 50, 51, 64,
  71, 81, *85*, 87, 96
Aucuba japonica 'Variegata' *177*
Azaleas 64
  in cold frame 86
  and compost 169
  deadheading 17
  taking indoors 159

Baby blue eyes 32, 49, 69, 87, 111,
  125
Bachelor's buttons 32, 49
Ballota pseudodictamnus 96, *131*
Balsam 32, 49
Bark ringing 75
Balm 32, 49
Bean crops 88
  see also individual beans
Bearberry, Red 61
Beauty bush 75
Bedding plants 82, *82*
  hardening off 54, 56, 62, 69
  and lawn 162
  planting 67, 79, 84, 86, 156
  preparing ground 142, 150
  removal of 67, 142, 150
  and shrubs 166
Beetroot 70, 84, 88, 96
Begonia rex 105
  semperflorens 31, 86, 108, 124, 138
Begonias 148
  after flowering 157
  boxing up 27
  cutting 135
  drying at roots 98
  feeding 76
  planting 40

Bellis perennis 64, 68, 71, 86, 87,
  108, 124, 138
Bells of Ireland 32
Beloperone guttata see *Justicia
  brandegeana*
Berberis candidula 72, 91
  darwinii 52, 72
  linearifolia 52
  x *rubrostilla* 72
  x *stenophylla* 72
Betula papyrifera 8
  papyrifera occidentalis 90
  utilus 8
Big bud mite 35
Birch
  Canoe 8, *90*
  Himalayan 8
  Paper 8, *90*
Blackberries 52, 84, 114, 150, 162
Blackcurrant bushes
  cutting shoots 129, 132, 156
  cuttings 160
  planting 35, 156
  pruning 132
  spraying 35
Black-eyed Susan 32, 49, 87, 111,
  125, 139, 157
Black locust 94
Black spot 24
Bladder senna 91
Bloodflower 11, 22, 33
Blue lace flower *21*, 31, 110, 124
Blueberry 'Colville' *159*
Bonemeal dressing 142
Border plants, supporting 106
Botanical gardens 178
Brachycome iberidifolia 31, 48, 68,
  86, 108, 124
Bridal wreath 61, *93*
Broad beans
  nipping out 88
  picking 96, 112
  sowing 36
  under cloches *67*
  watering 96
Broom
  Common 64, 73
  Genoa 64
  Mount Etna 122
  Spanish 91
  Warminster 64
  White 64
  White Portugal 78
Brussels sprouts
  picking 152, *161*, 170
  sowing 38, 49
  transplanting 70, 84
Budding *123*
Buddleia alternifolia 99
  colvilei 92
  davidii 'Emperor Blue' 113, 134
  d. 'Fortune' 107, 126
  d. 'Peace' 110, 130
  d. 'Royal Red' 107
  d. 'White Cloud' 110
  d. 'White Profusion' 110
  fallowiana 'Alba' 110, 130
  globosa 91
Bukhara fleece 118
Bulb-planter 157
Bulbs
  for Christmas flowering 131
  deadheading 42, 56
  drying off 37
  forcing 166, 169, 178
  in greenhouse 23, 171, 173, 177
  in lawn 22, *157*
  lifting 67, 79
  moving indoors 15, 23
  planting 110, 120, 146
  planting outdoors after
    flowering 38, 48
  potting up 148
  staking 17
  watering compost 11, 178, 181
Burning bush 32, 49
Busy Lizzy 109
Butterfly bush 107, 110, 113
Butterfly flower 95

Cabbages
  harvesting 14, 36, 54, 76, 84,
    158, 173, 183
  planting 142, 158
  sowing 54, 70, 102
  transplanting 102

  potting on 50
  sowing 21
Cacti *50*, *63*, *107*
Calceolaria 69, 86, 117
Calceolaria integrifolia; syn. C.
  rugosa 11, 22, 33, 108, 124, 138
Calendula officinalis 31, 48, *51*, 68,
  86, 108, 124, 138
Calico bush 92, *93*
Callistephus chinensis 31, 108, 124, 138
Calluna vulgaris 'Alba plena' 130,
  149, 162
  v. 'Beoley gold' 130, 149
  v. 'County Wicklow' 145
  v. 'Darkness' 126
  v. 'Gold haze' 130, 149
  v. 'H.E. Beale' 145, 159
  v. 'J.H. Hamilton' 126
  v. 'Peter Sparkes' 126, 145, 159
  v. 'Serlei' 130, 149, 162
  v. 'Tib' 126, 145
Calomel 142, 158
Calycanthus floridus 92
Calycinum 122
Camass, Common 88, 113
Camassia quamash; syn. C.
  esculenta 88, 113
Camellia, Common 25
Camellia japonica 25, 37, 58, 74
Campanula carpatica 115
  cochleariifolia 115, 130, 153
  medium 48, 68, 84, 86, 108
  portenschlagiana; syn. C. *muralis*
    96, 115, 133, 153
  poscharskyana 96, 115, 133, 153
Canary creeper 22, 33
Candytuft 32, 49, 69, 87, 110, 125,
  139
  Persian 81, 96, 115
Cane fruits, supporting 96
Cane spot 35
Canker 14, 180
Canna 11, 22, 33, *149*
Canterbury bell 48, 68, 84, 86,
  108, 114
Capsid bugs 95
Caragana arborescens 72
Cardoons, 60, 76, 123, 139
Carex stricta 'Aurea' *120*
Carnation
  border 132
  cuttings 22, 37
  layering stems 110
  moving 132, 152
  perpetual flowering 105, 152
  potting up 27
  spraying 95
Carpenteria californica 94
Carrots
  sowing 38, 54, 76, 79, 145
  thinning 56, 76, 79
Caryopteris x clandonensis 30, 134,
  151, 163
  x c. 'Arthur Simmonds' 134
  x c. 'Heavenly Blue' 134
  x c. 'Kew Blue' 134
Catalpa bignonioides 110
Catananche caerulea 22, 33, 51, 71,
  87, *109*
Cauliflowers
  harvesting 96, 117, 142
  planting 38, 84
  sowing 12, 30, 49
Ceanothus 'Cascade' 81
  'Delight' 81
  dentatus 81, 99
  'Gloire de Versailles' 99, 113,
    124, 134, 151, 163
  thyrsiflorus 81, 99
  t. repens *81*
  'Topaz' 113, 134, 151, 163
Cedar, Golden Himalayan 174
Cedrus deodara 'Aurea' 174
  d. 'Golden Horizon' 174
Celery
  earthing-up 117, 129
  lifting 10, 16, 158, 167, 176
  planting 70, 88
  preparing ground 38
  pricking out 44
  sowing 36
  tying stems 108
Celosia argentea plumosa 31, 48,
  108, 124
Centaurea cyanus 31, 48, 68, 86,
  108, 124, 138

INDEX

moschata 48, 68, 86, 108, 124, 138
Centranthus ruber; syn. *Kentranthus ruber* 51, 71, 87
Cerastium tomentosum 33, 51
Ceratostigma plumbaginoides 154
   willmottianum 113, 134, 151, 163
Cerdidiphyllum japonicum 154, 157
Cercis siliquastrum 74
Chaenomeles japonica 37, 58
   speciosa 'Cardinalis' 37, 58
   s. 'Crown of Gold' 37
   s. 'Fascination' 37
   s. 'Nivalis' 39, 78
Chafers 139
Chamaecyparis lawsoniana 'Aurea Densa' 174
   l. 'Lanei' 174
   l. 'Lutea' 174
   l. 'Minima Aurea' 174
   l. 'President Roosevelt' 8
   l. 'Stewartii' 174
   l. 'Winston Churchill' 8, 174
   obtusa 'Nana Aurea' 43
   pisifera 'Filifera Aurea' 174
Chamomile, Common 22, 33, 135
Chanomeles specosa 'Nivalis' 61
Checkerberry 110
Cheiranthus x allionii 68, 71, 86, 87, 108
   cheiri 71, 86, 87
   c. 'Easter Queen' 64, 68
   c. ''Mrs. John T. Scheepers' 64
   c. 'President Hoover' 64
   c. 'Red Emperor' 64
Cherry
   autumn-flowering 174
   bird 78
   in cold frame 86
   cornelian 18, 23, 24
   Japanese 60, 61
   Lombardy poplar 46
   picking 88
   spring 46
   weeping spring 46
   wild 61
   winter-flowering 21, 86
   Yoshino 37
Cherry pie 22, 33, 87, 110, 125, 139
Chicory
   harvesting 10, 25, 180
   planting 168, 176
   sowing 70
   storing 156
   thinning 84
Chilean fire bush 75
Chilean Potato Tree 111, 113, 136
Chimonanthus praecox; syn. *C. fragrans* 17, 26, 28
   p. 'Grandiflorus' 8, 13, 23, 34
   p. 'Luteus' 13
China tree 122
Chinese lantern 146
Chionodoxa gigantea; syn. *C. grandiflora* 22, 30, 53
   luciliae 22, 30
   sardensis 30, 53
Chionodoxas 28, 152
Choisya ternata 78, 94,
Christmas rose 8, 14, 172
Chrysanthemum 118
   boxing up 17, 21
   cutting down 169, 177, 183
   cuttings 32
   disbudding 114, 140
   and earwigs 129
   feeding 102
   lifting and dividing 56
   moving into greenhouse 148, 157
   moving outdoors 81
   planting 56, 67
   potting on 50, 59
   potting up 62
   protecting 146
   re-potting 56
   spraying 95
   stopping 70
   storing 156
   supporting 106, 132
   top-dressing 117
   watering 162
Chrysanthemum carinatum; syn. *C. tricolor* 31, 48, 68, 86, 108, 124
   maximum 51, 71, 71, 87

parthenium 22, 33
   ptarmicaeflorum 11, 22
Cinerarias 69, 98, 117, 123, 135
Cistus x anguilari 78, 94, 110
   x *corbariensis* 94
   x *crispus* 'Sunset' 131
   x *cyprius* 78, 94, 110
   x *purpureus* 74, 92, 107
   'Silver Pink' 92, 107
   x *skanbergii* 92, 107
Clarkia 131
Clarkia elegans 31, 48, 68, 84, 108, 124, 138
   pulchella 31, 48, 68, 84, 108, 124, 138
Clematis 100
   Mountain 78, 82
   Orange-peel 122
Clematis 'Barbara Jackman' 81, 99
   'Comtesse de Bouchard' 92, 107
   'Elsa Spath' 113, 134, 151
   'Ernest Markham' 126, 136, 145, 159
   flammula 130, 149
   'Gipsy Queen' 113, 134, 151
   'Hagley Hybrid' 92, 107, 126
   'Jackmanii superba' 99, 113, 134, 151
   'Lasurstern' 81, 99
   macropetala 81, 99
   'Mrs. Cholmondeley' 81, 99, 113, 134, 136, 151
   montana 78, 82, 95
   montana 'Rubens' 75, 92, 107
   'Nelly Moser' 92, 107
   orientalis 122, 140, 156
   'President' 99, 113
   tangutica 122, 140, 156
   'Ville de Lyon' 126, 136, 145, 159
   'W.E. Gladstone' 99, 113, 134
Cleome spinosa; syn. *C. pungens* 30, 31, 86, 108, 124
Clerodendron trichotomum 130, 136
Clethra anifolia 130, 149
Cloches 14, 22, 27, 36, 38, 67, 142, 145, 162, 172
Cocklebur 51
Colchicum autumnale 136, 144, 162
   speciosum 144, 162
Colchicums 110
Cold frame 54, 62, 69, 71, 72, 86, 102, 103, 135, 140, 145, 152, 159, 167
Coleus 40, 109, 135
Columbine, Alpine 81
Colutea arborescens 91, 104, 122, 140
Compost
   rooting 23
   watering 11, 44, 90
Conifers 162, 174, 178
Consolida ajacis 31, 48, 68, 86, 108, 124
Convallaria majalis 24, 167
Convolvulus cneorum 94, 110, 130, 149
   major; syn. Ipomoea purpurea 32, 49, 69
   tricolor; syn. *C. minor* 31, 48, 68, 108, 124, 138
Coreopsis tinctoria 31, 48, 68
Corn-cockle 126
Cornflower 31, 48, 68, 86, 108, 124, 131, 138
Cornea alba 14, 174
   a. 'Sibirica' 174
   florida 'Rubra' 92, 107
   kousa 94, 110
   mas 18, 23, 24, 34
Corokia cotoneaster 72, 91
Coronilla glauca 72, 91
Cortaderia selloana aka *C. argentea* 11, 174
Corylopsis pauciflora 34
Corylus avellana 'Contorta' 164
Cosmea 49, 68
Cosmos bipinnatus 49, 68, 124, 138
Cotinus coggygria 'Foliis purpureis' 154
Cotoneaster distichus 164
   lacteus 164
   x *watereri* 164
Cotula barbata 49, 68, 108, 124
Crab 46, 62, 78, 154, 164
Crataegus 154

Crataegus x grignonensis 164
   laevigata 'Alba Plena' 78
   l. 'Coccinea Plena' 74
   l. 'Rosea Pleno-flore' 74
   x *lavallei* 78, 94
   prunifolia 164
Crepsis incana 115, 133
Cress 33, 51
Crinodendron hookerianum 74, 92
Crinum x powellii 113, 129, 144
Crocus 18, 146, 152
   'Autumn' 136
   Scotch 18, 22, 30
Crocus biflorus 18, 22, 30
   chrysanthus 22
   kotschyanus 136
   susianus; syn. *C. angustifolius* 22
   tomasinianus 22, 30
   vernus; syn. *C. neapolitanus* 30
Crotons 112
Crown imperial 53, 124
Cucumbers
   clearing away 148
   feeding 105
   harvesting 112, 129
   picking 105, 112, 123, 127, 131, 148
   planting 69
   sowing 59, 70
   stopping 95, 96
   syringing 105
   thinning 84
   watering 105
Cunninghamia lanceolata 181
Cupid's dart 22, 33, 51, 71, 87, 109
Currant
   Buffalo 52
   Flowering 28
   Golden 52
   Red 42, 96, 160, 162, 176
   White 42, 96, 160, 162, 176
Curry plant 128
cuttings, taking 114
   see also under individual plants
Cyclamen
   checking for disease 159, 177
   drying 54
   feeding 159
   moving into greenhouse 148
   potting on 50
   potting up seedlings 40, 145
   pricking out 140
   removal of flowers 140, 159, 177
   repotting 86, 112
   sowing 17, 131
   syringing 109
   watering 177, 181
Cyclamen coum 10, 18, 22, 30
   hederifolium; syn. *C. neapolitanum* 129, 136, 144, 154, 162, 173, 173
   purpurascens; syn. *C. europaeum* 113, 129, 136, 144
   repandum 53, 72
Cypress, Summer 32, 49
Cytisus albus 64, 78, 94
   battandieri 64, 91, 104
   x *beanii* 64, 73, 91
   nigrans 122
   x *praecox* 64
   praecox 'Albus' 78
   purgans 52, 73
   scoparius 64
   s. 'Burkwoodii' 75, 92
   s. 'Golden Sunlight' 64, 73, 91
   s. 'Killiney Red' 75
   s. 'Killiney Salmon' 75
   s. 'Windlesham Ruby' 75

Daboecia cantabrica 'Alba' 94, 110, 130, 149, 162
   c. 'Atropurpurea' 99, 113, 134, 151, 163
Daffodils 18, 28, 28, 30, 35, 46, 53
   grading 143
   planting bulbs 143, 146
   taking indoors 15
   Wild 53
Dahlias 118, 154
   boxing up 21
   checking for decay 24
   cuttings 37, 40
   drying out 160
   and earwigs 129
   feeding 110

lifting 160
mulching 110
planting 38
preparation for 14
supporting 132
Daisy 64, 68, 71, 86, 87, 108, 124, 138
   African 31, 86, 108, 124, 138
   Barberton 32
   dwarf African 111
   Kingfisher 31, 49, 87, 110, 125, 139
   Livingstone 22, 33, 51, 87, 111
   Michaelmas 33, 51, 154
   Midsummer 51, 71, 87
   Shasta 51, 71, 71, 87
   Swan River 31, 48, 68, 86, 108, 124
   Transvaal 32
Damping off 131
Daphne x burkwoodii 'Somerset' 75, 92
   mezereum 18, 25, 37
   odora 25, 37
   o. 'Aureomarginata' 25
Darwin's berberis 52
Davidia involucrata 78
Deadheading
   see under individual plants
Delphinium consolida 'Stock Flowered' 120
   elatum 71, 87, 100, 103
   'Thunderstorm' 6
Delphiniums 82
   cuttings 48
   siting 100
   supporting 67, 84, 100
   thinning 67
Deutzia 'Magician' 92, 107
   x *rosea* 92, 107
   x r. 'Campanulata' 94, 110
   scabra 'Pride of Rochester' 94, 110
Deutzias 88, 114
Dianthus barbatus 71, 86, 87, 108
   chinensis; syn. *D. sinensis* 11, 22, 33
   deltoides 96, 115, 133, 153
Didiscus caeruleus see *Trachymene caeruleus*
Digitalis purpurea 71, 87
Dimorphotheca aurantiaca 31, 49, 68, 87, 110, 124, 138
   barberiae 'Compacta' 96, 115, 133, 153
   ecklonis 'Prostrata' 111
Diseases see individual diseases;
   see also under individual plants
Dogwood
   Flowering 92
   Red-barked 14, 174
   Westonbirt 174
Doronicum plantangineum 46
   p. 'Harpur Crew' 46
   p. 'Miss Mason' 46
Draba aizoides 50
   bryoides; syn. *D. rigida bryoides* 50
Draba rigida 50
Dracaenas 112
Dyer's greenwood 91

Earwigs 129
Earthworms 40, 112
Echinacea purpurea 142
Echinops ritro 51, 71, 87
Echium lycopsis; syn. *E. plantagineum* 31, 49, 68, 87, 110, 124
Edging-iron 76, 81, 173
Elaeagnus x ebbingei 162, 170
   macrophylla 162, 170
   pungens 'Maculata' 162, 164, 170
Embothrium lanceolatum 75, 92
Emilia flammea 31, 49, 68, 110, 125
Endive
   harvesting 117
   sowing 44, 67, 102
   thinning 56, 84, 112
   tying up leaves 108, 146
Eranthis hyemalis 18, 22, 30
Erica arborea alpina 51
   carnea see *E. herbacea*
   cinera 'C.D. Eason' 107, 126, 145
   c. 'Coccinea' 107

188

x darleyensis 28
x d. 'Arthur Johnson' 15, 25, 37, 58, 180
x d. 'Jack H. Brummage' 15, 25, 37, 58, 169, 180
x d. 'Silver Bells' 17, 26, 39, 61, 183
erigena see E. mediterranea 'W.T. Rackliff'
herbacea formerly E. carnea 28
h. 'Adrienne Duncan' 15, 25, 37, 58
h. 'Foxhollow' 15, 25, 37, 58, 169, 180
h. 'Myreton Ruby' 15, 25, 37, 58, 169, 180
h. 'Praecox Rubra' 15, 25, 37, 58, 169, 180
h. 'Ruby Glow' 15, 25, 37, 169, 180
h. 'Springwood Pink' 8, 15, 25, 37, 58
h. 'Springwood White' 8, 17, 17, 26, 39, 61, 183
h. 'Vivelli' 15, 25, 37, 58, 169, 180
h. 'Winter Beauty' (formerly 'King George') 14, 15, 169, 180
hibernica see E. mediterranea 'W.T. Rackliff'
lusitanica; syn. E. codonoides 17, 26, 28, 39, 61, 183
mediterranea 28
m. 'Brightness' 37, 58, 75
m. 'W.T. Rackliff'; formerly E. erigena or E. hibernica 17, 26, 39
vagans 'Lyonesse' 130, 149, 162, 166
v. 'Mrs. D.F. Maxwell' 107, 126, 145, 159
v. 'St. Keverne' 107
Erigeron speciosus 51, 71, 87
s. 'Strahlenmeer' 104
Erinus alpinus 32, 50, 81, 96, 115, 133
Erysimum alpinum 68, 84
Escallonia 'C.F. Ball' 107, 126, 145
'Donard Radiance' 92, 107, 126, 145
'Donard Star' 92, 107, 126, 145
x Iveyi 94, 110, 130, 149
'Peach Blossom' 92, 107, 126, 145
'Slieve Donard' 92, 107, 126, 145
Escallonias 114
Eschscholzia californica 6, 31, 49, 68, 87, 110, 125, 139
Eucryphia x nymensensis 130, 134
Euonymus 154
Euonymus fortunei 'Emerald 'n Gold' 164
f. 'Silver Queen' 164
Euphorbia veneta 55
wulfenii 55
Evergreens, cutting 180

Fairy thimbles 115, 130, 153
Fallopia baldschuanicum aka Polygonum baldschuanicum 110, 118
Felicia bergeriana 31, 49, 87, 110, 125, 139
Fencing 62
Fern, Maidenhair 25
Filipendula purpurea 139
Fir, Chinese 181
Flax
New Zealand 75
Scarlet 87, 110, 125
Fleabane 104
Flower-of-an-hour 32, 49, 68, 125, 139
Flowers, flower beds
checking soil 168
deadheading 13, 37, 42, 48, 102, 124
and frost 10
hoeing 120, 129
moving indoors 140, 179
mulching 120, 129
planning 12
preparing borders 166, 180
raking up leaves 168

removing supports 158
and snow 10, 12
sowing 52, 84, 124
spraying 84, 93, 132
thinning out seedlings 93
watering 93
Foam of May 61, 93
Foliage plants, keeping clean 179
Forget-me-not 64, 67, 69, 84, 103, 156
'Mrs. John T. Scheepers' 64
'President Hoover' 64
Forsythia 35
Prune 52
Forsythia 'Beatrix Farrand' 18, 34, 52
x intermedia 18
x i. 'Lynwood' 18, 34, 52
x i. 'Spectabilis' 18, 34
Fothergilla monticola 154
Foxglove 71, 87
Freesias 25, 127, 152
French beans 67, 108, 123
Fritillaria imperialis 53, 124
meleagris 53, 72
Frost
damage 10, 26
protecting blossom 42
and soil 12, 20
Fruit
planting 12
preparation of soil 12
protection from birds 102
spraying 35, 67, 79
storage 10, 24
see also individual fruits
Fruit cages 75, 102, 171
Fruit trees, bushes and birds 171
feeding 20, 22, 26
and fruit cage 75
planting 12
pruning 14, 170
removing blossom 75
spraying 10, 16, 48, 93
storing 10, 180
tying and staking 16
watering 79
weed control 24
Fuchsia cuttings 23, 37, 127
Fuchsia magellanica 126, 145, 159
Fumigating 37, 50, 98
Fungicides 62, 93, 132, 183
Furze 52
Fusarium 183

Gages 48, 120, 170
Gaillardia pulchella 32, 110, 125, 139, 157
Galanthus nivalis 10, 18, 22
Galega officinalis 149
Gall mite 35
Galtonia candicans; syn. Hyacinthus candicans 113, 129, 136, 144
Garden frame 59, 109, 152
Garden swing 105, 152
Garlic, Golden 88, 113
Gaultheria procumbens 110, 130
Gean 61
Genista 64
Genista aetnensis 122
cinerea 87
hispanica 73, 91, 104
januensis 64
lydia 73, 91
pilosa 64, 73, 91, 104
tinctoria 'Royal Gold' 91, 104, 122, 140
Gentian, Spring 81, 96
Gentiana sino-ornata 153, 160
verna 81, 96
Geranium cinereum 81, 96, 115, 133, 153, 160
farreri; syn. G. napuligerum 81, 96, 115, 133
subcaulescens 81, 96, 115, 133, 153, 160
Gerbera jamesonii 32
Germination 4, 15, 17, 31, 34, 49, 59, 62
Geum chiloense 51, 71, 87, 103
Gilia lutea 32, 49, 68, 87, 110, 125, 139
Gladiolus 136
Butterfly 113, 129
Byzantine 88

large-flowered 113, 129, 136, 144
lifting 142
miniature 113, 129
mulching 79
planting 26, 34, 48
primulinus 113, 129
supporting 70
watering 79, 106
Gladiolus byzantinus 88
Glory of the snow 22, 30, 53
Gloxinia (Sinningia) 148
after flowering 135, 157
boxing up 27
planting 40, 40
potting on 50
sowing 21, 117
Goat's rue 149
Godetia 131
Godetia grandiflora 32, 49, 87, 110, 125
Gold dust 33, 50, 96
Golden rain tree 122
Gomphrena globosa 32, 49
Gooseberries
checking shoots 42
Chinese 110
cuttings 162
feeding 48
'Leveller' 170
mulching 14
planting 166
pruning 30, 93
spraying 35
thinning fruits 79
Gooseberry mildew 35
Gorse 52, 64
Spanish 73
Grafting 181
Granny's bonnet 11, 22, 33, 51, 71, 86, 87, 108
Grape
Fox 164
Oregon 28
picking 123
Teinturier 82, 164
thinning 86, 95, 109
see also vines
Grape hyacinth 28, 53, 72
Greenfly 84
Greenhouse plants
boxing up 17, 21, 27
checking for pests and diseases 23, 37, 131, 167, 173
cuttings 23, 25, 32, 37, 40
damping off 131
deadheading 13, 17, 37
drying off 25
feeding 54, 98, 109
hardening off 40, 54
planting 40, 50
pollinating 25
position of 162, 181
potting on 105
potting up 27, 40, 50, 161
pricking out 32, 44
re-potting 25
sowing 11, 15, 17, 21, 25, 27, 32, 44, 50
spraying 50, 117, 131
stopping 32
taking indoors 148
ventilating 105
watering 11, 37, 44, 69, 90, 95, 98, 105, 109, 127, 140, 148, 157, 162, 167, 169, 179
Greenhouses
atmosphere 161, 171
and birds/cats 67, 81
checking for pests and diseases 62, 72
cleaning and maintenance 13, 117, 162, 179, 179, 183
and conifers 162
heating 15, 152, 159, 177
making space 72
shading 72, 109, 117, 127, 130, 140, 157
shelving 34, 50
ventilation 11, 20, 25, 44, 69, 109, 112, 127, 152, 157, 161, 167, 177, 181
watering 21, 95, 112
Growing-bags 50, 88
Guelder rose 95
Gypsophila elegans 32, 49, 68, 87,

110, 125, 139
paniculata 133
repens 96, 115
r. 'Fratensis' 96, 115

Hakonechloa macro 'Aureola' 106
Halesia carolina 78
Hamamelis mollis 8, 13, 13, 23, 34, 177
m. 'Brevipetala' 13
m. 'Pallida' 13
vernalis 8, 13, 23
virginiana 167
Handkerchief tree 78
Hanging baskets 40, 59, 76, 86
Hare's Tail Grass 162
Haricot beans 67, 112, 152
Harry Lauder's walking stick 164
Hawthorn 78
Hazel, Corkscrew 164
Heath, Cornish 107, 130, 166
Heather 24, 130
Bell 107
Hebe x andersonii 'Variegata' 118
armstrongii 94, 110
'Autumn glory' 113, 118, 134, 151, 151, 163
brachysiphon 110
'Carl Teschner' 99, 113
x Franciscana 'Blue Gem' 99, 113, 134, 151
'Great Orme' 107, 126, 145, 159
'Pagei'; syn. H. pinguifolia 'Pagei' 94
speciosa 'Gloriosa' 107
s. 'La Seduisante' 107, 126, 145, 159
s. 'Simon Deleaux' 107
Hedera canariensis 'Gloire de Marengo' aka H.c. 'Variegata' 164, 177
colchica 'Variegata' 164
Hedges
planting 170
trimming 102, 120, 129
Heel cuttings 107
Helianthemum nummularium; syn. H. chamaecistus 88, 96, 115
Helianthus annuus 32, 49, 68, 110, 125, 139
Helichrysum angustifolium 128
milfordiae; syn. H. marginatum 81, 96
Heliotrope 22, 33
cuttings 25, 40, 127, 140
Heliotropium x hybridum 22, 33, 87, 110, 125, 139
Helleborus niger 8, 14
Herbaceous border 82, 100
cleaning up 162
planning 34
preparing ground 26, 146
Herbaceous plants 100
cutting down 26, 142
deadheading 138
dividing perennials 147
and lawn 126, 162
lifting and dividing 34
planting 34
preventing frost damage 178
supporting 67, 84, 91, 138
Herbicides 62
Hesperis matronalis 51, 71, 87
Hibiscus rosa-sinensis 118
syriacus 118
s. 'Blue bird' 134, 151, 163
s. 'Coeleste' 134
s. 'Dorothy Crane' 130, 149, 162
s. 'Hamabo' 145, 159
s. 'Jeanne d'Arc' 130
s. 'Monstrosus' 164
s. 'Woodbridge' 145
trionum 32, 49, 68, 125, 139
Hoeing 22, 36, 56, 67, 70, 75, 84, 102, 106, 110, 114, 156
Hoheria glabrata 110, 130
Holly, Variegated 10, 164, 181
Hollyhock 11, 22, 71, 87
Honesty 69, 84, 146
Hop, Golden-leaved 100
Horse chestnut, Red 74
Hose-reels 103
Hosta elata 118
fortunei 'Albopicta' 85, 118
f. 'Aureo-marginata' 118
f. 'Obscura Marginata' 145

undulata 'Variegata' 118
Houseplants, potting up 161
Hoya carnosa 109
Humulus lupulus 'Aureas' 100
Hyacinth
  Common 53, 72
  forcing 169
  potting up 145
  summer 113, 129, 136, 144
  taking indoors 15
Hyacinthus candicans; syn. *Galtonia candicans* 113, 129, 136, 144
  orientalis 53, 72
Hybrid berries 52, 84, 114, 150, 162
Hydrangea
  climbing 100
  Common 118, *142*
  cuttings 76, 81
  Japanese climbing 95
  stopping 90
Hydrangea
  anomala 100
  arborescens 26
  a. 'Grandiflora' *27*
  aspera aspera 116
  hortensia 'Madame E. Mouillière' 110
  macrophylla 118, *142*
  m. 'Blue wave' 113
  m. 'Hamburg' 107, 126, 145
  m. 'Kluis Superba' 107
  m. 'Madame E. Mouillière' 130, 149
  m. 'Westfalen' 107
  paniculata 26, 110, 130, 149
  p. 'Grandiflora' 118
  petiolaris 95, 100, 110
Hypericum calycinum 91, 104, 140, 156
  patulum 'Hidcote' 104, *105*, 122, 140, 156
  polyphyllum 'Sulphureum' 115, 133, 153

Iberis sempervirens 81, 96,
  umbellata 32, 49, 69, 87, 110, 125, 139
Ilex x altaclarensis 'Golden King' 164
  x a. 'Lawsoniana' *181*
  aquifolium 'Golden Queen' 164
  a. 'Madame Briot' *177*
  a. 'Silver Queen' 164
Impatiens 135
Impatiens balsamina 32, 49
Indian bean tree 110
Indian shot 11, 22, 33
Indigofera gerardiana 92, 107, 126, 145, 159
Insecticides 48, 93, 123, 132, 135, 139
Ipheion uniflorum 56
Ipomoea purpurea; syn. *Convolvulus major* 32, 49, 69
  violacea; syn. *I. rubrocaerulea* 32, 49
Iris, Flag 96
Iris danfordiae 22, 30
  reticulata 18, 22, 30
  sibirica 'Tropic Night' *91*
Itea ilicifolia 130
Ivy
  Boston 164
  Persian 164
  propagating 109

Japanese angelica tree 130
Japanese pagoda tree 149
Japonica 37, 39
Jasmine
  rock 115
  winter 8, 18, 24, 174, *183*
Jasminium nudiflorum 8, 18, 24, 174, *183*
Jerusalem cross 33, 51, 71
Jonquil 53
Joseph's coat 48
Judas tree 74
June Berry 44, 61
Justica brandegeana; formerly *Beloperone guttata* 94

Kalmia latifolia 92, 93
Katsura tree 154
Kentranthus ruber; syn.

Centranthus ruber 51, 71, 87
Kerria japonica 52, 73
  j. 'Pleniflora' 52
Killarney strawberry tree 8
Kniphofia galpinii 154
Kochia scoparia 'Trichophylla' 32, 49
Kohlrabi
  harvesting 93, 117, 146, 161, 170, 180
  sowing 49, 67, 96, 132
  thinning 60, 108, 142, 161
Kolkwitzia amabilis 'Pink Cloud' 75, 92

Laburnum 64
Laburnum x waterei 72, 91
  x w. 'Vossii' 72
Lachenalias 127
Lady's Mantle 109
Lagurus ovatus 162
Larkspur 31, 48, 86, 108, *120*, 124
Lathyrus odoratus 11, 32, 49, 69
Laurel
  Mountain 92, *93*
  Spotted *177*
Laurustinus 8, 17
Lavandula spica; syn. *L. officinalis* 46, 113, 134
  s. 'Hidcote'; syn. *L. nana atropurpurea* 46, 113, 134, 151
  stoechas 113, 134
Lavatera trimestris aka *L. rosea* 32, 49, 69, *96*, 110, 125, 139
  t. 'Silver Oak' *48*
Lavender
  French 113
  Old English 46, 113
Lawn mowers 10, 12, 16, 25, 68, 86, 117, 167, 168, 176
Lawn rakes 148, 157, *159*, 180
Lawn rollers 44, 54, 72
Lawns
  aeration 27, 148, *152*, 157
  and ants 108
  brushing 180, 183
  bulbs in 22, 157
  and chamomile 135
  cutting 16, 25, 32, 68, 90, 105, 126, 135, 167
  and dogs 108
  drainage 158
  edges 12, 14, 32, 36, 76, 105, 126, 152, 162, 171
  feeding 54, 59, 62, 90, 123
  laying turves 72, 81, 145, *157*
  leaf removal 162, 178
  levelling 81, 152
  preparing for seeding 50, 54, 161
  repairing 79
  rubbish removal 40, 148, 157
  seeding 59, 62, 81, 98, 105, 145
  stepping stones on 20, 176
  watering 62, 68, 94, 112, 123, 129
  weed removal 72, 90, *117*
  and wheelbarrow tracks 171
  and worms 20, 112
Leaf miners 135
Leatherjackets 139
Leaves, fallen 135, 162, 168, 178, 182
Leeks
  harvesting 16, 27, 168, 178, 183
  planting 79
  sowing 49
Leptospermum scoparium 'Chapmanii' 75, 92
  s. 'Red Damask' 75
  s. 'Roseum multipetalum' 75
Lettuce 'Salad Bowl' 49, 67, 79, 93
Lettuces
  harvesting 36, 79, 88, 93, 108, 142, 156
  sowing 44, 49, 60, 67, 79, 96, 117, 132, 145, 158
  thinning 25, 27, 54, 70, 93, 112, 146, 162
  top-dressing 30
  watering 60, 76, 108, 129, 142
Leucojum 18
Lewisia cotyledon 96
Lilac 81
  Californian *81*
  Common 64, 75
Lilies 34, 48, 79, 106, 145

Lilium auratum 129, 136, 144
  candidum 82, 88, 113
  hansonii 82
  henryi 118, 129
  pyrenaicum 82
  regale 113
  rubellum 82
  speciosum 129, 136, 144
  tigrinum 129, 136, 144
Lily
  Arum 90, 127, 145, 157
  Belladonna 124
  Bourbon 88, 113
  Cuban 72, 88
  Golden-rayed 129, 136, 144
  Lent 55
  Madonna 82, 88, 113
  Peruvian 33
  Plaintain *85*
    Tiger 129, 136, 144
    Torch 112, 154
Lily leek 88, 113
Lily of the valley 24, 167
Limnanthes douglasii 32, 49, 69, 87, 110, 125
Limonium sinuatum 'Blue River' formerly *Statice sinuata* 141
Linaria maroccana 32, 49, 69, 87, 110
Ling 130
Linum grandiflorum 87, 110, 125
Lippia citriodora; syn. *Aloysia triphylla* 134
Liquidambar styraciflua 154
Lithodora diffusa; formerly *Lithospermum diffusum* 64, 96, 115, 133, 153, 160
  d. 'Heavenly Blue' 64
Lithospermum diffusum see *Lithodora diffusa*
Lobelia erinus 11, 22, 33, 68, 87, 110, 125, 139
  e. 'White Gem' 22
Lobularia maritima; formerly *Alyssum maritimum* 31, 48, 68, 86, 108, 124, 138
Lonicera fragrantissima 26, 28, 39
  japonica 'Halliana' 95, 110, 130, 149, 162
  periclymenum 'Belgica' 82
Love-in-a-mist 32, 49, 69, 87, 111, 125
Love-lies-bleeding 31, 48, 68, 108, 124, 138, 157
Lunaria annua 69, 84
Lupin 48
Lychnis, Scarlet 82
Lychnis chalcedonica 33, 51, 71, 82
  flos-jovis 134
  viscaria 32, 49, 68, 69, 87, 110
Lysichiton americanus 64

Magnolia, Star 28, *38*, 39
Magnolia denudata 28
  grandiflora 110, 130, 149
Magnolia liliflora 46
  l. 'Nigra' *58*
  x loebneri 'Leonard Messel' *35*
  sieboldii 78, 94
  x soulangiana 46, 61, 75, 78
  s. 'Alba superba' *61*
  s. 'Lennei' *46*, 58
  s. 'Nigra' *58*
  stellata 28, *38*, 39, 61
Mahonia aquifolium 28, 34, 52
  bealei 13, 23, *177*
  'Charity' 13, 23, 34, 167, *177*
  lomariifolia 13, 23, 34
  pinnata 23, 34, 52
Malcolmia maritima 32, 49, 69, 87, 111, 125
Mallow 32, 49, 69
Malus 'American Beauty' 46
  baccata mandshurica 46
  coronaria 'Charlottae' 74
  x eleyi 46, 58
  'Golden Hornet' 78, 164
  'John Downie' 78
  'Pink Perfection' 46, 74
  x purpurea 46
  'Red Sentinel' 78, 164
  x robusta 143
  x r. 'Red Siberian' *143*
  x r. 'Yellow Siberian' *143*, 164
  'Royalty' 74

'Snowcloud' 46, 78
'Van Eseltine' 74
Manuka 75
Maple
  Hedge 154
  Norway 154
  Paperbark 8
  Silver 18
Marigold 4, 111, 125, 139
  African 32, 111, 125, 139, 157
  English 31, 48, 68, 86, 108, 124, 138
  French *21*, 32, 87, 111, 139
  Pot 31, 48, *51*, 68, 86, 108, 124, 138
Mask flower 22, 33, 86, 108, 138, 157
Matthiola bicornis 32, 49, 69, 111, 125
  incana 32, 49, 84, 103
May 78
Meconopsis betonicifolia 82
Medlar 78
Melons
  cutting back sideshoots 109
  feeding 90
  harvesting 145
  planting 69
  sowing 59
Mentzelia lindleyi 32, 49, 69
Mesembryanthemum criniflorum 22, 33, *51*, 87, 111
Mespilus, Snowy 44, 61
Mespilus germanica 78
Mezereon 18, 25
Mignonette 32, 49, 69, 87, 111, 125, 139
Milkweed 11, 22, 33
Miscanthus sinensis 'Silver feather' 153
Mixed borders 100, *118*
Molucella laevis 32
Morning glory 32
Mulching *see under* individual plants
Muscari 28, 146
Muscari armeniacum 28, 53
  botryoides 28, 30, 53, 72
Myosotis sylvatica 69, 84, 103
Myrtus communis 130, 149

Naked boys 136, 144, 162
Narcissus
  cyclamen-flowered 18, 22, 30
  hoop-petticoat 18, 22, 30
  planting 146
  poet's 53
  potting up 145
Narcissus 30, 53
  bulbocodium 18, 22, 30
  cyclamineus 18, 22, 30
  jonquilla 53
  x odorus 53
  poeticus 53
  pseudonarcissus 53
  triandus albus 30, 55
Nasturtium 49, 69
National Trust gardens 178
Nectarines
  planting 146
  pollinating 25, 38
  pruning 60
  spraying 24
  thinning fruits 52, 93
Nemesia 131
Nemesia strumosa 32, 49
Nemophila menziesii 32, 49, 69, 87, 111, 125
Nerine bowdenii 136, 144, 162, *172*, 173
Nicandra physaloides 49, 69
Nicotiana alata; syn. *N. affinis* 32, 49, 87, 111, 125, 139
Nigella damascena 32, 49, 69, 87, 111, 125
Nitrogen in fertilizer 20, 26, 62, 90, 123

Olearia x haastii 110, 130, 149
  macrodonta 110, 130
  x scilloniensis 95, 110
Onions
  bending over tops 129
  harvesting 84, 112, 132, 142
  planting 44
  ripening *122*

sowing 22, 25, 30, 36, 56, 79
thinning seedlings 49
Orange
  Japanese bitter 78
  Mock 77
Orange-ball shrub 91
Orange blossom, Mexican 78
Orchards, grass in 79
Ornithogalum nutans 53
  umbellatum 53, 72
Osmanthus heterophyllus 162
Osmarea burkwoodii 61, 78

Pachysandra terminalis 26, 39
  t. 'Variegata' 26
Paeonia suffruticosa 'Rock's
  Variety' 88
Palm
  Chusan 90, 144
  Fan 90
Pampas grass 11, 174
Pansy 68, 84, 87, 103, 111, 120,
  150
Papaver alpinum 87, 103, 120
  nudicaule 87, 103, 120
  orientale 87, 103, 120
  rhoeas 32, 49, 69, 87, 111, 125
  somniferum 32, 49, 69
Parrotia persica 160
Parsnips
  harvesting 161, 170, 178, 183
  sowing 25, 30
  thinning 44, 129
Parthenocissus henryana 164
  inserta 164
  quinquefolia formerly *Vitis
    hederacea* 164, 164
  tricuspidata 164
Partridge-berry 110
Pasque flower 28
Passiflora caerulea 100
Passion flower, Common 100
Paul's double scarlet thorn 74
Paulownia tomentosa 81
Paving slabs 126
Pea tree 72
Peach, Common 58
Peach leaf curl 22, 24
Peach trees, peaches
  planting 146
  pollinating 25, 38
  pruning 60
  and soil 37
  spraying 22, 24
  thinning fruits 52, 93
Pear, Willow-leaved 53
Pear trees, pears
  bark ringing 75
  diseases 14, 180
  feeding 24
  grafting *181*
  picking 106, 138
  planting 166
  pruning 20, 30, 106, 132
  spraying 38
  staking 166
  storing 106, 172
  thinning fruits 96
Peas
  asparagus 67, 93, 117
  garden 38, 56, 79, 88, 93, 96, 112
  harvesting 93, 112, 158
  picking 117
  sowing 38, 56, 67, 79, 88
  supporting 56, 76, 93, 96
Pelargonium
  cuttings 23, 36, 37, 86, 127
  potting on 112
  Regal 86
Periwinkle
  Greater 62
  Lesser 42
Perovskia atriplicifolia 136
Pesticides 48, 62, 132
Pests *see* individual pests
Petunia x hybrida 11, 22, 33, 87,
  111, 125, 139
Pheasant's eye 31, 48, 68, 86, 108,
  124, 138
Philadelphus 88
Philadelphus 'Beauclerk' 95, 110
  'Belle etoile' 95, 110
  coronarius 'Aureus' 77
  'Virginal' 95, 110
Phlomis fruticosa 91, 104
Phlox, herbaceous 48

Phlox drummondii 32, 49, 87, 111,
  125
  subulata 'Alexander's Surprise'
    64
Phormium tenax 'Variegatum' *75*
Phosphate in fertilizer 62, 90, 123
Phygelius capensis 107, 126, 145
Picea abies 'Inverta' 43
  glauca 'Albertina Conica' 37
Pieris floribunda 39, 61, 78
Pilea 135
Pincushion plant 49, 68, 108, 124
Pine, Weymouth *124*
Pink
  Alpine moss 64
  cuttings 102
  Indian 11, 22, 33, 133
  Maiden 96, 115, 153
Pinus strobus 'Nana' 124
Piptanthus laburnifolius 73, 91
Planning of flower garden 12, 77
Plum trees, plums
  cherry 28, 37
  'Edwards' *159*
  feeding 24
  picking 120, *159*
  planting 170
  pruning 48
  supporting branches 120
  'Victoria' *159*
Plumbago, Hardy 113
Poached egg plant 32, 49, 69, 87,
  110, *125*
Poinsettia 178
Polyanthus 46, 156
Polygonum affine 'Donald
  Lowndes' 96
  baldschuanicum aka *Fallopia
    baldschuanicum* 130, 149,
    162
Poncirus trifoliata 78
Ponds 12, 162
Poor man's orchid 95
Poppy
  Alpine 87, 103, 120
  Blue Himalayan 82
  Californian *6*, 31, 49, 68, 87,
    110, 125, 139
  for decoration 146
  Field 32, 49, 69, 87, 111, 125
  Iceland 87, 103, 120
  Opium 32, 49, 69
  Oriental 87, 103, 120
  Shirley 32, 49, 69, 87, 111, 125
  Tree *109*, 110, 118
Potash in fertilizers 24, 62, 90,
  102, 106, 123
Potassium permanganate 112
Potatoes
  earthing-up 76, 88
  lifting 93, 102
  planting 44
  sowing 60
Potentilla arbuscula aka *P. fruticosa
  arbuscula* 154
  a. 'Abbotswood' 95, 110, 130,
    149
  aurea chrysocraspeda 96, 115, 133
  fruticosa 154
  f. 'Farreri' 73, 91, 104, 122, 140,
    156
  f. 'Katherine Dykes' 73
  f. 'Red Ace' 92, 107, 126, 145
Potting on, and stunted growth
  81
  see also under individual plants
Pride of India 122
Primula helodoxa 82
  pulverulenta 'Bartley Strain' 82
  rosea 28
Primulas 21
  in cold frame 86
  lifting and dividing 84
  sowing 69, 117
Prince of Wales' feather 31, 48,
  108, 124
Prince's feather 31, 124, 138
Privet, trimming 102
Propagation frame 25, 32, *39*, 105,
  140, 183
Pruning *see under* individual
  plants
Prunus 'Accolade' 58
  'Amanogawa' 46, 58
  x amygdalo-persica 'Pollardii' 37
  'Asano' 58

  avium 61
  a. 'Plena' 61
  cerasifera 'Nigra' 28, 37
  c. 'Pissardii' 28
  x cistena 61
  dulcis; syn. *P. amygdalus* 37
  glandulosa 70
  g. 'Sinensis' 58
  'Kanzan' 74
  padus 'Grandiflora' 78
  p. 'Purple Queen' 74
  'Pandora' 37
  persica 'Prince Charming' 58
  'Pink Perfection' 74
  sargentii 28, *36*, 37, 154
  serrula 78
  'Shirofugen' 74
  'Shirotae'; syn. *P.* 'Kojima' 61
  subhirtella 'Autumnalis' 174
  s. 'Autumnalis Rosea' 169
  s. 'Pendula' 46, *46*
  s. 'Pendula Plena Rosea' 46, 58
  tenella 'Fire Hill' 58
  triloba 37, 58, 70
  'Ukon' *60*, 61
  'Umeniko' 61
  x yedoensis 37
Pteris 25
Pulsatilla vulgaris 28
Purple Cone Flower 142
Puschkinia scilloides 30, 53, 72
Pygmy torch 31, 124, 138
Pyracantha atalantioides 95
  crenulata 95
Pyrus nivalis 61
  salicifolia 'Pendula' 53, 61

Queen Anne's lace *21*, 31
Quince
  Japanese 37, 39
  Maule's 37

Radishes 30, 60, 70, 96, 117, 132,
  145
Ranunculus 26, 34
Raspberries, raspberry canes
  cutting back canes 22, 24, 26
  cutting out 142
  feeding 56
  mulching 67
  planting 38, 158, 168, 182
  pruning 26
  preparing ground 158
  supporting *169*
  tying 70, 93
  weed removal 56
red hot poker *112*, 146
Red spider mite 95, 123
Reseda odorata 32, 49, 69, 87, 111,
  125, 139
Rhododendron 'Blue Diamond' *40*
  'Christmas Cheer' 18
  'Tessa' 18
Rhododendrons 8, 18, 46
Ribes alpinum 52
  aureum 52
  laurifolium 28
  sanguineum 28
  s. 'Pulborough Scarlet' 58, 75
  speciosum 58, 75
Robinia hispida 75
  pseudoacacia 94
Rock gardens 64, 67, 88, 182
Romneya coulteri 110, 118, 130, 149
  trichocalyx *109*, 118
Rooting frame *39*
Rooting powder 76
Rosa 'Albertine' 82
  banksiae 'Lutea' 82
  eceae 'Helen Knight' 82
  'Meg' *84*
  'Ophelia' 82
Rose
  aphids on 75
  and black spot 24
  budding 123
  bush 38
  climbing 38, 82
  feeding 102
  planting *43*
  pruning 38, *44*, 132, 138, 156, 176
  rambler 70, 132, 138, 156
  Rock 88
  sucker growth, 96, 106, 129
  tying 70
Rose of Sharon 91, *105*

Rosemary 81
Rosmarinus officinalis 81, 99
  o. "Miss Jessop's Upright' 81
Rowan 78
Rubus x tridel 'Benenden' 78
Rudbeckia fulgida 'Goldsturm' *100*
  hirta 125, *139*, 157
Runner beans
  harvesting 117, 129
  mulching 108
  preparing for 36
  sowing 67
  supporting 67
  watering 108

'Saffron, Meadow' 136
Sage
  Jerusalem 91
  White 115
Saintpaulias 92, 109
Salix alba 'Chermesina' 174
  a. 'Vitellina' 174
  lucida 90
  matsudana 'Tortuosa' 8
Salvia nemorosa (*S. x superba*) 118
  patens 11, 22, 33, 125, 139
  splendens 11, 22, 33, 111, 125,
    139
Sandwort 71, 87
Santolina chamaecyparissus 91, 104,
  122
Sarcococcoa humilis 26, 28
Saxifraga x apiculata 32, 50
  x borisii 32, 50
  burserana 22, 32, 50
  'Cranbourne' 32, 50
  x kewensis 22, 32
  oppositifolia 32, 50
  paniculata; syn. *S. aizoon* 96, 115
  'Riverslea' 32
Saxifragas 18
Scab disease 38
Scabiosa atropurpurea 49, 69, 111,
  125, 139
Scabious, Sweet 49, 69, 111, 125,
  139
Schizanthus 32, 44
Schizanthus pinnatus 95
Scilla bifolia 30
  peruviana 72, 88
  sibirica 30
Scillas, potting up 152
Seakale 10, 36, 44, 49, 54
Sedum 'Autumn Joy' 136, *138*
  cauticolum 133
  dasyphyllum 96
  spathulifolium 81, 96
  spectabile 'Carmen' *150*
  spurium 115, 133
Seed catalogues 183
Seeds, seedlings
  equipment 181
  pricking out 32, 44, *55*, 62, 123
  sowing 11, 21, 27, 32, 34, 44,
    56, 57, 59, 75, 84, 102, 124
  thinning 87
  watering 49
  and weeds 79
Sempervivum octopodes 96, 115
Senecio greyi 174
  'Sunshine' 82, 104, 122, 174
Shallots 22, 108
Shell flower 32
Shoo fly plant 49, 69
Shrimp plant 94
Shrubs 100
  and bedding plants 166
  cuttings 140, 158
  and frost 10, 182
  planting 33, *167*, 170
  potting up 158
  pruning 88
  re-firming 182
  and snow 10
  in tubs 168
  weeding 172
Silene acaulis 81, 96
  schafta 115, 133, 153, 160
Silver lace 11, 22
Silver leaf disease 48
Simazine 178
Sinningia *see* Gloxinia
Skimmia japonica 78
  'Fragrans' 61
Skunk cabbage 64
Slugs 14

INDEX

Smoke tree 154
Snake's head fritillary 53, 72
Snapdragon *see* Antirrhinum
Snowball bush 95
Snow-in-summer 33, 51
Snowdrop
  Common 10, 18, 22
  lifting 30
  planting 146
Snowdrop tree 78
Snowflake 18
Soft fruit
  cuttings *140*
  hoeing 102
  watering 110
  weed control 75
Solanum capsicastrum 21
  crispum *111*, 113, 134, 136, 151, 163
  c. 'Glasnevin' aka 'Autumnale' 136
Solanums 169
Solidago 'Crown of rays' *133*
  'Leraft' *149*
Sophora japonica 149
Sorbus 154
Sorbus aria 78
  aucuparia 78
  hupehensis 164
Spartium junceum 91, 104, 122, 140
Spider flower *30*, 31, 86, 108, 124
Spinach
  harvesting 67, 84, 102, 139
  sowing 38, 44, 56, 76, 93
  thinning 38, 60, 93, 123
  winter production 161
Spiraea x arguta 61, 78, 93
  palmata 139
  thunbergii 39, 61
Spring star flower *56*
Sprinklers 94, 112
Spur blight 35
Squill
  Siberian 30
  striped 30
  two-leaf 30
Stachyrus chinensis 25
  praecox 34
Staking *see under* individual plants
Star of Bethlehem 53, 72
Star of the veldt 31, 49, 68, 87, 110, 124, 138
Stardust 49, 68, 87, 110, 125, 139
Statice sinuata see Limonium sinuatum
Stepping stones 20, 176
Sternbergias 110
Stock
  Brompton 84, 103
  East Lothian 32
  night-scented 32, 49, 69, 111, 125
  perpetual-flowering 49
  ten-week 49
  trysomic 49
  Virginian 32, 49, 69, 87, 111, 125
Stranvaesia davidiana 95
Strawberries 16
  clearing 114
  covering 22, 24, 38
  hoeing 70, 110, 114, 156
  mulching 156
  picking 88
  planting 106, 124
  preparation for planting 12
  removing runners 67, 110
  and straw 70
  weed control 178
Strawberry tree, Grecian 39
Striped quill 53, 72

Sulphate of ammonia 36, 52
Sulphate of potash 48, 56
Sunflower 32, 68, 110, 125, 139
Swedes 112, 129, 180
Sweet corn 76, 122
Sweet gum 154
Sweet pea 11, 32, 49, 69
  cordon-grown 124
  hardening off 40
  mulching 84
  picking 120
  removing sideshoots 67
  watering 84
Sweet pepper bush 130
Sweet peppers *127*
Sweet rocket 51, 71, 87
Sweet sultan 48, 68, 86, 108, 124, 138
Sweet William 71, 82, 86, 87, 108, 114
Syringa microphylla 'Superba' 75
  vulgaris 64, 75, 81, 92, 99
  v. 'Blue Hyacinth' 64, 81
  v. 'Charles Joly' 75
  v. 'Congo' 64, 75
  v. 'Elinor' 75
  v. 'Firmament' 81
  v. 'Katherine Havemeyer' 81
  v. 'Massena' 64
  v. 'Maud Notcutt' 64, 78, 95
  v. 'Michael Buchner' 81
  v. 'Sensation' 75
  v. 'Souvenir de Alice Harding' 64
  v. 'Souvenir de L'Spath' 75
  v. 'Vestale' 64, 78

Tagetes erecta 32, 111, 125, 139, 157
  patula 87, 111, 125, 139
  p. 'Glowing Embers' *21*, 32
  tenuifolia; syn. *T. signata* 32, 111, 125, 139
Tamarix tetrandra 92
Tessel flower 31, 49, 68, 110, 125
Tea tree 75
Teucrium fruticans 99, 113, 134
Thistle, Globe 51, 71, 87
Thrift 81, 96, 115
Thrips 95
Thunbergia alata 32, 49, 87, 111, 125, 139
Thyme, Wild 96, 115, 133
Thymus hirsutus doerfleri; formerly *T. doerfleri* 96, 115
  nitidus 81, 96
  serpyllum 96, 115, 133
Tickseed 31, 48, 68
Toadflax 32, 49, 69, 87, 110
Tobacco plant 32, 49, 87, 111, 125, 139
Tomatoes, greenhouse
  'Alicante' 88
  clearing away 148
  feeding 62, 95, 117
  picking 95, 105, 117, 123, 127, 131, 148
  planting 50
  removing lower leaves 123, 131
  removing sideshoots 59, 62, 72, 95, 105
  sowing 15, 25
  spraying 98
  watering 95, 117
Tomatoes, indoor
  and cloches 142
  planting 88
  removing sideshoots 102, 123
  sowing 50
  staking 88
  stopping 117
Top-dressing 30, 36
Touch-me-not 32, 49

Trachelospermum jasminoides 110, 130
Trachycarpus fortunei 90, 144
Trachymene caeruleus; formerly *Didiscus caeruleus* 21, 31, 110, 124
Tradescantia 135
Trees
  in borders 100
  and frost 10
  planting *167*, 170
  pruning 14
  re-firming 182
  and snow 10
  supports 178
  in tubs 168
  see also fruit trees; individual trees
Trellis-work 100
Tropaeolum majus 49, 69
  peregrinum 22, 33
Tulip 46
  cottage 72
  Darwin 72
  lifting 106
  lily-flowered 72
  parrot 64, 72
  storing 106
  triumph 72
  water-lily 28
Tulipa 53
  fosteriana 30, 53
  greigii 53
  kaufmanniana 28, 30
  'Keizerskroon' 64
Turnips 112, 180

Ulex europaeus 52, 64, 73
  e. 'Plenus' 52, 64

Vaccinium corymbosum 159
Valerian 51, 71, 87
Vegetables, vegetable plot
  covering 10
  harvesting 10
  lifting 10
  preparing plot 20, 173, 176
  rubbish removal 146
  and soil 84
  thinning seedlings 87
  top-dressing 36
  watering *102*, 129
  and weeds 79
Verbascum 'Gainsborough' 82
Verbena
  cuttings 40
  Lemon-scented 134
Verbena x hybrida 11, 22, 33, 87, 111, 125, 139
  x h. 'Sparkle Hybrids' 22
Veronica cinerea 96, 115, 133
  prostrata 81, 96, 115
Viburnum 154
Viburnum 'Anne Russell' 28, 39, 61
  x bodnantense 8, 17, 26, 28, 39, 61, 183
  x burkwoodii 78
  carlesii 61, 78
  farreri; syn. *V. fragrans* 8, 17, 26, 28
  opulus 95
  o. 'Sterile' 95
  plicatum 78, 95
  rhytidophyllum 78, 95
  tinus (Laurustinus) 8, 17, 26, 39, 183
Vinca major 62, 81, 99, 113
  m. 'Elegantissima'/'Variegata' 62
  minor 42, 62, 81, 99, 113
  m. 'Atropurpurea' 42

  m. 'Azurea Flore-pleno' 42
  m. 'Bowles Variety' 42
Vines
  Japanese crimson glory 164
  Mile-a-minute 110, 118
  nipping back young growth 62
  pruning 177
  Russian 110, 118
  Siberian 118
  and soil 37
  spraying 37, 123
  syringing 23
  and tar oil winter wash 177
Viola 'Maggie Mott' 82
  x wittrockiana 68, 84, 87, 103, 111
Violas 64, 120
Violets 70
Vipers bugloss 31, 49, 68, 87, 110, 124
Virginia creeper 164, *164*
Vitis coignetiae 164
  hederacea see Parthenocissus quinquefolia
  labrusca 164
  vinifera 'Purpurea' 82, 164

Wallflowers 46, 64, 67
  alpine 68, 84
  fairy 68, 84
  planting 156
  Siberian 68, 71, 86, 87, 108
  transplanting 114
Walls 100
Water-lilies 60, *98*
Weed killer 72, 90
Weeds
  control of 26, 30, 50, 67, 75, 161, 166, 172, 178
  and hoeing 102, 106, 129
  and seedlings 79
Weigela 'Abel Carriere' 75, 92
  'Bristol Ruby' 75, 92
  florida 92
  f. 'Foliis Purpureis' 92
  'Newport Red' 75, 92
Weigelas 88, 114
Wheelbarrows 171
Whin 52
White fly 98
Whitebeam, Common 78
Willow
  Golden 174
  Pekin 8
  Scarlet 174
  Shining *90*
Windflower
  Blue winter 18, 22, 30
  Grecian 18, 22, 30, 53
Winter aconite 18, 22, 30, 146
Winter-green 110
Winter sweet 8, 13, 17, 28
Wire-netting bush 72
Wisteria 82, 100
  Chinese 81
  Japanese 81
Wisteria floribunda 81, 99
  f. 'Alba' 78
  f. 'Macrobotrys' 81
  sinensis 99
  s. 'Alba' 78, 81
  venusta 78, 95
Witch hazel
  Chinese 8, 13, *13*
  Common 167
  Ozark 8, 13
Woodruff, Annual 31, 48, 68, 108

Yarrow, Woolly 115, 133

Zebrina 135
Zinnia elegans 32, 49, 111, 125, 139
  'Persian Carpet' *131*